THACKERAY
A RECONSIDERATION

J. Y. T. GREIG

THACKERAY

A RECONSIDERATION

ARCHON BOOKS
1967

First published 1950
Reprinted with permission
OXFORD UNIVERSITY PRESS
in an unaltered and unabridged edition

Library of Congress Catalog Card Number: 67-19515
Printed in the United States of America

PREFACE

I_N a country like South Africa it is not easy to come by all the material required for the preparation of a book like this. I wish to thank especially the Witwatersrand Council of Education for a grant, which helped me to search for and purchase books not readily available in South African libraries, and Mr. Percy Freer, Librarian of the University of the Witwatersrand, for his co-operation. Without his help I should often have been brought to a stand.

I am also indebted to the Harvard University Press and to Mr. Gordon N. Ray for permission to quote from his edition of *The Letters and Private Papers of William Makepeace Thackeray.*

J. Y. T. G.

JOHANNESBURG

August 1949

CONTENTS

I. THE INDECISIVE THACKERAY

He is a big fellow, soul and body; of many gifts and qualities (particularly in the Hogarth line, with a dash of Sterne superadded), of enormous *appetite* withal, and very uncertain and chaotic in all points except his *outer breeding*, which is fixed enough, and perfect according to the modern English style. I rather dread explosions in his history. A big, fierce, weeping, hungry man; not a strong one. (Carlyle to Emerson on Thackeray in 1854. D. A. Wilson, *Carlyle to Threescore-and-ten* (1853–65), p. 90.)

§ 1

ON All Fools' Day 1862, Thackeray, who was then at the height of his fame, and had just resigned the editorship of *The Cornhill Magazine*, turned up at the weekly dinner of the *Punch* Table. Although he had long ceased to write and draw for *Punch*, he was still regarded as an honorary member of the Table and would come to dinner every now and then.

The talk drifted to Bishop Colenso and his sceptical opinions on the Pentateuch; and Thackeray, as anyone might have foreseen who had previously listened to him on the subject of the Old Testament, took the Bishop's part, repudiated the authority of Genesis, and dismissed as fables Joshua's interference with the sun at Gibeon and the maritime adventures of the prophet Jonah. The debate grew warm.

Nineteen months later he again visited the Table, and for two dinners running. And again the talk drifted to the Bishop and his heresies. But Thackeray, it seemed, had revised his opinions. On 2 December 1863 he took his stand, most unexpectedly, upon the Book of Genesis; on

9 December he admitted that the whole affair puzzled him. Leaving after dinner, he dismissed it airily with a *¿ Quién sabe ?*[1]

These are his last recorded words at the *Punch* Table. Two weeks later he was dead.

§ 2

Any monument to Thackeray the novelist might have this *¿ Quién sabe ?* suitably engraved upon it. The question speaks the man. It was no accident that he veered during the discussions on the Pentateuch; for he had been veering all his life on religion, morals, politics, and art, and, indeed, on the men and women that he met in the actual world or invented for his fiction. What he lacked was a stable and undeviating mind.

It is this mutability, perhaps more than any other quality of the man, which serves, on the one hand, to mark him off from the bulk of his contemporaries, and, on the other, to account for his declining fame in the present century. To the men of his own day he was enigmatic and disturbing; to the men of ours he appears hesitant, irritating in his vacillations, even poor-spirited.

The early Victorians believed in character. They also believed in characters. They took it for granted that a man (and especially a 'great' man) should become this or that, and remain this or that—not oscillate between the two. What is more, they were many of them able to achieve this stability. Hence that self-assurance which we see in Charlotte Brontë no less than in Martin Tupper, in Charles Dickens no less than in his Pecksniff and Gradgrind, Podsnap and Pumblechook, in John Henry Newman and Charles Kingsley, in the Chartists no less than in the ironmasters. Looking back upon them now, we can see the early Victorians, not without envy, as a solid, practical, enduring, and determined people. They did things. As a rule, they were well aware of what they wished to do, and they gave their full mind to doing it.

This stability, at its worst smug and coercive, but at its

2

best the foundation for the highest enterprises, implied the existence of a Code, comprehensive and generally accepted. The trouble with Thackeray was that he could never bring himself either to accept the Code and go steadily to work on that foundation, or to set the Code aside and declare himself a rebel. Had he done either, his contemporaries would have known how to take him. But he wobbled, wobbled interminably. As in the conversations at the *Punch* Table, so in the writing of his books; he suggested doubts, then withdrew them, finally retiring with a *¿ Quién sabe ?* Readers and acquaintances alike felt uneasy in his company. Not only when he wrote a novel, but also when he dined with men in clubs or conversed with women in their drawing-rooms, he insinuated doubts concerning the established Code that they were all living by. It was not the doubts that disturbed them most; it was Thackeray's manner. He was evasive; he was timid even while affecting boldness; he was not concrete; he had not 'grown together'. How could they be sure of him?

Sure of him they were not. One of Carlyle's judgements is recorded at the opening of this chapter. Alongside it we may put that of the sharp-tongued Douglas Jerrold of *Punch*: 'Thackeray is the most uncertain person I know. To-day he is all sunshine—to-morrow he is all frost and snow.'[2] From any full collection of contemporary judgements on the man, no clear picture will emerge at all: every feature emphasized in one is obliterated by another.[3]

Nor does the picture grow clearer when we turn from man to author. It was not by chance that *The Times* never fully approved of Thackeray, and on more than one occasion disapproved pretty strongly; for *The Times*, under the editorship of Delane, became the acknowledged mouthpiece of that stable and self-assured Victorianism which the unstable and self-distrusting Thackeray offended. It was not by chance either that the Rev. Whitwell Elwin, sometime editor of the *Quarterly*, and for a year or two Thackeray's admiring Boswell, thought it a duty, though an irksome one, to defend him against charges of heresy and cynicism.

The cry of 'Cynic' becomes wearisome by iteration in Victorian journals and memoirs. No less wearisome are the attempts, by Elwin, Marzials, and Dr. John Brown of Edinburgh, for example, to rebut the charge. For in nearly all of them we can hear special pleading. Thackeray's partisans are distinctly ill at ease. Deliberately or out of blindness, they evade the issue. It is little use quoting sentimental passages from his writings to persuade us he is no cynic; since what we have a right to complain of is that the sentimental in Thackeray alternated with the satirical. There was no fusion, no reconcilement of the two.

Was the author of *The Book of Snobs* himself a snob, a toady, a tuft-hunter, a Major Pendennis? Here was another question the Victorians endlessly and inconclusively debated.[4] Some said one thing, some another; and it comes as a slight shock to the reader of the present century to learn that even Edward Fitzgerald, one of Thackeray's oldest and closest friends, could not give a firm answer. 'Yes' and 'No' were, of course, both right; for in his social dealings, as in the novels that he wrote, Thackeray remained equivocal. He was not this *or* that *or* the other; he was usually this *and* that *and* the other. He was unintegrated. His personality was scattered, one might almost say dissociated. And since the business of the artist, in the phrase of Coleridge, is to bring 'the whole soul of man' into activity, Thackeray, being scarcely ever in command of a whole soul, could not, despite his insight and his indisputable dexterity with words, produce, except in snatches and fragments, work stamped with that integrity and coherence which we find even in seemingly shapeless novels by Dickens and Hardy, Dostoievsky and Tolstoy. He had great gifts, but they were not co-ordinated, not fused.

No man since the late George Saintsbury has written on Thackeray with more understanding and sympathy than Lord David Cecil in *Early Victorian Novelists*; but even he seems to shoot wide of the mark when he speaks of the author of *Vanity Fair*, *Pendennis*, and *Esmond*—the only works in the canon comparable with, let us say, *David Copperfield*, *The Return of the Native*, *The Idiot*, and *Anna Karenina*—as 'imposing a moral order on experience'.[5] It is surely an overstatement to say that 'Thackeray is the first novelist to do what Tolstoy and Proust were to do more elaborately—use the novel to express a conscious, considered criticism of life . . . to present the reader with a systematic philosophy of human nature.'[6] This critical judgement is open to two serious objections. In the first place it ignores Henry Fielding, who, a century before Thackeray, used the novel 'to present the reader with a systematic philosophy of human nature', and, at any rate in *Tom Jones*, used it very well. In the second place it implies that Thackeray resembled Fielding, Tolstoy, and Proust in having a systematic philosophy of human nature to present. This implication is false. No doubt Thackeray wished to have one. At times also he thought he had. But a systematic philosophy was beyond his powers. He had no sooner stated a conviction than he wanted to insert a question-mark; no sooner taken up an attitude than he wondered if he wasn't being insincere, foolish, or extravagant; no sooner underlined a moral than he cocked a snook at it. Greatly as he admired Fielding, he had little of Fielding's stability of purpose; and in the end all that was left to him was the paralysing thought, 'Vanity of vanities, all is vanity.' Even this moral he had too little resolution to maintain without evasions.

§ 3

Puzzling and uncertain as a man, puzzling and uncertain as an author, Thackeray tempts the biographer. He once tempted Mr. Frank Swinnerton, who, after arguing that criticism could no longer be 'aesthetic' only, but, at best, must become 'psychological' as well, noted that Thackeray offered a very promising subject for the method which he recommended, largely 'because his work is so full of disguised autobiography, and so perplexing in some of its characteristics'.[7] That is the very point. Thackeray as a novelist was beyond reason egocentric; it was only at times that he attained to the 'anonymity' demanded by Mr. E. M. Forster. He allowed his private life to dictate to him when he wrote fiction. He could not push it away far enough to enable him to gain the mastery of his material. The business of the novelist is to reshape experience of the world of fact and embody it in a world of fiction. This, Thackeray could do, but by no means always. He became master of his material only when his personal feelings, prejudices, and ill-sorted articles of faith were in no way engaged. Again and again he allowed himself to be dominated by the actual—by people to whom as a man he had stood closely and emotionally related, by episodes in which, still as a man, he had found himself deeply and emotionally implicated.

This book is not a biography of Thackeray.[8] It might be called the study of a novelist *manqué*. I shall try to show how fact interfered with fiction; or (to put it in another way) how Thackeray the artist failed to overcome Thackeray the man.

II. MOTHER AND SON

It gives the keenest tortures of jealousy and disappointed yearning
to my dearest old mother (who's as beautiful now as ever) that she
can't be all in all to me, mother sister wife everything but it mayn't
be—There's hardly a subject on wh. we don't differ. And she lives
away at Paris with her husband a noble simple old gentleman who
loves nothing but her in the world, and a jealousy after me tears &
rends her. Eh! who is happy? When I was a boy at Larkbeare, I
thought her an Angel & worshipped her. I see but a woman now, O so
tender so loving so cruel. My daughter Anny says O how like Granny
is to Mrs. Pendennis Papa—and Granny is mighty angry that I should
think no better of her than that. (Thackeray to Mary Holmes, 25
February 1852. Ray, iii. 12–13.)

§ 1

It is indisputable that the person who exerted the most
powerful influence on Thackeray, both man and writer,
was his mother. She dominated him all his life, even from
a distance. Though they had sharp disagreements on religion, the upbringing of children, houses, the competence of
physicians, and so on, it is not true that he ever reached
such detachment as to see her but as a woman; the length
and occasional vehemence of his letters to her during a
disagreement point to his emotional dependence on her
even in revolt. She had a far stronger will than he; she had
convictions and was stubborn; she suffered tortures of
jealousy when he turned to some other woman for com-
panionship; she never let go of him until his death; and
only then—the fact is significant—did she mellow into
some degree of toleration of the religious and other heresies
that his children had acquired under his tuition. For years
Anny and Minny Thackeray had 'terrible religious discus-

sions' with their grandmother, and used to feel positively
ill in consequence. But a year after her father's death,
Anny notes in her diary: 'I went for a little walk with
Grannie, she said she had changed her mind about many
things, especially about religious things, and that she
could now sympathise far more than she had done, with
what my father used to think and say.'[1]

Old habits do not usually cease to operate suddenly. For
years the old lady had clung stubbornly to power by en-
gaging her wayward son in a struggle for the immortal
souls of his daughters.

§ 2

We know a good deal, from Thackeray's letters and the
memoirs of Lady Ritchie, about the Mrs. Carmichael-
Smyth of mid-century, that gracious, tall, handsome,
strong-willed matron in Paris, who had once been Mrs.
Richmond Thackeray in Calcutta, and before that, Anne
Becher, a reigning beauty. We know less (though perhaps
enough) about the same woman in her early years.

Though the Bechers were traditionally a naval family,
Anne's father had spent twenty-one years in the service of
the East India Company when he died in Calcutta in the
year 1800. Some years before that, his wife had caused
a scandal by eloping with a Colonel Butler, whom she
married as soon as her husband's death made it possible.
Like other Anglo-Indian children, Anne was sent back to
England while still very young, being entrusted for her
upbringing to her paternal grandmother, who 'lived for
scores and scores of years in a dear little old Hampshire
town [Fareham] inhabited by the wives, widows, daughters
of Navy captains, admirals, lieutenants'—a town very like
those in the Jane Austen novels.[2] Besides the grandmother
(an imperious old lady if ever there was one) the Fareham
house contained the original of Martha Honeyman in
The Newcomes—Aunt Becher, whom her mother always
addressed as 'Miss Becher' and presumably despised as a
hopeless old maid. Life there seems to have been made up

of tea parties, naval gossip, netting silk-purses, and the straitest Evangelical proprieties.

But even at the age of fifteen Anne had a will of her own. During a visit to Bath she met, danced with, and fell in love with Henry Carmichael-Smyth, an ensign in the Bengal Engineers who had already distinguished himself in battle. Unfortunately, though he came of good family, he had no fortune, and Mrs. Becher decided, once and for all, that her granddaughter must have nothing more to do with him. Anne had other views. Though whisked away to Fareham and kept a close prisoner in the house there, she continued a clandestine correspondence with her ensign, and might have followed in her mother's footsteps and eloped with him had her Evangelical grandmother not substituted flat lies for exhortations and threats. Henry Carmichael-Smyth was bluntly told that Anne no longer cared for him and had requested the family to return his letters, unopened; as for Anne, she was told that her lover had been carried off by a sudden fever. So ended (Mrs. Becher thought) a romantic folly.

But the effect on Anne's health was disastrous, and not long after she was shipped off to Calcutta, where there were plenty of young and eligible civilians to assist her recovery. It appears that she became a toast there at once.

Among these eligible civilians was an elegant Etonian, very tall and slim, uncommonly handsome, a Corinthian in appearance and habits, delighting in parties and good living, able to make a few gentlemanly flourishes as an amateur in painting, with a cultivated taste in horses, *objets d'art*, engravings, and saloon organs, and nevertheless with very good prospects of rising in the service to the highest posts. His name was Richmond Thackeray. He had a Hindu mistress, of course; but then so had all the other young men in Calcutta; and Anne, herself an Anglo-Indian by birth, was not likely to be troubled much on that score. Richmond Thackeray snapped her up from under the noses of eager rivals, and they were married in the Old Cathedral on 13 October 1810.

The first and only child of the marriage, the novelist-to-be, was born on 18 July 1811, and received the names of his paternal grandfather, William Makepeace, who had been famous in his day as 'the elephant-hunter of Sylhet'. A few months later Richmond Thackeray got further promotion in the service, being appointed Collector in the district lying round the capital—always regarded as a 'plum' by the younger civilians. He and his wife and child moved into the official residence at Alipur.

It was to this house that Richmond Thackeray one evening brought back to dinner a captain of the Bengal Engineers whom he had just met at the Club and taken a fancy to: an episode as dramatic as any the infant then in his cradle could have wished for later, when he gave his mind to prose fiction. Taken completely off their guard, Henry Carmichael-Smyth and Anne Thackeray did not attempt for long to conceal the past from Richmond. It seems to have been a pretty severe shock to him.

§ 3

Richmond Thackeray died on 13 September 1815, when his son was just over four years of age. The consequences for the child were serious. Had the father lived, and taken his share in the upbringing of William Makepeace the younger, it is probable that the boy would have grown up less sensitive, less self-distrusting, less woman-ridden; what he might have lost in sensibility, he would almost certainly have gained in sense. Being without a father from the age of four, he became too dependent on his mother.

And, contrary to all probability, this dependence was in fact aggravated by his separation from her when, at the age of six, he was sent home to England. Perhaps, like young Clive Newcome when he parted from his father, 'he was at play with a dozen of other children on the sunny deck of the ship' half an hour after she had weighed anchor. One suspects not, however. He felt the separation keenly. The memory of it stayed with him, hardening into a fixed attitude of mind.

As a man he betrayed an excessive, almost a pathological antipathy to saying good-bye. On both occasions when he left England for America it cost him bitter pangs to part from his daughters, and even to say farewell to friends that he seldom met, like Fitzgerald;[3] and on both occasions when he left America for England, he slipped away unawares to avoid the discomfort of saying farewell to friends whom he had known but a month or two. The process of saying good-bye, he confessed, was horrible to him.

Both *The Newcomes* and the *Roundabouts* handle this topic in a manner that betrays the survival into middle age of a childish attitude. After recounting the departure of Colonel Newcome for India, Thackeray bursts out: 'Ah, pangs of hearts torn asunder, passionate regrets, cruel, cruel partings! . . .'[4] Still more significant is the passage in the *Roundabout* entitled 'On Letts's Diary':

In one of the stories by the present writer, a man is described tottering 'up the steps of the ghaut', having just parted with his child, whom he is despatching to England from India. I wrote this, remembering in long long distant days, such a ghaut, or river stair, at Calcutta; and a day when, down those steps, to a boat which was in waiting, came two children, whose mothers remained on the shore.[5]

The two children, of course, were William Makepeace Thackeray and his cousin, Richmond Shakespear. What is more important for our present purposes is to note the exaggeration, the stridency, in the writing, as soon as Thackeray surrenders himself to a heavily loaded memory of this kind. One of the surest signs of it always is the repetition of an adjective—'cruel, cruel partings', 'long long distant days'. Another is exaggeration in the description of an action: the bereaved father 'totters' up the steps. We shall see other examples of the same kind of false writing later.

Possibly the mere parting from his mother would not have produced the effect it did on the child Thackeray, had his life for a year or two after arriving in England been less unhappy. Loneliness, frustration, and actual bullying

11

drove him in upon himself, and so riveted his devotion to
the distant mother. From the age of six to the age of ten
he seems to have missed her with all the acuteness and
concentration of feeling possible only in a child who is re-
buffed by circumstance and ignored or roughly handled by
the grown-ups around him. He built up an image of her in
his mind, and turned to it persistently, as to a refuge. He
prayed that he might dream of her at night; and he lived
more and more in the dream by day. The image possessed
and frustrated him; it delayed the normal, healthy pro-
cesses of adjustment to a changing world, and it thereby
intensified the misery that he was trying to escape from.
Compensations do not always compensate.

Of the rough handling he received at school more will be
told later. For the present, a word or two must be said
about the relatives that he was sent to.

Both his Thackeray grandparents, who had retired from
India as early as 1776, and ten years later had settled on a
small but charming estate at Hadley Green in Middlesex,
were now dead. Peter Moore, Lord of the Manor at Hadley
Green and a bustling Whig politician who was then riding
for a financial crash, had been named by Richmond
Thackeray in his will as one of the guardians of his son;
but there is nothing to show that Peter Moore ever gave
the child a thought. It fell to Richmond Thackeray's
favourite sister, Mrs. Ritchie, to receive young William
Makepeace when he first set foot in England. And this at
least she did with sympathy and understanding.

Thackeray, in whose writings we may find many a
savage thrust at 'a man's relations', always exempted
Aunt Ritchie from his diatribes. She remained for him the
perfect aunt: gracious, overflowing with kindness, fun, and
laughter, always tolerant and easy-going. 'I think', he
once wrote to her daughter Charlotte, 'that Southampton
Row [where the Ritchies were living in 1817] was the only
part of my youth that was decently cheerful. All the rest
strikes me to have been as glum as an English Sunday.'[6]
Unfortunately, Uncle Ritchie, who may well have given

12

the novelist suggestions for the character of Mr. Sedley in *Vanity Fair*, was already losing money in his business, and rumours of his troubles were already ascending from the counting-house on the ground floor to the parlour and the drawing-room above. With the best heart in the world, Aunt Ritchie could not do as much for her brother's rather forlorn little son as she would have liked to.

Her brother-in-law, a crochety lawyer named Langslow, handled some of the business arrangements needed for placing young William Makepeace in his various schools. In later years Thackeray did what he could for this uncle-in-law of his, who had fallen on evil days; but in the years 1817–21 it does not seem as if he found the man sympathetic.

As for Great-Grandmamma Becher, to whose house in Fareham he was soon dispatched from Bloomsbury, she had now reached the age of seventy-seven, but had lost nothing of her imperial manner. The mature Thackeray of the *Roundabouts* recalled her as 'a most lovely and picturesque old lady, with a long tortoiseshell cane, with a little puff, or *tour*, of snow-white (or was it powdered?) hair under her cap, with the prettiest little black-velvet slippers and high heels you ever saw'. She took snuff from an old gold snuff-box.[7] Her house stood in the middle of the town, and contained a low-pitched parlour, a shallow, carved staircase made fragrant with pot-pourri in a large blue jar, and a high roof, with dormer windows. Outside was a garden full of flowers.

It all looks very picturesque and charming—as seen through the eyes of the elderly Thackeray, casting back in memory through forty-odd years. One wonders how a timid and restless little boy fitted into this setting. Great-Grandmamma Becher had grown up in the naval traditions of the eighteenth century: 'she had a grandson, a lieutenant in the Navy; son of her son, a captain in the Navy; grandson of her husband, a captain in the Navy';[8] and no one will pretend that discipline in the Navy was particularly gentle to the young. Besides, Great-Grandmamma Becher ought to have been troubled in conscience.

She had lied like a diplomat in order to protect 'Miss Nancy' from a penniless adventurer. Not only had she failed; for Mrs. Thackeray was now on the point of marrying the adventurer in Calcutta. Great-Grandmamma had also been exposed as a cruel liar; which was much more galling. Somehow, I do not think I should have enjoyed being her great-grandson if, at the age of six or seven, I had carried gouts of mud into her trim parlour on my boots.

§ 4

Three years dragged by somehow for the child Thackeray, and in 1821 his mother, now Mrs. Carmichael-Smyth, returned to England with her husband. The reunion between the handsome, dignified lady of twenty-eight and the timid, withdrawn little boy of ten proved affecting, and, in her own description of it, most revealing.

He was not at Chatham when we arrived, but Mr. Langslow brought him from Chiswick the next morning. . . . He had a perfect recollection of me; he could not speak, but kissed me and looked at me again and again. I could almost have said, 'Lord, now lettest thou thy servant depart in peace, for mine eyes have seen thy salvation'.[9]

Mrs. Carmichael-Smyth struck the very note with the biblical quotation. For her, the incident came near to being a religious ceremony; for the child, it was that precisely. His dream image had descended from on high; his dream mother had been made flesh.

For the rest of his life Thackeray was never separated from his mother for a longer period than a year, and wherever she might be—in the same house with him, a few streets away, across the English Channel, or even across the Atlantic Ocean—and whether he was conscious of her influence or not, he remained subject to it. She was always present; if not in person, then as an image, a tutelary spirit, sometimes sharp in outline, sometimes blurred, nearly always powerful.

§ 5

The tutelary spirit was active, controlling his pen, when

he related how Arthur Pendennis, summoned home from
school on his father's death, met his mother in the silent,
darkened house at Fairoaks.

What passed between that lady and the boy is not of import.
A veil should be drawn over those sacred emotions of love and
grief. The Maternal passion is a sacred mystery to me. What
one sees symbolized in the Roman churches in the image of the
Virgin Mother with a bosom bleeding with love, I think one
may witness (and admire the Almighty bounty for) every day.[10]

As a piece of emotive writing, this passage is not likely
to find favour now, though it may have moved many of
the readers it was meant for. When Thackeray wrote it, the
artist in him had been overwhelmed by a bewildered,
adolescent worshipper confronted with a mystery too sacred
to be looked into or recorded. He had been false to his craft;
for what, in the name of heaven, is a writer for, but to
attempt the expression of mysteries through language?

It is a test passage, but there are many others like it in
Pendennis. Thackeray never denied that he had drawn
Helen from his mother; indeed, he rather boasted of it.
As a result of taking his mother for the model, he has a way
of stumbling out of the world of fiction, where the writer
must remain master of his scene, into the world of life,
where the writer may be only a forlorn and bewildered
child. When he decided that Helen must die, everything
began to go awry. There was no good reason in the novel
why death should come to Helen; and indeed, on one
occasion later, Thackeray forgot that he had killed her,
and in *Philip* (written many years afterwards) spoke of her
as still alive after the marriage of Arthur and Laura. But
on reaching Chapter LVII of *Pendennis* the thirty-nine-
year-old man was again overcome by childish sentiment,
and began luxuriating, as a day-dreaming child will, in a
delicious, self-imposed form of torture. His real mother (not
Helen Pendennis, though he regularly got the two mixed
up) was to die, he fancied; and he, wretched child, would
be left alone in a terrifying world. Sham, day-dreaming
grief led to sham writing:

He led her, tottering [another totterer, to be sure], into her room, and closed the door, as the three touched spectators of the reconciliation looked on in pleased silence. Ever after, ever after [repetition again], the tender accents of that voice faltering sweetly at his ear—the look of the sacred eyes beaming with an affection unutterable—the quiver of the fond lips smiling mournfully—were remembered by the young man. . . .[11]

It would be almost an outrage on the author to continue the quotation farther.

Do not let us try to account for such maudlin stuff by the fashion of the day. That other contemporary writers, led by Charles Dickens, wrote in the same manner is beyond question. But Thackeray knew better. For years he had been pouring ridicule on the mawkish, the namby-pamby, the counterfeit-sentimental. No doubt he surrendered more and more to the fashion as he grew in popularity; no doubt his artistic conscience dulled as the money (which he badly needed) poured in fast and faster; no doubt there is more fustian in *The Virginians* and *Philip* than in *Vanity Fair, Pendennis,* and *Esmond.* But none of this explains his uncontrolled mawkishness when 'Mother and Child' becomes his theme. He cannot discuss Alexander Pope and his mother without false sentiment.[12] Amelia Osborne and young George in *Vanity Fair* drive him into rhapsodies on the 'blind, beautiful devotions which only women's hearts know'.[13] Let a painter take a young mother as his subject, and Thackeray's judgement pitifully fails him. He comes upon a picture by Decaisne entitled *Guardian Angel,* and after admitting that its colouring is not good, goes on: 'A little child and a nurse are asleep: an angel watches the infant. You see women look very wistfully at this sweet picture; and what triumph would a painter have more?'[14] It is difficult to believe that this, from the author of 'Strictures on Pictures' and many another swashbuckling attack on the popular painters of his day, is not meant to be ironical. That it is not seems certain when we recall the absurd sentiments put into the mouth of his successful painter, J. J. Ridley, in *Philip,* as soon as J. J. begins to paint Charlotte Firmin and her baby. J. J. is an obvious wish-fulfilment. He is not intended for a fool.

§ 6

When Pendennis at the age of sixteen left Grey Friars, he continued a few months at Fairoaks in the West Country, studying Greek and mathematics with the local curate, reading Shakespeare and *The Christian Year* to his mother, and Byron, Pope, and Moore to himself, writing short melancholy poems for the *County Chronicle*, riding to hounds on his mare Rebecca, undertaking a little mild electioneering in the Tory interest, and, most important episode of all, losing his heart to Milly Costigan, better known as the Fotheringay, of the Theatre Royal, Chatteris. And so the time passed till he went up to Oxbridge. When Thackeray at the same early age left the Charterhouse, he continued eight months at Larkbeare, in Devonshire, studying mathematics with his stepfather, and writing for the *Western Luminary*, published at Exeter, at least one poem on a political topic.[15] And so the time passed till he went up to Cambridge.

What else Thackeray did in the interval between school and university is uncertain. There is no evidence good enough to support Merivale's belief that he fell in love with a Fotheringay. That he had a mild love affair with his cousin, Mary Graham, is probable enough. But of that, later.

Saintsbury, who in general doubts the propriety of arguing from Thackeray's books to events in Thackeray's life, is willing to accept Pen's reading of *The Christian Year* to his mother as a fragment from the author's biography. Nothing is more probable. This vade-mecum of devout Victorians had appeared in 1827, only a year before Thackeray was removed from the Charterhouse. We know, too, that by this time Mrs. Carmichael-Smyth had turned more than usually devout, inclining to the stricter forms of Evangelicalism; and since we learn from *Pendennis* that the principal occupations of her counterpart in the novel were 'to love and to pray', we may reasonably infer that this represents yet another memory of Larkbeare, rather than an invention for Fairoaks. Indeed, we have other evidence. In a letter Thackeray wrote to his daughter Anny when she was fifteen, at a time when she was having somewhat painful arguments with her grandmother on religion, he told her: 'When I was of your age I was accustomed to hear and read a great deal of the Evangelical (so called) doctrine and got an extreme distaste for that sort of composition—for Newton, for Scott, for the preachers I heard & the prayer-meetings I attended.'[16]

Thackeray's attitude to religion proved to be hardly less ambiguous than his attitude to other matters commonly disputed. Unlike many another youngster who had been brought up under the Evangelical discipline, he did not swing away afterwards to the opposite extreme: he did not utterly reject his early teaching; he became neither Puseyite nor thorough sceptic. As his custom was, when confronted with a vexatious choice, he was prepared to alternate and temporize. The narrowness and austerity of Evangelicalism repelled him; for he believed very heartily in the pleasures of life, and accepted with gusto nearly anything that came his way. Hence what appears to be pointed dislike of the Evangelicals—Lady Southdown and her daughter Emily in *Vanity Fair*, the Simcoes in *Pendennis*, and the Clapham Sect in general in *The Newcomes*. But this dislike is hesitant and temperate in comparison with Dickens's, for example: nowhere does it issue in a Stiggins or a Chadband. What is more important, the cult of duty, which has been rightly called the central power of Evangelicalism in the nineteenth century, took such a hold upon him in his early years that he never afterwards escaped from it completely. He might flout it, being careless, dilatory, fond of good wine and rich food, and extravagant with money; but he never questioned its authority. Though he rejected the doctrines of Puritanism, he remained all his life something of a Puritan at heart.

§ 7

This comes out clearly when, in the course of a story, he is forced to touch on sexual passion. Once again he vacillates. His occasional grumbles over the prudery of his time are familiar. Never since the time of Fielding and *Tom Jones*, he complains in the preface to *Pendennis*, has an English novelist 'been permitted to depict to his utmost a MAN'; readers will not hear 'what moves in the real world, what passes in society, in the clubs, colleges, and messrooms—what is the life and talk' of their sons. He implies here that, but for the restrictions imposed upon him by his public, he would have written Pen's history as frankly and fully as the robust Fielding wrote Tom's. This echoes a passage in *Vanity Fair* in which, after remarking that 'a polite public will no more bear to read an authentic description of vice than a truly-refined English or American female will permit the word *breeches* to be pronounced in her chaste hearing', he claims to have bowed to the fashion and to have only hinted at the wickedness of Becky Sharp 'in a light, easy and agreeable manner, so that nobody's fine feelings may be offended'.[17] And again (but this time in a private letter to the Perry sisters) he deplores English prudery, which ties his hands and prevents his having what he calls 'fun' in the book that he is planning (*The Newcomes*).[18]

All this may have been sincere enough at the time of writing, though I doubt it. Thackeray, posing as a man of the world to readers and to 'kind female correspondentesses', could be insufferably arch. At other times, his attitude is different. To look for consistency is hopeless; nor are we justified in concluding that he simply gave weak-stomached readers what they could digest, and refrained from giving them the stronger meat that he preferred himself. The truth is that he never really preferred strong meat. He seemed to be almost as squeamish as his public. It is very unlikely that he would ever have made *Pendennis* very different from what it is. Public or no public, he could no more have told the whole truth about a young man's sexual life than he could have crossed the North Atlantic in a winter gale and avoided being sea-sick.[19]

In his novels, he betrayed something very like a phobia about 'irregularities'. 'Wild' his youthful heroes were allowed to be; 'wicked', never. And it is characteristic of him (as of English Puritans in every age) that by 'wickedness' he means fornication and adultery. The 'purity' of his heroes is almost as obtrusive as King Charles's head in the compositions of Mr. Dick. Arthur Pendennis must recoil with horror from the notion of seducing Fanny Bolton, partly, it may be, because many readers of the monthly numbers would have stopped buying them if he had given way to this temptation—some did stop, Thackeray tells us, merely because he honestly admitted that the young man *was* tempted—but principally because the very notion of seduction always drove the author into a kind of panic.[20]

The scruples of Arthur Pendennis may not be incredible, but the scruples of Harry Warrington, the Fortunate Youth of *The Virginians*, are. Harry is allowed to dine, wine, and gamble with Lord March and other well-known pleasure-seekers of the 1750s, but he is presented as being deeply chagrined at the rumour that he has had a love-affair with a stage dancer. The matter is dragged in, quite needlessly, in order to make the point that, drunk or sober, in Virginia or in England, Harry Warrington has remained 'pure'. In fact, all through this book, Thackeray conducts a half-hearted debate with himself on the question, 'Does the obvious change in manners between 1756 and 1856 mean a genuine improvement in morals or only an increase in squeamishness?', and the conclusion that he reaches is that the first is true.

No sensible reader would be much troubled about all this, were it not that Thackeray protests too much. Having a divided and perplexed mind, he must be talking. The words *pure* and *purity* occur so often in his writings that we cannot help remarking them. Then we begin to notice

20

their irrelevance. Goldsmith 'obstinately bore in his breast', not merely a kind heart, but a 'pure kind heart';[21] Lord Kew's mother in *The Newcomes* offered 'pure supplications' for him;[22] when Pen left home for Oxbridge, Helen's 'pure blessings' followed him;[23] 'pure fragrance' is one of the chief qualities of any 'good woman';[24] the portrait of Titania in Leslie's picture is 'gracious, pure and bright';[25] portraits of saints and martyrs have 'pure eyes turned heavenward';[26] and, most absurd of all, Mathilde, in the first of *Love-Songs made Easy*, is alleged to have 'pure feet'—and not, as the ribald might suppose, in jest.[27] Thackeray's repeated emphasis, in *Vanity Fair* upon Amelia's purity, in *Pendennis* upon Helen's and Laura's, in *Esmond* upon Rachel Castlewood's, in *Philip* upon Charlotte's, and indeed, his emphasis on the purity of all 'good' women when he pauses in his narrative to talk about them, is so pointed and ridiculous that we have to ask why. Why can't he take their purity for granted? Nobody has questioned it.

Again, no doubt, the answer must be sought in Mrs. Carmichael-Smyth. Thackeray protests too often and too loudly about 'purity' because he is still on edge about it, and he is in this state because, emotionally, he is still little better than adolescent: his mother, by 'possessing' him, has arrested his emotional growth, and at forty he is still almost as firmly tied to her as he was at fourteen. The clue is to be found in what he says of Helen Pendennis. 'To love and to pray' were her main occupations. Had the emphasis fallen only on the praying, Pen's attitudes might have proved different when he grew to manhood. Boys have a way of recovering from the religiosity of their mothers. But Helen bound him to her by a great deal more than prayers and preaching; by her possessiveness she planted his standards for him so firmly that he could not shift them afterwards even if he wished to. So, I believe, did the case stand with Thackeray as well. Whenever in his later life he found himself drifting very far in conduct or in thought from the sexual standards that had been established for him by the gracious (but intolerably rigid) mother that he worshipped as a child, the memory of her pulled him back again. His head may have told him one thing, but his heart, still that of an unemancipated adolescent, told him another. Hence the falsity and at times puerility of his writing when his story brought him within sight of sexual 'irregularities'. Hence, too (as I hope to show later), some of the vacillations, extravagances, and futilities of his own abortive love-affair with Jane Brookfield.

§ 8

Evangelicalism suited Mrs. Carmichael-Smyth pretty well. It gave her authority to do exactly what she felt impelled to do—to guard, reprove, guide, and control her affectionate but wayward son. It empowered her to keep watch and ward upon his soul. She had now acquired a divine sanction for possessing him. She was even warranted in being cruel if the safety of his soul required it. And cruel (with paws like velvet and a sanctimonious air) she often was. He knew it as a boy; and his daughters knew it after him.

Priests and women, remarks Harry Esmond parenthetically, are 'tyrants by nature'.[28] One fact had certainly impressed itself firmly on the mind of Thackeray: that 'good' women can be singularly hard. The classic instance is the cruelty of Helen Pendennis to the unhappy little Fanny Bolton. (Writing to Mrs. Brookfield about this, Thackeray remarked: 'My mother would have acted in just such a way if I had run away with a naughty woman—that is I hope she would—though praps she is prouder than I am myself.'[29] Why the 'I hope she would'?) Other instances from the novels are only less striking. The tender-hearted Rachel Castlewood in *Esmond*, when her conscience pricks her, can behave like a sleek panther: she is brutal to Harry and to her own daughter, Beatrix, and she provokes even the infatuated Harry to the comment: 'There are some moments when the tenderest women are cruel, and some triumphs which angels can't forgo.'[30] The same trait

22

is to be seen in her second daughter, Mrs. Esmond-Warrington of *The Virginians*,[31] and in the stout-hearted Mme Duval of the last, unfinished novel. Mme Duval, says Thackeray, 'loved her own way, was jealous of all who came between her and the objects of her love, and no doubt led her subordinates an uncomfortable life'.[32] Once again, it would seem, he was thinking chiefly of his own mother.

The key word is *jealous*. Very daringly, in a novel written for Victorians, Thackeray admits the existence of sexual jealousy in Helen Pendennis when her son is philandering with Blanche Amory. 'I have no doubt', he says, again parenthetically, 'there is a sexual jealousy on the mother's part, and a secret pang.'[33] Later in the same book, during the episode of Fanny Bolton, he elaborates the point:

There is a complaint which neither poppy, nor mandragora, nor all the drowsy syrups of the East could allay, in the men of his time, as we are informed by a popular poet of the days of Elizabeth; and which, when exhibited in women, no medical discoveries or practice subsequent—neither homoeopathy, nor hydropathy, nor mesmerism, nor Dr. Simpson, nor Dr. Locock can cure, and that is—we won't call it jealousy, but rather denominate it rivalry and emulation in ladies.[34]

As it happens, homoeopathy, mesmerism, and hydropathy were all at one time or another fads of the Carmichael-Smyths.

But here again we see the vacillation, or perhaps it would be truer to call it the alternation, of Thackeray. At one moment he is dominated and controlled by his tutelary spirit, his mother; at the next, he is free, and in a flash of humour and unexpected psychological insight, puts his finger on one of the causes of danger in the relations between himself and her. But the two attitudes remain disconnected, dissociated.

§ 9

Thackeray never succeeded in sorting out the muddle in his mind between 'to love' and 'to pray', since both activities were emotionally loaded for him by his tutelary spirit. The failure shows very plainly in the chapter on Jerusalem which he wrote for *From Cornhill to Cairo*. This, by far the best of his travel books, was written up from notes made during his tour of the Mediterranean and Palestine in 1844. In general, it shows a sustained ease and vivacity which Thackeray had not achieved before. Some parts of it, indeed, and especially his account of the voyage through the Ionian Sea, are unsurpassed as examples of his mature, colloquial, well-mannered style. But the chapter on the Holy City is very different from the rest. It is laboured and disjointed.

And no wonder. Thackeray was prevented from writing it as he wished to, by reluctance to hurt his 'dear old Gospel mother'.

'Titmarsh at Jerusalem', said Fitzgerald, when he heard of Thackeray's proposed tour in the Levant, 'will certainly be an era in Christianity.'[35] Doubtless he believed that the tourist would be stirred into ridicule of the shams there. And the tourist was. But Fitzgerald did not allow for another side of the man, the sentimentally religious one, which, perhaps, he had not become aware of very often in their easy-going friendship. Nor did he allow for what was hopelessly entangled with this—Mrs. Carmichael-Smyth.

Jerusalem in 1844, with its jostling Jews, Copts, Arabs, Armenians, Orthodox Christians, Catholic Christians, Protestant Christians, rubbernecks, guides, beggars, and rogues, might be an unholy muddle, but Thackeray brought a muddled mind to it. Unholy in appearance, it yet remained for ever memorable because of its associations with the divine person of Jesus Christ, to whom Thackeray's devotion was at all times emotional, non-rational, rooted in childhood memories, but quite unshakable. This was the aspect of the Holy City that he found it hardest to represent in the book, but, of course, it was the only aspect of the Holy Land that his mother could conceive of. And so, when he wrote of Bethlehem and the Church and Grotto of the Blessed Nativity, he addressed her directly: 'But you, dear M——, without visiting the place, have imagined one far finer; and Bethlehem, where the Holy Child was born, and the angels sang, "Glory to God in the highest, and on earth peace and goodwill towards men", is the most sacred and beautiful spot in the earth to you.'[36]

On the other hand, Jerusalem, as Thackeray saw it, was also the battleground of warring, intriguing, bribing sects, and the stage for 'deceits too open and flagrant', 'inconsistencies and contrivances too monstrous', 'grovelling credulity', 'sanctified grimaces',[37] and all manner of other disgusting by-products of religious fanaticism and ecclesiastical hypocrisy; and all this excited in him that 'pert little satirical monitor' (his own phrase[38]) which had a sharp eye for humbug, and which always threatened to overthrow that other daemon of his, the sentimental comforter. As usual, head and heart remained at variance, and Thackeray, uneasily turning over notes and memories of 'ten days passed in a fever' at Jerusalem,[39] fell under the dominance now of the one and now of the other.

I have only just found time to finish my book [he writes to his mother on 26 July 1845], and am here at an Inn at Chelsea for that purpose: looking out on the river and working away tant bien que mal. But I am gravelled with Jerusalem, not wishing to offend the public by a needless exhibition of heterodoxy: nor daring to be a hypocrite. I have been reading lots of books—Old Testament: Church Histories: Travels and advance but slowly in the labour. I find there was a sect in the early Church who denounced the Old Testament: and get into such a rage myself when reading all that murder and crime wh. the name of the Almighty is blasphemously made to Sanction: that I don't dare to trust myself to write, and put off my work from day to day.[40]

This letter seems to have driven Mrs. Carmichael-Smyth into something like a panic. She replied immediately with what, writing to his cousin, Charlotte Ritchie, he described as 'a letter so full of terror and expostulation. and dread of future consequences for my awful heresy',[41] that he cancelled what he had said about Jerusalem and

began again. But to his mother he was blunter than usual.
No doubt annoyance at having wasted so much 'copy'
found a vent in the surprisingly direct attack he made on
her.

We don't know what orthodoxy is indeed. Your orthodoxy
is not your neighbour's—Your opinion is personal to you as
much as your eyes or your nose or the tone of your voice. . . .
Why be unhappy then about the state of another's opinion? . . .
What right have you to say that I am without God because I
can't believe that God ordered Abraham to kill Isaac or that
he ordered the bears to eat the little children who laughed at
Elisha for being bald. You don't believe it yourself. You fancy
you do: you search out explanations to reconcile these awful
things to your mind—the Belief is gone, directly the explanation is necessary. What did the Saviour mean by searching the
Scriptures?—that a man was to read them to the best of his
own reason or to take his neighbours? What did he do himself
by the Old Testament—he repealed it. . . . Why do I love the
Saviour? (I love and adore the Blessed Character so much that
I don't like to speak of it, and know myself to be such a rascal
that I don't dare)—Because He is all Goodness Truth Purity—
I dislike the Old Testament because it is the very contrary:
because it contains no Gentleness no Humility no forgiveness—
nothing but exclusiveness and pride curses and arrogance . . .
why is my dear old Mother to weep and be unhappy because
my conclusions & her's don't tally? . . . But the Great Intelligence shines far far above all mothers and all sons—the Truth
Absolute is God—And it seems to me hence almost blasphemous: that any blind prejudiced sinful mortal being should
dare to be unhappy about the belief of another; should dare
to say Lo I am right and my brothers must go to damnation—
I Know God and my brother doesn't. And now I'll stop scold-
ing my dearest old Mother about that favourite propensity of
hers to be miserable. God bless all.[42]

§ 10

It is not surprising that Thackeray's friends contradict
one another when they discuss his attitude to religion.
Locker-Lampson,[43] Merivale,[44] and Dr. John Brown[45] all
present him as a man fundamentally religious; Jeaffreson[46]
and others, as the opposite. Among later commentators,

Saintsbury finds his utterances on religion 'rather trying', because the man obviously knew so little about it that he ought at least to have held his tongue;[47] Mr. Ellis dismisses him as 'essentially unreligious';[48] and Elton, with his customary sure judgement, says of him that 'his creed, though orthodox, seems to be little doctrinal; his piety is deep, emotional, and generous; but he has no turn for abstract ideas, and does not trouble about the mental vexations of his time'.[49]

A systematic study of theology would have wearied Thackeray to death. It is evident, nevertheless, that he did follow some of the religious and philosophical controversies of his time with interest, though without any great understanding of them, and certainly without troubling to think matters out to conclusions of his own. On the whole, he tended to sympathize with the heretics and sceptics, but again for emotional rather than intellectual reasons. He praised Clough for throwing up his Fellowship at Oxford on religious scruples,[50] and praised John Stuart Mill for a 'noble' article in the *Westminster Review* which, as it happened, was written not by Mill but by James Martineau.[51] Temperamentally, he was anti-authoritarian, and this tendency was often reinforced by personal dislike of the authorities. After the reference to Mill, which occurs in a letter to Mrs. Brookfield, he continued:

It is time to begin speaking truth I think—Lady Ashburton says not—Our Lord spoke it and was killed for it: and Stephen and Paul who slew Stephen. We shuffle, and compromise, & have Gorham controversies, and say let things go on smoothly, and Jock Campbell writes to ye Mo^r Superior and Milman makes elegant after-dinner speeches at the Mansion House—Humbugs all—I am become very stupid and rabid—Dinner time is come —Such a good dinner truth be hanged let us go to Portland Place.[52]

The conclusion of this passage is characteristic enough. Thackeray might sympathize with the heretics, and privately admit distaste for the Christianity of his day, which he dubbed 'Gothic'; but he was content to praise

27

the martyrs from a safe distance, and under his breath; he was no more prepared to speak out than Macaulay; and the longer he lived the stronger became his consciousness of the pious readers who were buying his novels in order to read them aloud in the family circle. Good dinners must be eaten. He had neither time nor inclination to devote himself to the study of doctrine, and if the only way to be reasonably comfortable in both mind and body was to shuffle and compromise, shuffle and compromise he would, like his friend Lady Ashburton. We need not take too seriously either the outburst to Mrs. Brookfield just quoted—which she bowdlerized when she first printed it— or his simulated anger at himself (in the person of Pendennis) for continuing a Sadducee.[53]

Nevertheless, when it came to his own children, the Sadducee roused himself to do his duty occasionally. It would seem that they got involved pretty often in painful arguments with their grandmother, and, naturally enough, turned to him for support. He generally gave it, even though it led him into sharp conflicts with the imperious old lady.

In so far as Thackeray had a faith at all, it was a simple one, the core of which was devotion to Jesus Christ and the doctrine of love. When he tried to express this in untheological terms, he found himself ringing the changes on three words, *fun*, *truth*, and *love*. Like others before and since, he assumed that everybody knew what the words stood for—a large assumption—and he therefore believed that he was saying something important when, in the last sentence of the 'Snob' papers, he urged *Punch* (in which these papers had appeared) not to forget 'that if Fun is good, Truth is still better, and Love best of all'. He elaborated on this a little in his lecture on 'Charity and Humour'. After referring to a hostile notice of his work in *The Times*, where the reviewer had accused him of being 'a dreary misanthrope' who saw 'only miserable sinners round about him', he went on:

So we are; so is every writer and reader I ever heard of; so was every being who ever trod this earth, save One. I cannot

28

help telling the truth as I view it, and describing what I see. To describe it otherwise than as it seems to me would be falsehood in that calling in which it has pleased Heaven to place me; treason to that conscience which says that men are weak; that truth must be told; that fault must be owned; that pardon must be prayed for; and that love reigns supreme over all.[54]

It was in trying to apply this threefold creed that he fell into difficulties and muddles—like those which beset him when he had to write his chapter on Jerusalem. And the cause of them all was the loving but strong-willed mother, the tutelary spirit of the years 1817–21, whose dominion over his mind he was never able afterwards to break entirely. How far Mrs. Carmichael-Smyth made Thackeray the novelist, it is hard to say. That she did much to mar him is beyond question.

III. SATIRE AND SYMPATHY

Whenever he writes, Mephistopheles stands on his right hand and Raphael on his left; the great doubter and sneerer usually guides the pen, the Angel, noble and gentle, interlines letters of light here and there. (Charlotte Brontë on Thackeray, Shorter, p. 418.)

§ 1

Most readers of the present century greatly prefer the satirical Thackeray, the connoisseur in rascals, the unveiler and chastiser of humbugs, to the sentimental Thackeray, who simpered over Amelia and agonized over the death of Helen Pendennis; and they are apt to assume that the satirist was the true Thackeray and the sentimentalist a regrettable accident. Many of his contemporaries, however, took a different view. James Hannay, who worked with him, insisted that he 'had rather an original tendency towards the soft and lachrymose and sentimentally religious view of life';[1] Brown and Lancaster quoted with approval a writer in *Le Temps* who preferred Thackeray as a satirist to Dryden, Swift, and Pope, and distinguished him from these writers by adding: 'Sa colère . . . n'est au fond que la réaction d'une nature tendre, furieuse d'avoir été désappointée';[2] Brown, too, liked to quote a speech on Thackeray delivered by Lord Neaves in Edinburgh, in the course of which he referred to 'Satire and Sympathy rising in his deepest and highest nature, and rising together, though they each took their several ways';[3] and Arthur Hugh Clough, after travelling in the same ship with Thackeray from Liverpool to Boston, gave it as his opinion: 'Thackeray doesn't sneer; he is really very sentimental; but he sees the

30

silliness sentiment runs into, and so always tempers it by a little banter or ridicule.'[4]

Perhaps the ultimate motive behind all satire is defence. Whether this is true of Dryden as well as Pope, of Fielding as well as Swift, and of Burns as well as Byron, I will leave an open question. I am sure it is true of Thackeray. Charlotte Brontë was mistaken in assigning the right hand to Mephistopheles and the left to Raphael. James Hannay and the writer in *Le Temps* came nearer the truth; for the satire of Thackeray was, at bottom, only the reaction of a sensitive, sentimentally religious nature, furious at having been thwarted.

It all goes back to the six-year-old child, cut off from his mother, and tossed by well-meaning but somewhat indifferent relatives into one savage school after another.

§ 2

The first was the Polygon, at Southampton, where, very young, and strange to England though he was, he had to board. Thackeray never forgot or forgave 'the olivey little blackguard' (Arthur by name) who kept this school, and who starved and caned his small pupils in a manner strongly reminiscent of the amiable Mr. Squeers—at the same time writing fulsome letters to their parents and guardians.[5] 'I can remember George coming and flinging himself down on my bed the first night', Thackeray wrote long afterwards to George's sister, a Shakespear cousin;[6] and twice in *Roundabouts* he vented the indignation he had nursed for some forty years.[7] It is little wonder that he would kneel by his bed at night, and pray to be comforted by a dream of his mother.[8]

The second school, Walpole House, Chiswick Mall, was kept by a relative of Thackeray's, Dr. Turner, and seems to have been an improvement on the first. But the boy disliked it almost equally.

Not that he said so openly. In his first extant letter to his mother, written under the strict eye of his Great-Aunt Becher, he declares that he likes Chiswick; adding a reason

31

that must surely have been hers, not his: 'there are so many good Boys to play with'.[9] So far from enjoying Walpole House, he attempted an escape from it. Slipping out un-observed, he got as far as the junction of Chiswick Mall and the Hammersmith Road; then, frightened by the noise and the traffic, he returned, still unobserved, to the house of bondage. One is almost tempted to regret that he did not get clear away. It would probably have made a difference to his life and to his fiction afterwards. But perhaps, unlike Dickens, he could never have survived had he been then subjected to the brutal education of the London streets.

The responsibility for sending her ten-year-old son to the Charterhouse (then in Smithfield) must remain with Mrs. Carmichael-Smyth, who had returned to England by then. In January 1822 Thackeray stood for the first time in the Headmaster's room, trying to answer the questions barked at him. The results were not encouraging to him or credit-able to the Walpole House that he had just left. Dr. Russell soon dismissed him with, 'Take that boy to the Matron, and make my compliments to the Junior Master and tell him that the boy knows nothing and will just do for the lowest form.' This formed his introduction to the school that for many years after he had quitted it he preferred to call 'the Slaughter House'.

He had reason to be savage. He began his six years as a Carthusian in Mr. Penny's house, which stood in Wilderness Row. There were fifty boys there, who 'had to wash in a leaden trough, under a cistern, with lumps of fat, yellow soap floating about in the ice and water'.[10] Two of these fifty succeeded between them in disfiguring the young Thackeray for life. One, George Stovin Venables, broke his nose in a fight, and another, unnamed, broke it again before it had properly set. This calamity had a greater effect upon Thackeray than most of his biographers have been ready to admit. He could joke about his broken nose in after-life, but if anyone else referred to it pointedly, he was apt to take the joke amiss.

Needless to say, it distressed Mrs. Carmichael-Smyth as

well. She hastily removed her son from the tender super-
vision of the Rev. Edward Penny, and sent him to board
with a Mrs. Boyes in a neighbouring square. Mrs. Boyes
does not seem to have been all angel, but she must have
been some improvement on Mr. Penny, for Thackeray
stayed on with her for the remainder of his time at the
Charterhouse.

Bullying from other boys he certainly endured. The same
Venables who broke his nose the first time speaks of him as
having been 'a pretty, gentle, and rather timid boy';[11] and
Devile's bust, modelled about 1822, confirms the gentleness
and the timidity, though perhaps not the prettiness. He
also suffered from short sight, which prevented him from
playing outdoor games.

It was not, however, the physical hardships and physical
pains that he remembered afterwards most vividly; it was
the stupidity in the teaching and the blundering, coarse-
grained bullying of the masters. Sixteen years after he
escaped from the Slaughter House, he visited Athens for
the first time, and so powerful were his memories of school
that the visit prompted him to a savage pasquinade on the
so-called 'Classical' education he had undergone. This outburst shocked Charles Whibley. He called Thackeray a
'mutinous Cockney'.[12] It might have been fairer to call him
a 'mutinous and unforgiving schoolboy'. The whole passage (which occurs in *From Cornhill to Cairo*), with its
reference to 'ten years' banishment of infernal misery,
tyranny, annoyance' at a public school under 'vulgar bullies', is more significant than its bantering tone suggests.[13]

The chief of the vulgar bullies must have been Dr. Russell himself, whose translation from life into fiction in the
early pages of *Pendennis* is a good deal less vicious than it
might have been. It is evident from Thackeray's own
letters, written while he was still at school, that the invented harangue in the novel, being softened by humour,
fell short in brutality of the actual harangues that he suffered from many years before. Russell, indeed, came near
to destroying the Charterhouse; and in the end the Board

of Governors had to request his resignation. It must be recorded, as among his errors, that he drove Thackeray out of the school before the age of seventeen, with only verbal memories of Horace, a profound distaste for the Greek poets and historians, a bitter hatred of the public-school system, and a strong tendency himself to find victims to be bullied in their turn.

The persecuted turned persecutor is a familiar figure; and though Thackeray cannot be exonerated for his brutality to Bulwer and others, or his occasional vindictiveness when someone less well established in the literary world ('Deady' Keene and Edmund Yates are the outstanding examples) attacked him in the Press, it has to be admitted that one cause of this brutality is to be found in his own sufferings under 'vulgar bullies' at school. He had old scores to pay off; he had been a victim too long; and he revenged himself when the occasion served. Once he had the power that had been denied him earlier, he used it. It was not admirable conduct. It was the sort of conduct, all the same, to be expected from a rather timid, sensitive, and uncertain creature with a grudge.

Remember your own young days at school, my friend [he wrote in a *Roundabout*], the tingling cheeks, burning ears, bursting heart, and passion of desperate tears, with which you looked up, after having performed some blunder, whilst the Doctor held you to public scorn before the class, and cracked his great clumsy jokes upon you—helpless and a prisoner! Better the block itself, and the lictors, with their fasces of birch-twigs, than the maddening torture of those jokes.[14]

And yet, the maddening torture of jokes was precisely what he employed himself when he got the chance to hit back at the savage world.

§ 3

The ambagious Mr. Batchelor, in *Lovel the Widower*, relates how, when he first came upon the town, he was cozened like Moses Primrose; only, it was not a gross of green spectacles he bought, but a commodity equally unprofitable, namely, 'that neat little literary paper, the *Museum*'. His cozeners were the Rev. Charles Honeyman and a wine-merchant named Sherrick, both of whom had figured in *The Newcomes.*

I dare say I gave myself airs as editor of that confounded *Museum*, and proposed to educate the public taste, to diffuse morality and sound literature throughout the nation, and to pocket a liberal salary in return for my services. I dare say I printed my own sonnets, my own tragedy, my own verses. . . . I dare say I wrote satirical articles, in which I piqued myself upon the fineness of my wit, and criticisms, got up for the nonce out of encyclopaedias and biographical dictionaries; so that I would be actually astounded at my own knowledge. I dare say I made a gaby of myself to the world: pray, my good friend, hast thou never done likewise?[15]

This must come pretty close to the actual events in the year 1833. For the *Museum* read the *National Standard and Journal of Literature, Science, Music, Theatricals, and the Fine Arts*, a weekly; and for Honeyman and Sherrick read F. W. N. Bayley, a journalist, and one or two rather shady characters who are not named. Thackeray and his stepfather bought the paper, and Thackeray took over the editorship in May, announcing his arrival with a pun in doubtful taste: 'We have got free of the Old Bailey, and changed the Governor.'

Journalism in the 1830s was a rough-and-tumble business, still doubtfully becoming to a gentleman (which Thackeray assumed himself to be). Not a few of its practitioners were, at best, pretty shabby Bohemians, and, at worst, thoroughly dishonest; for it was not until later that the Victorian Code deodorized the traditions of eighteenth-century Grub Street. Thackeray knew his men when, in *Pendennis*, he portrayed London journalists as he had seen them in the thirties. There were honest men among them, certainly, but a good many pretty sorry rogues as well.

Honest or not, they had no tradition of restraint. Some of them who lived on into the respectable sixties looked back on the vivacious thirties with regret. James Hannay was one of these. So far from deploring 'a Bohemian

35

gaiety and riotousness of ridicule' that pervaded the magazines of those days, he maintained that the satire, for all its
ferocious air, laid about it 'with less essential malignity'
than later in the century.[16] Readers of *Pendennis* will recall
how the 'smashers' of the rival newspapers, the *Dawn* and
the *Day*, blazed away at each other with the greatest gusto
but remained good friends in private, and, indeed, sometimes composed their most scurrilous articles after a friendly
collaboration over a dish of kidneys and a glass of stout.
This was no wild exaggeration. Smashing articles had become a sort of game, with ill-defined rules, but with a
general understanding that immediately the players walked
out of the arena, they would drop hostilities. On the upper
levels of the Press, it is true, there were unwritten laws:
for example, you were expected not to write leading articles
for two rival papers at the same time.[17] On the lower, there
was greater freedom of action, and the William Maginns,
Theodore Hooks, and F. W. N. Bayleys would write simultaneously for both political parties if the pay was good
enough.

Nor were many of the papers mealy-mouthed, never
mind what their standing was. When Macaulay and Sheil
were created Privy Councillors, the upper-middle-class
Times exploded: 'These men Privy Councillors! These men
petted at Windsor Castle! Faugh! Why, they are hardly
fit to fill up the vacancies that have occurred by the
lamented death of her Majesty's two favourite monkeys.'[18]
On the other side the *Morning Chronicle* thought nothing
of referring to *The Times* as 'a squirt of filthy water'.[19]

When considering Thackeray, then, as a journalistic
swashbuckler and artilleryman in the years 1833–50, we
must remember that he did what the fashion of the day
allowed, nay, encouraged. He was paid to shoot, and shoot
he did. It was only afterwards, when he became prominent
enough himself to be worth others' shot, that he took to
wondering if the ethics of that sort of warfare was beyond
reproach. He came in the end to regret his 'militating'. At
any rate, he said so. But these regrets, too, coincided with

a change of fashion. By 1860, the review that scarified an author was no longer quite respectable.

§ 4

The early swashbuckling of the *National Standard* is of no account. We pass from ephemeral journalism to at least the fringes of permanent literature five years later, when we come to the 'Yellowplush Papers' in *Fraser's Magazine*.

Charles James Yellowplush's first victims, John Henry Skelton and Dr. Dionysius Lardner, may be passed over too. Thackeray had his fun with them, but the fun was good-natured on the whole, and there was nothing specially interesting or Thackerayan about it. Good nature was *not* evident in the treatment given to the chief victim in this series of articles—the novelist, Sir Edward George Earle Lytton Bulwer, Bt., otherwise known as 'Sawedwadgeorgearllittnbulwig'.[20] Him, Thackeray baited without mercy.

It all began when Thackeray reviewed Bulwer's *Ernest Maltravers* in January 1838. At this time—or so he asserted many years later—the reviewer had seen Bulwer only once, and then in public, and 'had no sort of personal dislike' for him. But he could not stomach the popular novelist's 'sentiments', 'big words', and 'premeditated fine writing'.[21] Consequently, when he hit, he hit hard. Bulwer's genius, he said, is for the 'low', though he will believe that he has gifts for the 'sublime'; Bulwer 'prates'; he is a sort of Beau Tibbs; if he indulges himself much longer in politics and Plato, the 'natural' will disappear altogether from his writings. To sum up: 'Mr. Bulwer's philosophy is like a French palace— it is tawdry, showy, splendid; but *gare aux nez sensibles*! ONE IS ALWAYS REMINDED OF THE SEWER.'[22]

This is offensive, to be sure. Yet we cannot say that it is more offensive than was common in the journals of the time; nor does it appear more brutal than the bludgeoning that Thackeray gave in the same article to Mrs. Trollope for her *Vicar of Wrexhill*.

When he returns to the attack under the mask of

Yellowplush the footman, Thackeray derides Bulwer for
cant, humbug, careless writing, and excessive vanity. In
'Mr. Yellowplush's Ajew', Bulwer himself is given the task of
dissuading the footman from turning author, and the words
in which he does it are a remarkably clever parody of his
style at its most pretentious. In 'Epistles to the Literati'
(January 1840), it is Yellowplush who takes the floor,
rating Bulwer, not only for writing a poor play (*The Sea
Captain*), but also for publishing it when he openly admitted that it *was* a poor play.

> The play *is* bad—your right—a wuss I never see or read. But
> why kneed *you* say so? If it was so *very* bad, why publish it?
> *Because you wish to serve the drama!* O fie! Don't lay that flatter-
> ing function to your sole as Milton observes. . . . You wrote it
> for money—money from the maniger, money from the book-
> seller—for the same reason that I write this. Sir, Shakespeare
> wrote for the very same reasons, and I never heard that he
> bragged about serving the drama. Away with this canting about
> great motifs![23]

Bulwer, the footman continues, suffers from the 'diddlu-
sion' that he is an important public figure; yet what he
writes is often sheer nonsense. The lines—

> Girl, beware,
> The love that trifles round the charms it gilds
> Oft ruins while it shines,

may be repeated 'backards, forards, and in all sorts of
trancepositions', such as—

> The love that ruins round the charms it shines,
> Gilds while it trifles oft;

and these 'trancepositions' are all 'as sensible as the fust
passidge'. Then Yellowplush yields the floor to his friend
and fellow footman, John Thomas Smith, who sums up the
objections to Bulwer as 'a careless habit of writing, and a
peevish vanity which causes him to shut his eyes to his
faults'.[24]

All this occurred more than a hundred years ago, and
to-day no one will deny that Thackeray had grounds for

disparaging Bulwer—who was a dandy and a fop, excessively vain and sensitive to criticism, apt to believe himself the victim of persecution, and, as a writer, often tawdry, pretentious, and verbose. Mr. Michael Sadleir has made out the best case he can for Bulwer, but even he has to admit:

> Indeed, taken in bulk and at his worst, [Bulwer] is so rich a mine of the faults and many of the actual phrases common to the baser journalism of to-day that 'Bulwerese' might with advantage have had a general article in *Modern English Usage*, so expressive and so valuable would be a cautionary list of his excesses.[25]

This, however, leaves several questions still open. Granted that Bulwer's literary errors were deserving of censure, did they justify the virulence of Thackeray's attacks? Were the critic's motives all literary, or at least moral? Was there no animus against Bulwer as a person, or as a successful novelist and a public figure? Was the humbug all on Bulwer's side?

Faced with these questions, Mr. Sadleir does not hesitate. He calls Thackeray a 'hypocrite', 'a snob who worked anti-snobbery to death'; finds 'moral inconsistency' both in his reviewing of novels and in his criticism of painting; roundly accuses him of treating several of his fellow authors shabbily; and, as to Bulwer, concludes that Thackeray treated him viciously as long as he believed that it would pay to do so, and then, seeing that his victim could not be dislodged either from public esteem or from the friendship of certain people whom Thackeray himself wished to stand well with, apologized insincerely, positively cringing to the man whom he had previously attacked with unwarranted venom. Further, Mr. Sadleir believes that it was Maginn, then editor of *Fraser's*, who prompted these venomous attacks, and that Thackeray did not pause to consider who was right and who wrong in this rather dirty quarrel.[26]

It is a damning indictment. Nor does it lack evidence to support it. *Fraser's* had long ago singled out Bulwer as an author to be baited. The game had been going on since April 1830, and when Thackeray first took a hand in it, he conformed very closely to the rules laid down by his predecessors, chief among them the editor himself. It is also unlikely that he did not know the game to be a dirty one; it is unbelievable that he was ignorant of the current gossip—that Bulwer had thwarted Maginn in an attempt to seduce Letitia Elizabeth Landon, and that Maginn was furious at this interference. Thackeray was no longer the greenhorn who had worshipped Maginn in 1832. By 1838 he must have known his Maginn pretty well. He would have done better, undoubtedly, to ask himself what the devil he was doing in *this* galley. It is no use protesting that your motives are as pure as pure, if you choose to keep the wrong company.

So far, Mr. Sadleir is right. He goes to the root of the matter also, when he calls attention to certain likenesses between Thackeray and Bulwer. The two men, he says, were so alike that 'a very slight dislocation of their similarity could make the one more odious than if he had been of a wholly different type'.[27] This is an acute judgement. Both men were 'gentlemen'—which is more than could be said of Maginn or many of his associates; both nursed dandiacal affectations and sentimental obsessions; both were too sensitive for a rough world; and both derived their principal obsessions from the same source—domination by a mother in their early years.[28]

It is quite probable that Thackeray, who was desperately poor and fighting hard for recognition between 1835 and 1845, envied Bulwer his success as writer, politician, clubman, and dandy. It would be surprising if he hadn't. But envy alone is not quite sufficient to explain his rancour.

A better explanation is to be found in an irritating half-awareness of the likeness between himself and his victim. Thackeray had it in him to be as sentimental or pretentious as Bulwer, and indeed, when one of his obsessions mastered him, there was little to choose between them. But he had an intermittent gift of humour, which Bulwer lacked. James Hannay says that this gift kept the other tendencies in check. That is putting the matter too simply. There was hardly any fusion of humour and sentiment in Thackeray; satire and sympathy were apt to operate independently. It was a case of 'Pull devil, pull baker'. And so, in flagellating Bulwer, Thackeray was flagellating himself, flagellating those tendencies in himself which he was half-conscious of but could not face openly and deal with rationally. His attitude to Bulwer was throughout ambivalent. Hence its malevolence.

§ 5

A similar ambivalence or instability of attitude spoiled two other early works of Thackeray, *Catherine* and *Barry Lyndon*. The first set out to be a parody of the Newgate School of Fiction, and especially of Harrison Ainsworth's *Jack Sheppard*, which, as novel and play, had beaten all best-selling records since the days of Walter Scott. Once again envy of a successful author who was coining money while Thackeray often could not tell where his next £5 was coming from, may have been another motive at the back of this parody. But I do not think it was the only one.

At the end of Chapter I of *Catherine* Thackeray states his case. He must apologize, he says, for introducing his readers to characters 'so utterly worthless' as the heroine and her associates; he knows what the public likes, and having resolved to be in fashion, has chosen a story out of the *Newgate Calendar*; but this at least he can say on his own behalf, that he proposes to 'follow it out to edification'.

We say, let your rogues in novels act like rogues, and your honest men like honest men; don't let us have any juggling and thimblerigging with virtue and vice, so that, at the end of three volumes, the bewildered reader shall not know which is which; don't let us find ourselves kindling at the generous qualities of thieves, and sympathising with the rascalities of noble hearts.[29]

This is very well. No doubt Thackeray believed that he generally acted on this principle when he wrote his fiction; and certain of his friends and admirers heartily commended him for it. Brown and Lancaster, for example, find 'no topsyturvification, like Madame Sand's, in his moralities'.[31]

41

They must have read his books with most inadequate
spectacles. For in any criticism of life the burden of which
is *Vanitas vanitatum*, topsyturvification in the moralities
is certain; the sharp distinction between right and wrong
that the Victorian Code delighted in just disappears; it is
irrelevant; and the spectator of the panorama comes in the
end to the point of view of Lear—'None does offend, none,
I say, none'. Hence the charge of cynicism levelled at
Thackeray time and time again after he had become famous
enough to be worth the attention of moralists.

The ethical absolutism that he professed at the beginning of *Catherine* did not govern his practice even in that
story. In writing it he might have followed either of two
methods: to tell his tale plainly, as a sort of moral emblem,
interspersing it with sermons and apostrophes for the
simple-minded reader; or, in imitation of Swift, Fielding,
or Voltaire, to tell it with sustained irony, and allow the
reader, if intelligent enough to perceive and understand the
irony, to extract his own moral. What he did was to oscillate between the two, and confuse the whole business.

We have good reason to regard Thackeray as a master
of irony—'that handsome kind of raillery . . . when in a
grave and serious tone we express that to which inwardly
we express no regard or assent'.[30] Even in this very early
work, *Catherine*, he reveals his quality.[31] But the irony is
intermittent. The sustained irony of Swift or Voltaire was
beyond him. He was neither cool enough nor equable
enough. At any moment his sympathy might overflow his
satire, quenching the glow in it, and reducing the embers
to a damp paste. He kept on remembering his early pro-
mise—to follow the story out to 'edification'.

Still worse, he could not help feeling 'a sneaking kindness for his heroine', and indeed for certain of the other
rogues, too; and this was the very error he had roundly
condemned in the work of the Newgate School. Once the
story was finished, he admitted his failure. 'It was not
made disgusting enough', he told his mother,[32] being ap-
prehensive of her censure.

The main defect of *Catherine*—that it lacks 'keeping'—shows again in *Barry Lyndon*, and, indeed, in all the greater novels. It derived from a central weakness in the man himself.

Barry Lyndon is more readable than *Catherine*. Written four years later, it marks a clear advance in the arts of story-telling and satire. Smooth narrative passes before an historical background that is full, accurate, and realized; breaks now and then into eloquence, as in Barry's defence of play, or is brought into sharper focus for a memorable 'discriminated occasion' (to take Henry James's term), like Barry's return to Castle Brady after many wanderings; and is interrupted only here and there, in order that the author may interpolate a short story in the manner of the eighteenth-century novelists. 'A great feat of ventriloquism' is Elton's judgement on the book.[33] That is just. But from time to time the ventriloquist forgets what his business is, forgets that he is using a particular voice, and descends to a voice and manner that are moralistic, sententious, or mawkish.

To succeed completely, *Barry Lyndon* should have begun, continued, and ended as a cool, hard, crystalline performance. Swift or Voltaire might have so fashioned it, and Fielding, though less capable of sustained irony than they, would, one assumes, have accomplished something just as good as his own *Jonathan Wild*. The task was beyond Thackeray. He was too infirm of purpose.

§ 6

For much the same reason, Thackeray was incapable of doing justice to the man Swift. The savage impropriety of his portrait of this great satirist in *The English Humourists* and *Esmond* is notorious, and, when used to throw an oblique light on Thackeray himself, not unimportant.

If you had been his inferior in parts (and that, with a great respect for all persons present, I fear is only too likely), his equal in mere social station, he would have bullied, scorned, and insulted you; if, undeterred by his great reputation, you had met him like a man, he would have quailed before you, and not had the pluck to reply, and gone home, and years after written a foul epigram about you—watched for you in a sewer, and come out to assail you with a coward's blow and a dirty bludgeon. If you had been a lord with a blue riband, who flattered his vanity, or could help his ambition, he would have been the most delightful company in the world. He would have been so manly, so sarcastic, so bright, odd and original, that you might think he had no object in view but the indulgence of his humour, and that he was the most reckless simple creature in the world. How he would have torn your enemies to pieces for you! and made fun of the Opposition! His servility was so boisterous that it looked like independence; he would have done your errands, but with the air of patronising you; and after fighting your battles, masked, in the street or the Press, would have kept on his hat before your wife and daughters in the drawing-room, content to take that sort of pay for his tremendous services as a bravo.[34]

Thackeray makes out the Dean of St. Patrick's to have been a hypocrite in religion, a sceptic who only pretended to believe what he preached. His sermons 'have scarce a Christian characteristic'. His cassock poisons him. 'He goes through life, tearing, like a man possessed with a devil.' Not a word can be said in his favour for his conduct towards Stella and Vanessa. As for the 'moral' of *Gulliver*, it is 'horrible, shameful, unmanly, blasphemous'. 'Giant and great as this man is,' Thackeray concludes, 'I say we should hoot him.'[35]

All this in the lecture. It is no use excusing the lecturer on the ground that he had much less information at hand than we have, a century later. He had quite enough information. But he suppressed facts that were not to his purpose, and distorted others. He had so vicious a bias against Jonathan Swift that he made him out (as James Hannay admitted) 'not a man but a monster'.[36]

The distortion shows up the more plainly by contrast with what Thackeray in the same lecture has to say about the literary qualities of Swift's work. Here, he is excellent.

It is evident that he entertained for Swift the man— who had been in his grave more than a century—

something like the personal hatred that he might have
entertained for a contemporary of his own who had
deeply injured him. This is an attitude of mind that
requires explaining.

Hannay has two explanations. First, he says, Thackeray
repented of his own early 'militating'; secondly, as he did
not cease to be a novelist when he took to lecturing, 'there
were times when the desire to present a striking character
led him away from the soberer task of patient research and
analysis'.[37]

Hannay knew his man. In these two explanations, however, he is groping after something that eludes him. There
is a very simple objection to the first. It is this: Thackeray's
judgement of Swift was formed, not in 1850, when he
might have begun to regret early 'militating' of his own,
but at least eight years earlier, while he was still actively
'militating' in the London Press; for in the first chapter of
The Irish Sketch Book he refers to Swift as 'the scoffer and
giber', 'the fiery politician', 'equally ready with servility
and scorn'. There is also a simple objection to Hannay's
second explanation. It is this: even if true, it explains too
much; since it might apply equally well to the other portraits in *The English Humourists*. It does, of course. The
portraits of Pope and Addison, Steele and Congreve, Fielding, Goldsmith, and Sterne are all novelist's portraits. But
the question that we have to answer is: Why did Thackeray
turn, not merely unjust, but savagely unjust, to Jonathan
Swift rather than to other men of letters of the eighteenth
century?

Saintsbury has the answer: 'Thackeray himself, when
the "Shadow of Vanity" was heaviest on him, felt the
danger of actual misanthropy, and thus revolted from its
victim with a kind of terror.'[38]

Taking our cue from this, we may see in Thackeray's
injustices to Swift the counterpart of his injustices to
Bulwer. Just as he might have become a Bulwer, so he
might have become a Swift. Let us recall the saying of Lord
Neaves quoted earlier: satire and sympathy in Thackeray

'each took their several ways'. That was the whole trouble,
though Lord Neaves meant his saying to be complimentary.
It is by the fusion of the tendencies represented by satire
and sympathy that the great humorists are fashioned—
Cervantes, Shakespeare, Fielding. In Thackeray there was
no fusion. And so, when he surrendered to the one for a
time, he was engaged in fighting the other, in himself, and,
by projection, in whatever other author he was then considering. Hannay, as we saw, insisted that the tendency
'towards the soft and lachrymose and sentimentally religious view of life' was the original one in Thackeray; and
this is almost certainly correct. This was the tendency
buttressed and fortified in him by his mother-worship. Had
his conduct been wholly directed by this tendency, Swift
would have had no terrors for him, Swift would just have
proved incomprehensible. But the other tendency, towards
satire, also directed his conduct as a man and as a writer,
and when he observed it as dominant in Swift, he revolted
from it 'with a kind of terror'. When pulled by the devil, he
hated the baker; when pulled by the baker, he hated the
devil.

The resemblance between Swift and Thackeray did not
escape Thackeray's contemporaries. Once, at the *Punch*
Table, when he was absent, Percival Leigh likened him to
Swift, adding significantly: '[He] despises Vanity Fair, and
despises himself for taking pleasure in it.'[39]

There you have it—the Thackeray of ambivalent attitudes. Both Bulwer and Swift made him acutely uncomfortable because, like a pendulum, he was for ever swinging
between them.

IV. CONSUMPTION OF THE PURSE

In later times, a vulgar national prejudice has chosen to cast a slur upon the character of men of honour engaged in the profession of play. . . . They cry fie now upon men engaged in play; but I should like to know how much more honourable *their* modes of livelihood are than ours. The broker of the Exchange who bulls and bears, and buys and sells, and dabbles with lying loans, and trades on State secrets, what is he but a gamester? . . . A gallant man who sits him down before the baize and challenges all comers, his money against theirs, his fortune against theirs, is proscribed by your modern moral world. It is a conspiracy of the middle classes against gentlemen: it is only the shopkeeper cant which is to go down nowadays. (*Barry Lyndon*, p. 112.)

§ 1

IN a letter of July 1861 to George Smith, the publisher of the *Cornhill*, in which the novel *Philip* was then running as a serial, Thackeray admits the correspondence between his fiction and his life. He says: 'Philip is unfortunately going into poverty and struggle, but this can't be helped; and as he will, *entre nous*, take pretty much the career of W. M. T. in the first years of his ruin and absurdly imprudent marriage, at least the portrait will be faithful.'[1]

The wording is a little odd. Why the word *unfortunately* in the first line? Presumably because some readers of the magazine would prefer the course of true love to run smooth, and the monthly sales might diminish for a time. If so, why couldn't it be helped? Thackeray, as author of the story, could direct its course as he pleased. Or couldn't he? George Smith probably knew his editor well enough by this time to be reconciled to his limitations, the chief of which was his inability, when his feelings were engaged, to depart very far in fiction from the course of events which had happened in his own early life. It was not so much that he lacked powers of invention; it was rather that these powers were circumscribed by his inability to recollect in tranquillity people and events that had deeply stirred his emotions as a man, not an artist. His 'absurdly imprudent marriage' meant Isabella Shawe and Isabella Shawe's mother. These were women between whom and himself he could not interpose the 'aesthetic distance' needed for artistic creation. If he decided to use them for his fiction (as he did more than once), his memories and the old emotions they aroused took charge of him, instead of becoming just material to be reshaped to a new pattern. Anonymity failed almost as completely as it did when he let the image of his mother take possession of his mind.

I shall try to show this in the next chapter. For the present, in order to point a contrast, I shall take events and people associated in memory with the financial 'ruin' to which he also refers in his letter to Smith. One might have expected this, too, to be carrying a load of emotion for him. But his work shows that the contrary is true. His adventures and misadventures with money as a young man made him a better, not a worse, novelist. They did become material for fiction; they did not merely stir him into adolescent day-dreaming.

§ 2

Richmond Thackeray left his son about £20,000, most of it invested in an Indian bank or banks. The trustees, until the son reached the age of twenty-one, were Peter Moore of Hadley Green, who does not seem to have acted at all, and who died in 1828, the Rev. Francis Thackeray, Richmond's brother in England, and Robert Langslow, the lawyer, Richmond's brother-in-law, who left England before his ward reached the age of twenty-one.

The knowledge that in 1832 he would come into a regular income of between £500 and £600 a year, whether he earned anything by his own labour or not, encouraged

William Makepeace Thackeray as a boy in the indolent and easy-going habits that came naturally to him. He grew up in the belief that he would always be comfortable, and with rather lordly views on the value of a guinea. Nor, it would seem, did either his mother or his stepfather, who were both well off themselves, do very much to discountenance these views. His education was being paid for out of the interest on his capital, and if this was not enough, the capital, apparently, could be drawn on also.

It is evident, therefore, that when he went up to Cambridge in February 1829 he did not see any reason why he should stint himself of the pleasures open to him as a 'pensioner' at Trinity College. At this period the University was in pretty poor shape. Many of the dons took their duties very lightly, being less distinguished for scholarship than for after-dinner drinking in the Combination Room; and the undergraduates, unofficially divided into Reading Men, Boating Men, Dandies, Loungers, Varmint Men, and Sporting Men, spent a large portion of their time drinking, fighting pitched battles with the bargees and other snobs of the town, hack riding, playing billiards, gambling, and visiting the districts of Barnwell and New Zealand, where they found plenty of accommodating Cyprians.

When Thackeray went up, he began working with the best of good resolutions. But he found little inspiration in either Whewell, his tutor, or Fawcett, his coach; and, like his hero, Arthur Pendennis, he seems to have drifted pretty soon out of the company of Reading Men, whom he found rather dull, into that of Dandies, whose habits pleased him better; and from the Dandies he descended to the Loungers at last.

This was all quite in character. We may discover the same Thackeray for several years afterwards—always planning optimistically, gaily deceiving himself that as soon as he had made a plan he had almost done the job itself, tiring pretty soon of both plan and job, enjoying himself lightheartedly until a new plan occurred to him, and then, amiable and unashamed, starting on the same pleasant round again.

E   49

What Thackeray did learn at Cambridge was to carry his wine like a gentleman; to play cards and billiards, and to win or lose at these games with a smiling face; to play the host at dinner-parties; to go for long walks and rides in the country; to sketch churches; to fence (but probably very ill); to listen to speeches in the Union and attempt, not with much success, to deliver some himself; to read and discuss poetry and novels; to found an essay club; to tolerate various Thackeray cousins at King's College; to write prose and verse (of no value) for at least two university magazines. Daring opinions on religion, politics, and literature broke through the thin crust of piety which his mother had endeavoured to protect his mind withal.

It was at Cambridge, too, that he started gambling on a fairly big scale. Gambling fascinated him, then and later. It also delivered him, greenhorn that he was, into the hands of two card-sharpers, who, learning that he had an inheritance coming to him, took rooms opposite Trinity College, scraped acquaintance with him, and invited him to dinner. Unlike Pendennis, he had no worldly-wise uncle-major to identify a scamp at sight, and so, having dined, wined, and played écarté with his new-found friends, he returned to Trinity College poorer by some £1,500.

This escapade, together with others of the same sort during visits to Paris (one of which was surreptitious), proved too much for Thackeray's guardians. The debts of honour were paid out of the estate no doubt, but the culprit, who had made no sort of showing academically at the University, was removed, and in the autumn of 1830 dispatched to Germany to acquire the language. He remained about a year in Weimar.

Either because he had got a fright or because there were few opportunities for gambling in the little grand-ducal town, Thackeray took a greater interest there in the court theatre and in court balls than in hazard, écarté, and roulette. He even fell temporarily and not very seriously in love with Fräulein Melanie von Spiegel. It looks as if, for a year or so, he lived frugally enough.

On returning to England in the autumn of 1831, however, he backslid. Having entered himself as a student of the Middle Temple, rented chambers at 2 Brick Court which had once been Goldsmith's, and paid over a premium of 100 guineas to a special pleader and conveyancer, Taprell by name, for the privilege of perching on a high stool before a blazing fire in a small dark room at 1 Hare Court, he began, without enthusiasm, study of the law—'one of the most cold blooded prejudiced pieces of invention that ever a man was slave to'.[2] It completely failed to catch his interest. Although, after a few weeks, he continued to look in at Mr. Taprell's every now and then for form's sake, he used his desk mainly as a receptacle for drawings that he had made; and when, in June 1832, he walked down the stairs for the last time, he probably knew hardly any more about English law than he had nine months before.

In these months London went to his head. The parks to stroll in; the jolly taverns to eat and drink in; the theatres, with Duvernay 'prancing in as the Bayadère', and 'the exquisite young Taglioni, and Pauline Leroux, and a host more';[3] Grub Street, with its 'low literary men',[4] who talked, smoked, drank, and borrowed money—the whole colourful, noisy, good-natured, and not oppressively virtuous London into which an easy-going young man of twenty, not pinched for money, could precipitate himself, intoxicated Thackeray and drew off his attention from the 'old calculating codgers' who sidled in and out of legal chambers. He had plenty of friends. Some of them, like Edward Fitzgerald and Charles Buller, dated from Cambridge; others dated from the Charterhouse; others again, like Father Prout and William Maginn, belonged to the group of 'low literary men'. The last-named wheedled £500 out of him as a loan. Even the baby-faced, twenty-year-old Thackeray, with the lordly air (which was defensive) and the monocle fixed in the right eye (which he hoped would impress), must have known that this alleged loan was in fact a gift.

The young man's diary for the period, now printed in

full by Ray, shows how little work he was doing and how seldom he was to be found in his chambers. It also shows that he had become familiar with more than one of the gambling-houses of the West End. He records his day-to-day expenses, which from time to time include such items as 'Lost at play £8. 10. 0', 'broke my vow & one [*sic*] five pounds at play at 60 Quadrant', and 'spielte und verlierte acht pfund'. By comparison with his loss of £1,500 at Cambridge, the losses are small, but one wonders if his diary is to be entirely trusted. It is quite evident that a good deal of ordinary and perfectly legitimate expenditure (for rent, clothes, laundry, &c.) has been omitted, and one can only conclude that an uncertain amount of illegitimate expenditure has been omitted also.

§ 3

The entry in the diary for 18 July 1832 is worth quoting in full: 'Here is the day for wh. I have been panting so long, wh. now though it is come has not brought with it any sensations peculiarly pleasant. But I am a man now & must deal with men—Drew on Lubbock for £25.' It was a modest sum to draw on one's twenty-first birthday, but Thackeray soon made up for this modesty.

In a letter to his mother, dated on 25 June preceding, he had given expression to some very pretty sentiments:

I have been lying awake this morning meditating the wise & proper manner I shall employ my vast fortune when I am of age—wh. if I live so long will take place in 3 weeks—First I do not intend to quit my little chambers in the Temple, because £30 a year is better to pay than 90 the general price for good chambers—& the other 60 will do excellently well for poor Mrs. Blechynden. Then I will take a regular monthly income wh. I will never exceed. &c.[5]

Needless to say, these good intentions were not carried out. Thackeray always meant to do something for Mrs. Blechynden, his father's daughter by an Indian mistress and therefore his half-sister, but apparently he never did; for an entry in his diary for 6 August 1841 notes her death, and adds: 'It is the sorest point I have on my conscience never to have taken notice of her.'[6] Nor, of course, did he keep to a regular monthly income.

Abandoning the law, and giving as an excuse that he ought to study French literature, he hurried over to France, where he remained till the end of November. He merely exchanged the London parks and Piccadilly for the Champs-Élysées and the boulevards, the London playhouses for playhouses where he could sit enraptured by Mlle Mars, Mlle Déjazet, and other dazzling figures of the French stage, and the gambling-houses of Leicester Square and the Quadrant for others equally accessible in Paris. Entries on two successive days in his diary are in point:

[17, 18 August] There is a vow recorded in this book & God knows how it has been kept. May Almighty God give me strength of mind to resist the temptation of play, & to keep my vow that from this day I will never again enter a gaming house—
[19 August] I broke the vow I solemnly made yesterday—& thank God lost the last halfpenny I possessed by doing so— At first I had won back nearly all my losings & went away but the money lay like fire in my pocket & I am thank heaven rid of it—[7]

Back in London in 1833, he continued his gambling, one evening losing the sum of £668.[8]

This year saw the silly venture of the *National Standard*, in which both Thackeray and his stepfather lost money— how much, nobody knows. It also saw Thackeray engaged in the not very reputable business of bill-discounting. The whole affair still remains somewhat obscure. He became associated with a firm in Birchin Lane, and kept an account-book (still extant) in which he entered not only bills discounted but also such items as 'Bought 10 doz. Wine £19. 0. 0', 'Paid Phillips rent £28', and 'Sold 1000 Belgian Bonds £851. 5. 0'.[9]

The final crash came before the end of 1833. Between 1830 and 1834 Indian banks in Calcutta failed to the tune of £17 millions, and in one or more of these, which closed their doors in the autumn of 1833, the sum of £11,325 belonging to William Makepeace Thackeray disappeared. This left him with an income of £100 a year, and it looks as if even this had also vanished by the time he married in the year 1836.

§ 4

Both Saintsbury and Whibley, the one an Oxonian and the other a Cantabrigian, have praised with warmth and discrimination the narrative of Arthur Pendennis's adventures at the University of Oxbridge. We can see in it, says Whibley, 'the true aspect of the University, mellowed by a knowledge of the larger world'.[10]

That is a precise and accurate statement, and the fact stated is a little surprising. Every university man who has tried to write a novel of university life, or to include a section on the university within a novel with a wider range, knows how difficult it is to avoid turning sentimental. Memories of those halcyon days stand out, pretty clear for most of us, but isolated. We can reproduce them, possibly; but the temptation is to reproduce them either as they appeared to us at an age between eighteen and twenty-three, measured by a scale of values which the larger world cannot but regard as limited, or apologetically, patronizingly, as the follies of our irresponsible and shallow youth. To hit the balance; to make what was vivid and immediate vivid and immediate still, and yet to present it all mellowed (not distorted) by a knowledge of the larger world—*hic labor hoc opus est.* Yet that is what Thackeray did, the unintegrated, ambivalent Thackeray. The Oxbridge chapters of *Pendennis* are mature, balanced, of just the right length, and in just the right tone. If Thackeray had always written like this, one would not hesitate to rank him with Tolstoy—the Tolstoy of *Anna Karenina* and *War and Peace.*

Arthur Pendennis is recognizably William Makepeace Thackeray, but Thackeray the author has been able to withdraw to a suitable distance from Thackeray the green youth of 1829–30 and to look at him with critical sympathy, but without illusions. Helen Pendennis is mercifully off stage. The hero has become a character in his own right, and what he does or fails to do, his relations with other characters, his ideas and his feelings—these are determined by the novel itself, not by the private experience of Thackeray some twenty years before. Thus neither Foker nor the scamp Bloundell-Bloundell seems to have been reproduced from actual undergraduates who were up with Thackeray himself; Foker derived from Andrew Arcedeckne, a later acquaintance of Thackeray's and a fellow member of the Garrick Club, and Bloundell-Bloundell, although he may well have acquired some traits of the card-sharper who went off with £1,500 of Thackeray's inheritance, has his own personality. It was a clever stroke to bring Major Pendennis to visit his nephew at St. Boniface, for the Major is not only startlingly human himself but also the cause that humanity is in others; in this book even the stock characters seem to come alive in the Major's presence.

It comes to this: the people and events of Thackeray's short residence in Cambridge had been incorporated in his memories and taken their appropriate place there and acquired their appropriate value in the whole. There was nothing recalcitrant and unassimilated by the time he came to write *Pendennis*.

§ 5

The same is true of his financial follies and misdemeanours between 1829 and the end of 1833. They were temporary worries at the time, and they left no permanent twist or distortion in his mind. And so, when he took to fiction, they became material, very suitable material, which he handled coolly and with the right distribution of emphasis. Out of his experience with the card-sharpers in Cambridge, together with whatever other experience in gaming-houses in London and Paris proved relevant, came Deuceace of *The Yellowplush Papers*. The wretched Dawkins who lost

£4,700 to Deuceace was not an attempted portrait of William Makepeace Thackeray, but unless Thackeray had lost considerable sums to one or more originals of Deuceace his stories of gambling and of pigeoning would not have had the ring of truth that we can hear in them.

To be sure, the events of his own early life seem to have got somewhat mixed in his memory with the events that he had invented in *Yellowplush*, *The Paris Sketch Book*, and other publications. For, some time in the fifties, he and Sir Theodore Martin were strolling through a gaming-house at Spa, and came upon 'a tall man, in a seedy brown frock-coat', who had the appearance of a broken-down gentleman. Thackeray called Martin's attention to the man, and then, walking away, remarked: 'That was the original of my Deuceace; I have not seen him since the day he drove me down in his cabriolet to my broker's in the City, where I sold out my patrimony and handed it over to him.'[11]

This is a memory of what happened to the fictitious character Dawkins, not of what happened to Thackeray himself. Or perhaps it is a case of muddled recollection by Sir Theodore Martin.

As for the failure of the Indian banks, that provided Thackeray with material from which he could work out the ruin of Colonel Newcome.

V. MARRIAGE

That excellent and facetious being [Thackeray] ... has fallen in love, and talks of being married in less than twenty years. What is there so affecting as matrimony! I dined yesterday with his object, who is a nice, simple, girlish girl; a niece of that old Colonel Shawe whom one always meets at the Sterlings'. (Henry Reeve's Diary for January 1836: Laughton, *Memoirs of Henry Reeve*, i. 59.)

§ 1

DURING 1834 and 1835 Thackeray lived mainly in Paris, studying painting. Since he no longer had any money of his own to speak of, he depended for his support partly on his mother and stepfather, and partly on his maternal grandmother, the quick-tempered Mrs. Butler. She had an *appartement* in Grande rue de Chaillot, and for a time he lived with her there, at her expense. But they did not get on well together, and in the end he chose independence rather than material comfort, and moved into 'a little den' in the rue des Beaux Arts. There (as he confided to his diary) he intended 'to work hard & to lead a most pious sober & godly life'.[1]

It was during his stay with his grandmother that, visiting some friends of hers in a *pension* not far away, he met and instantly fell in love with Isabella Creagh Shawe, a red-polled[2] Irish girl of seventeen who sang and played the piano with rather more skill than was usual in a duly accomplished young woman. She was the daughter of the late Colonel Matthew Shawe, who had served with the Marquis of Wellesley in India, and whose pension did not serve to maintain his widow and five children in the state to which at least the widow thought them entitled. It was cheaper, however, in France than in England. That was why Mrs. Shawe lived in a Paris *pension* with her two daughters. Her sons, two of whom had entered the Army, seem to have lived elsewhere.

Mrs. Shawe was vain, selfish, and unbalanced, and evidently led her daughters, Isabella and Jane, a painful life of it. When she discovered that Thackeray was in love with one of them, she at first made him welcome as a possible son-in-law, and proceeded to cultivate his grandmother. What Isabella thought and felt at this stage, it is difficult to say. She had little will of her own, but apparently did what her domineering mother told her to do, and accepted the addresses of the impetuous young art student. By the beginning of 1836 they were formally engaged, and Thackeray gave her a ring in which a diamond was set between two opals in black enamel. In his ignorance, he had bought a mourning ring instead of an engagement one. But Isabella wore it. She was still wearing it thirty years after his death.

The first of Thackeray's extant letters to Isabella is dated 10 April 1836. He was then on his way to England for a brief visit. It is evident that by this time he has taken the measure of her subservience to her mother, and is somewhat uneasy. He writes to her as to a child, lectures her, scolds her gently, but is obviously a little exasperated because she does not take their engagement very seriously.

My father [he writes from London on 14 April 1836] says I could not do better than to marry, my mother says the same. I need not say that I agree with the opinion of my parents—so, dearest, make the little shifts ready, and the pretty night caps; and we will in a few few months, go & hear Bishop Luscombe read, and be married, and have children, & be happy ever after, as they are in the Story books—Does this news please you as it does me? Are you ready and willing to give up your home, & your bedfellow [her sister Jane], and your kind mother, to share the fate of a sulky grey headed old fellow with a small income, & a broken nose?—Dear little woman, think a great deal on this now, for it seems to me that up to the present time

(& considering the small chance of our union you were wise) you have avoided any thoughts as to the change of your condition, & the change of sentiments & of duties, wh. your marriage with me must entail.[3]

This letter must have been shown to Mrs. Shawe. Mrs. Shawe made a scene. This horrid brute of a penniless art student was threatening to take her beloved daughter away from her, to destroy the sacred love between them, to bring down the mother's head with sorrow to the grave—and so on and so on and so on. We have no record of what Mrs. Shawe said on this occasion, but we have enough evidence about her to be sure that it was something like the foregoing. Further, she professed to be shocked that a man should be gross enough to mention a bed to her innocent child.

In later letters from London, Thackeray had to try to smooth things over. In one dated 25 April, he exclaims:

. . . but what in God's name have I been saying to hurt you (for I see you are hurt) and your Mother?—What a scoundrel should I be were I to endeavour to weaken such a tie as exists between you two—The separation to wh. I alluded did not go farther than the bedroom—If I recollect rightly this was the chief object of my thoughts at the moment, and I opined that you would be unwilling to quit your bedfellow, and your present comfortable home for another with me. If you are my wife you must sleep in my bed and live in my house—voila tout. . . .[4]

But things were not to be smoothed over, if Mrs. Shawe could help it. By this time she had probably decided that Thackeray was not a good enough match. There may have been somebody else in prospect. (Remembering the story of *Philip*, one is tempted to believe so.) At any rate, things went wrong between Isabella and her William, and in July there appears to have been a violent quarrel between him and Mrs. Shawe, after which he was forbidden the house.

Looking back now, after more than a hundred years, *we* may wish that Thackeray had accepted his dismissal, put Isabella Shawe out of his head as soon as might be, and waited till he found a wife more suited to his temperament.

But he didn't. He forced a reconciliation somehow; for a time carried on a clandestine correspondence with Isabella through servants; finally placated the mother; and married the girl of his choice in the house of the British Ambassador on 20 August 1836.

'Absurdly imprudent' it certainly was. Thackeray had failed at law, journalism, and painting; he had dissipated a tidy fortune with remarkable speed; and for the last three years he had been living somehow, light-heartedly enough, to be sure, but with no settled income. Though he had just received an appointment as Paris Correspondent of a new Radical daily in London, the *Constitutional,* and for this would receive a salary of £400 a year, how long could anyone expect so irresponsible a man to retain the job?

There is evidence that, except for his mother and step-father (who probably hoped that marriage would steady him), his 'dear relatives' thoroughly disapproved of his action. But it is characteristic of him that, having once taken the step, he ever afterwards defended it, and ever afterwards defended others who committed a similar imprudence. To Mrs. Brookfield he praised an old acquaintance, Longueville Jones, 'because he flung up his Fellow- and Tutorship at Cambridge to marry on nothing a year'.[5] The 'dear relatives' of George Warrington in *The Virginians* (who is another projection of Thackeray) were shocked when he and Theo Lambert married on a small, insecure income; but George himself was convinced that he had done wisely.[6] When Philip married on an income of £450 a year, and Arthur Pendennis (the supposed narrator of the story) took the worldly view of this folly, Laura and Mrs. Mugford put him in his place. 'I'm sure', said Mrs. Mugford, 'if a man won't risk a little he don't deserve much.'[7] This was precisely Thackeray's own opinion, as delivered in letters of 1852 to W. W. F. Synge, then an attaché at the British Legation in Washington.

Je vous félicite, Monsieur: moi aussi j'ai aimé—j'ai eu vingt-cinq ans. . . .

I married at your age with £400 paid by a newspaper, which

failed six months afterwards, and always love to hear of a young fellow testing his fortune bravely in that way. And although my own marriage was a wreck as you know, I would do it again, for behold Love is the crown and completion of all earthly good. The man who is afraid of his fortune never deserved one.[8]

§ 2

All this illustrates again the egocentric Thackeray. He has the air of being a social philosopher, but he isn't; for there is no system in his thinking. He is generalizing from a particular experience which had engaged his emotions very deeply. Something that *he* had done must be justified, and therefore he justified it unreservedly. As a man of the world, as a man, that is to say, not unlike his Major Pendennis,[9] he knew very well that such marriages as his own, George Warrington's, Synge's, and Philip Firmin's might be quite as selfish and even more disastrous than the loveless marriages that drove him into furious rages—Barnes Newcome's, for example, or Agnes Twisden's (in *Philip*), or the one that Ethel Newcome very nearly entered into with the Marquis of Farintosh. But it was a marriage of the first sort (imprudent, but for love) that he had made himself. Moreover, he had made it in spite of the opposition of his mother-in-law. Therefore a marriage of this sort was right for all. He erected an emotional quiddity into a principle of social conduct.

His anger over 'marriages of convenience' is indeed intemperate. When his theme is 'the most godless respectable thing', the Marriage Market,[10] his tone of cool irony is no longer audible; he begins to rant. This is evident when he tells the story of Jack Spiggot and Letty Lovelace in the 'Snob' paper which appeared in *Punch* on 5 December 1846. The apostrophe at the end is very Thackeray:

What cursed frost was it that nipped the love that both were bearing, and condemned the girl to sour sterility, and the lad to selfish old-bachelorhood? It was the infernal Snob tyrant who governs us all, who says, 'Thou shalt not love without a lady's maid; thou shalt not marry without a carriage and horses; thou shalt have no wife in thy heart, and no children on thy knee, without a page in buttons and a French *bonne*; thou shalt go to the devil unless thou hast a brougham; marry poor, and society shall forsake thee; thy kinsmen shall avoid thee as a criminal; thy aunts and uncles shall turn up their eyes and bemoan the sad, sad manner in which Tom or Harry has thrown himself away.[11]

It is still more evident in *The Newcomes*, which, of course, is written round this very theme.

Oh me! what a confession it is, in the very outset of life and blushing brightness of life's morning, to own that the aim with which a young girl sets out, and the object of her existence, is to marry a rich man; that she was endowed with beauty so that she might buy wealth, and a title with it; that as sure as she has a soul to be saved, her business here on earth is to try and get a rich husband. . . . The article of Faith in her catechism is, 'I believe in elder sons, and a house in town, and a house in the country!' They are mercenary as they step fresh and blooming into the world out of the nursery.[12]

We have to remember, also, that this ranting of Thackeray's—and there is far more of it in *The Newcomes* than the reader of to-day can easily put up with—though it can be traced back in the end to his defensive-aggressive attitude about his own imprudent marriage in 1836, had been stimulated afresh by another personal and private experience. He had been recently in America, and there he had come very near to falling in love with young Sally Baxter of New York, memories of whom contributed a good deal to his portrait of Ethel Newcome. Not long after he started *The Newcomes* he was deeply shocked at the rumour that Sally was on the point of entering into a marriage of convenience herself.[13]

§ 3

Of all Thackeray's novels, *Philip* is probably the least often read now. It may therefore be worth while to show how closely some of it follows the events of Thackeray's own wooing and marriage.

Philip was the Paris correspondent of an English newspaper, just as Thackeray was; and one day in Boulogne he fell in with the Baynes family, who were on their way to Paris from England. They consisted of General Baynes, a stout but henpecked old warrior who had seen service in India but had now retired, and was struggling to bring up his children on a depleted income; Mrs. Baynes, a termagant and a snob; Charlotte Baynes, with whom Philip fell in love; and other smaller children who do not matter much. Notice that for his novel Thackeray departed from life only at one important point: although in fact Colonel Shawe, Isabella's father, was dead before he met her, the novelist preferred to keep alive the 'opposite number', General Baynes. It was a wise decision. The collisions between General Baynes and his shrew of a wife add to the drama.

Philip's Charlotte, when we first meet her disembarking at Boulogne, was a tall girl. Nobody knows why, unless it was that Thackeray had resolved not to reproduce life in all its details. If so, life was too strong for him. Within a few pages Charlotte had become 'little', and 'little' she remained—obviously because Isabella Shawe was 'small and slight'.[14] Immediately after the Channel crossing Charlotte's ringlets were 'brown'; not long after, they became a 'rich chestnut'—and we have already heard Thackeray call Isabella 'red-polled'.[15]

In the novel, Philip soon became engaged to Charlotte; and for a time he believed himself in heaven.

French people are very early risers; and, at the little hotel where Mr. Philip lived [obviously on the south side of the river, and probably, if the truth were known, in or near the rue des Beaux Arts], the whole crew of the house were up hours before lazy English masters and servants think of stirring. At ever so early an hour Phil had a fine bowl of coffee and milk and bread for his breakfast; and he was striding down to the Invalides, and across the bridge to the Champs Élysées, and the fumes of his pipe preceded him with a pleasant odour. And a short time after passing the Rond Point in the Elysian Fields, where an active fountain was flinging up showers of diamonds to the sky—after, I say, leaving the Rond Point on his right, and passing under umbrageous groves in the direction of the present Castle of Flowers, Mr. Philip would see a little person. Sometimes

a young sister or brother came with the little person. Sometimes only a blush fluttered on her cheek, and a sweet smile
beamed in her face as she came forward to greet him.[16]

There is a ring of actuality in this. Though Isabella Shawe
had.no young brothers or sisters in Paris when Thackeray
knew her, she had young friends in the boarding-house, to
whom Thackeray refers in some of his letters to her.

But Mrs. Baynes in the novel soon decided that Philip
was not a good enough match for her daughter, and set
about getting rid of him. Her opportunity came when, at
an Embassy ball, he lost his temper and knocked another
man into a fountain. Shocking manners like these were not
to be tolerated in a future son-in-law; General Baynes was
goaded into agreeing that Philip must be dismissed; Charlotte was peremptorily told she must give him up, and,
when she showed fight, was locked in her room and not
allowed to see him; and Philip, after a painful scene with
the parents, was sent about his business. But of course it
all came right in the end.

The main difference between this and the story of
Thackeray and Isabella Shawe lies in the attempted re-
sistance of Philip's Charlotte. This itself is significant.
Looking back, Thackeray could hardly be expected to
present his fiancée as meekly giving him up on the orders
of her masterful mother; so Charlotte had to resist. I am
afraid such evidence as there is in the Thackeray correspondence does not indicate that Isabella resisted very
stoutly. This probably hurt Thackeray at the time, and
since in retrospect it could not be regarded as flattering to
him, he altered it into something more romantic for the
novel.

§ 4

Though Mr. Ray's edition of the Thackeray Correspondence contains a number of hitherto-unpublished letters
from Isabella Thackeray dating from the years 1836–40,
she still remains a somewhat shadowy figure. Eyre Crowe
speaks of her 'charming grace and modesty';[17] Thackeray

himself, writing, twelve years after his marriage, to her sister Jane, refers to her as 'that dear artless sweet creature who charmed us both so', and recalls her sweet singing voice and her 'anxious little soul', which had always been afraid lest the flattery of his friends should corrupt her husband.[18] He also tried to impress on her children how humble-minded she had been.[19]

Essentially simple, rather colourless, frightened of her fury of a mother, malleable, but often puzzled by the volatile, quick-witted, and impulsive man that she had married—that is the impression one gets of Isabella Thackeray during the four years she lived with him. Now and then she seems to have felt, being his wife, that she ought to write clever letters; but her attempts at them are rather pitiful. She bore three children in quick succession, and seems to have been an affectionate, cheerful, but not, perhaps, very sensible mother. It is evident, too, that despite the comparative poverty in which they had to live at Great Coram Street, Bloomsbury, she never really understood why her husband must be left undisturbed when writing; she would drift in and out of his room, and be genuinely surprised and hurt when he remonstrated. All too often he had to escape elsewhere, hide himself at the Garrick Club, or even farther off still, in order that he might earn the rent or the doctor's fees for the wife and children who were always interrupting him.

It is not surprising, therefore, that the three characters in his fiction for whom he used his wife as the only or the chief model are the insipid and essentially selfish Amelia in *Vanity Fair*, the weak and stupid Rosey Mackenzie in *The Newcomes*, and the vaguely charming but empty-headed Charlotte in *Philip*.

§ 5

The year 1839 brought sorrow to the Thackeray household, through the death of their second child. Both parents seem to have recovered from this sorrow pretty quickly—especially the mother.

The year 1840 brought disaster from which Thackeray never wholly recovered.

In May, Isabella gave birth to her third child, who was christened Harriet Marion, but was generally known in the family as Minny. Nothing went wrong at first. After a week or two Thackeray danced off to Belgium with a light heart, in search of local colour for an article he was writing; but on his return, after only a little while away, he found his wife sinking into 'a strange state of languor and mental inactivity'. Very soon it became clear that this was no simple illness, but a grave one, touching the patient's mind.

He broke up the household, sent his children to Paris to his mother, borrowed money to meet the new and heavy expenses that had fallen upon him at a time when he had no reserves, and, with a faithful Scots servant, Jessie Brodie, to help him, devoted himself to nursing his wife. First he took her into Kent. She improved a little there, then relapsed. It occurred to him that a visit to her old home in Ireland might very well break the melancholy that was settling like a fog upon her mind. He put her on board a ship at Southampton, and they sailed for Cork. But while off the Isle of Wight Isabella Thackeray climbed through a porthole and threw herself into the sea. She was rescued after having floated, like Ophelia in the brook, for twenty minutes, and though she tried to kill herself a second time on board ship, she was prevented, and reached Cork alive, though 'very low'.

The visit to Ireland did the patient no good, and merely involved Thackeray in new and terrible quarrels with his she-devil of a mother-in-law (who, to be sure, seems to have been hardly sane herself). He brought his wife back, via Bristol, to London, and then to Paris. He consulted doctor after doctor, and tried cure after cure, but to no purpose. In the end he had to admit to himself that his wife had gone insane.

She never recovered. But she lived till the year 1893— thirty years after Thackeray himself was dead.

§ 6

'A dead sorrow is better than a living one', Thackeray once said bitterly.[20] He was right. This disaster was by far the worst that befell him. It renewed his dependence on his mother, and confirmed in him those tendencies that made for weakness, vacillation, and self-distrust. We cannot be sure that even if she had remained sane and happy Isabella Thackeray could have helped her husband to build himself up into a compacted and self-reliant personality; she was probably too simple and shallow for that. But his courage and determination during the years 1837–40 show that it might have been possible, had the circumstances of his life been a little more favourable. There is no reason to doubt that he was passionately in love with her. After she went insane, he was lost again. He was neither married nor unmarried—a condition of peculiar difficulty for a man of Thackeray's history and tempera- ·ment. It is small wonder that for a time he clung more than ever to his strong-willed and affectionate mother, and then, as time passed, turned to other women for support and sympathy. His relations with them, however, could never be satisfying, could never, as things were in the Victorian age, stabilize him. Jane Brookfield was married, though unhappily, and was selfishly respectable; he fell hesitantly in love with her, and she, so far as she possessed a heart at all, with him; and then, since they were both fettered by the Victorian Code, there was misery for a time, followed by a smug pride in their having stayed virtuous. Sally Baxter in America was extremely young, little better than a child; and although it flattered her to be admired (and avuncularly kissed) by a distinguished man of letters, there is nothing to show that she ever took him very seriously except as a middle-aged friend of the family. Of all his women friends in later life the Perry sisters proved the most helpful; for here, so far as we can tell, the friendship never became uneasy and equivocal.

Had Thackeray lived in England in the middle of the

eighteenth century—to which period at least half his mind belonged—or, though still a man of the nineteenth, lived in a country where the sexual code did not press heavily upon him, he might have attained to a greater measure of self-possession and symmetry, and have written novels equal to the best of Fielding, or Flaubert, or Turgenev. For him it was a misfortune, and for the literature of England, a disaster, that he fell a victim to the Victorian Code.

VI. THE MOTHER-IN-LAW

But to this day, when he [Philip] is enjoying good health and competence, it is not safe to mention mothers-in-law in his presence. He
fumes, shouts, and rages against them, as if they were all like his;
and his, I have been told, is a lady perfectly well satisfied with
herself and her conduct in this world; and as for the next—but our
story does not dare to point so far. (*Philip*, p. 616.)

§ 1

THE modern reader of Thackeray is not apt to agree very
often with the Laura Pendennis of *The Newcomes* and
Philip, that smug and excessively virtuous matron. But
he probably will, for once, when she reproaches her husband for 'always attacking mothers-in-law'. 'Oh, how
stale this kind of thing is, Arthur', she tells him very justly,
'from a man *qui veut passer pour un homme d'esprit!* '[1] The
mother-in-law, always selfish, grasping, interfering, snob-
bish, domineering, ruining the peace of her daughter's
household, is a stereotype in Thackeray, an obsession in
his mind. How often he is ridden by this hag is evident, not
merely from the long list of actual representatives—
Mrs. Shum, Mrs. Gam, Mrs. Gashleigh, Mrs. Budge, Mrs.
Cuff, Lady Southdown, Lady Kicklebury (renamed Mrs.
Baker for *Lovel the Widower*), Lady Stonehenge, in addition
to the two most famous ones, Mrs. Mackenzie (the Campaigner) in *The Newcomes*, and Mrs. Baynes in *Philip*—but
from his *obiter dicta* also.[2] It was as much of himself as of
Philip he was speaking in the passage quoted at the opening of this chapter.

69

§ 2

By itself, such an obsession would point to a model in actual life. But we are not dependent merely on that. Speaking to James Russell Lowell in 1856 about the Campaigner in *The Newcomes*, Thackeray said: 'That's my she-devil of a mother-in-law, you know, whom I have the good luck to possess still.'[3] And if the Campaigner was drawn from Mrs. Shawe, so were the rest of the mothers-in-law. They have all too strong a family resemblance to be unrelated.

As I pointed out in the last chapter, Mrs. Shawe did her best to break Thackeray's engagement to her daughter. This must have been the first major cause of his dislike. But as time passed he found plenty more. Isabella's dowry seems to have been fixed at £100 a year, payable quarterly; but after paying the first two instalments, Mrs. Shawe, it appears, paid no more, although there were times between 1836 and 1840, as she very well knew, when William and Isabella Thackeray were down to their last £5 note. No wonder he wrote in some exasperation to his mother in 1840, a few months before the birth of his third child: 'When the confinement comes I shall certainly apply to Mrs. Shawe. She has no business to be ordering fallals & leave her daughter without her allowance.'[4]

When the first child was born (in the Carmichael-Smyths' house in Albion Street, Hyde Park), Mrs. Shawe was staying in the house. That, perhaps, was only natural. But evidently the two grandmothers (both possessive women) did not hit it off, and to avoid similar unpleasantness on the next confinement, Thackeray and his wife, who were by this time installed in Great Coram Street, gave Mrs. Shawe no warning as to when the child was expected. Writing to her to say that the child had in fact arrived, and that all was well, Thackeray said, plainly enough, that last time there had been 'too many cooks'.[5]

In the spring of 1840, when the Thackerays were more than usually pinched for money, he tried to persuade his grandmother, Mrs. Butler, to come and live at Great

Coram Street, contributing to the rent and other household expenses. 'If she don't come', he told his mother, 'I must ask Mrs. Shawe and if I ask Mrs. Shawe, storms, whirlwinds, cataracts, tornadoes will be the result.'[6]

But what turned Thackeray's dislike for his mother-in-law into a furious and permanent obsession of hatred was her behaviour to Isabella and himself when he took the invalid to her old home in Cork, in the hope that this might restore her to mental health. As a story it is almost incredible, and makes what often seem the exaggerations of Mrs. Mackenzie and Mrs. Baynes almost natural by comparison.

At first, matters seemed to go well. 'Jane & her mother', Thackeray reports, 'have done my poor patient a great deal of good.' He had taken lodgings next door to Mrs. Shawe, and left his children with her sometimes while he helped Jessie Brodie with the nursing of his wife.[7] Before long, however, we hear a different note in his letters to his mother. 'Mrs. Shawe', he says, 'as usual brags bustles bothers prates incessantly of her great merits & sacrifices, but is good in the main—one must not judge too hardly a woman who is really & truly demented.'[8] Later in the same letter he adds: 'We have just had a scene—fancy that— in the midst of all this trouble she can't keep her monstrous tongue quiet. Don't *you* however come forward. It would only make matters worse.' A few days later again he has worse to report:

I don't like to tell you of the conduct of Mrs. Shawe: so unmotherly has it been. As far as bringing her daughter tea and dinner & sitting by her bedside she is well enough: but she has a spare room in her house and refused to receive her on account of her nerves (she has been very ill that's certain) & those of her darling Jane. She abused me for bringing her away from London, said her daughter had been denied to her in time of health to be thrown on her in sickness, and so on. She tried to pump out from Brodie whether I had been ill-treating her or not, and I scarcely get a meal at her home but I am obliged to swallow an insult with it.—but why talk of it? the woman is mad, more desperately self-deceived than any I ever knew. . . .

What a fool I was to ⟨believe that such a⟩ woman would behave decently, and give a shelter ⟨to her daughter. I⟩ declare to God when she refused, and talked about ⟨her nerves, God forgive⟩ her; responsibility; and her darling Jane, I was quite ⟨sick at heart, and⟩ yet this woman humbugs herself, and has I am pe⟨rsuaded no thought⟩ at this minute but that she is performing her duty ⟨in the most perfect &⟩ admirable way! It would do you good to hear Brodie ⟨express her scorn &⟩ hatred of her.[9]

Some three weeks later, Thackeray could stand things no longer in the neighbourhood of Mrs. Shawe, and, without warning, removed his wife and children, and sailed for Bristol. There, he wrote Mrs. Shawe a nine-page letter, telling her what he thought of her. Whether he ever posted it or not is uncertain. Unfortunately, it does not seem to have survived.[10]

§ 3

The mother-in-law of Thackeray's fiction is a woman who marches in, bag and baggage, to the undefended citadel of her daughter's house, and, once established there, takes possession; who insidiously assumes control, especially when the daughter is about to have a child; who harries the servants, summons her own physicians and apothecaries, quarrels with the tradesmen, and raises the expenses of the household to a level far beyond the struggling husband's means; who disapproves of all Radicals, and nags at the husband for his private opinions; who patronizes or insults the husband's friends, and discourages them from coming any more to the house; who (if Irish) keeps on boasting of her own ancient family; who insists on the husband's calling her 'Mamma', however he may dislike doing so; and, worst of all, who begins to cultivate suspicions of him in his wife's rather simple mind. And, if there happens to be another grandmother, there is everlasting friction in the handling of the children.[11]

Another recurring element in Thackeray's stories about mothers-in-law is an unpleasant brother-in-law, petted and

·encouraged at the expense of the husband. Captain Baker in *Lovel the Widower* is perhaps the best example; but there are others. Once again the correspondence of fiction to fact is significant; for Isabella's brother Henry, a lazy, good-for-nothing officer in the Army, stayed for a long time at Great Coram Street, and in the end had to be sent about his business. He went to the dogs, mainly through liquor. Years afterwards, when he was destitute in France, Thackeray tried to help him—but with what success, there is no record.

Let Lady Stonehenge, mother-in-law to Arthur Rowdy, of the firm of Stumpy, Rowdy, & Co., Lombard Street, bankers, stand for all mothers-in-law as portrayed by Thackeray.

When Rowdy went to live in Mayfair, what a wretched house it was into which he introduced such of his friends as were thought worthy of presentation to his new society! The rooms were filled with young dandies of the Stonehenge connection—beardless bucks from Downing Street, gay young sprigs of the Guards—their sisters and mothers, their kith and kin. They overdrew their accounts at Rowdy's bank, and laughed at him in his drawing-room; they made their bets and talked their dandy talk over his claret, at which the poor fellow sat quite silent. Lady Stonehenge invaded his nursery, appointed and cashiered his governess and children's maids; established her apothecary in permanence over him; quarrelled with old Mrs. Rowdy, so that the poor old body was only allowed to see her grand-children by stealth, and have secret interviews with them in the garden of Berkeley Square; made Rowdy take villas at Tunbridge, which she filled with her own family; massacred her daughter's visiting-book, in which Lady Cleopatra, a good-natured woman, at first admitted some of her husband's relatives and acquaintance and carried him abroad upon ex-cursions, in which all he had to do was to settle the bills with the courier. And she went so far as to order him to change his side of the House and his politics, and adopt those of Stonehenge, which were of the age of the Druids, his Lordship's ancestors; but here the honest British merchant made a stand and con-quered his mother-in-law, who would have smothered him the other day for voting for Rothschild. If it were not for the counting-house in the morning, and the House of Commons at night, what would become of Rowdy? They say he smokes there, and drinks when he smokes. He has been known to go to Vauxhall, and has even been seen, with a comforter over his nose, listening to Sam Hall at the Cider Cellars. All this misery and misfortune came to the poor fellow for marrying out of his degree. The clerks at Lombard Street laugh when Lord Mistletoe steps out of his cab and walks into the bank-parlour; and Rowdy's private account invariably tells tales of the visit of his young scapegrace of a brother-in-law.[12]

VII. FRANCE AND IRELAND

I can hardly bring my mind to fancy that anything is serious in
France—it seems to be all rant, tinsel, and stage-play. Sham liberty,
sham monarchs, sham glory, sham justice—*où diable donc la vérité
va-t-elle se nicher? (Sketch Books,* &c., p. 38.)

Never was a truer saying than that those people [the Irish] are
foreigners. They have neither English notions, manners, nor morals—
I mean what is right & natural to them, is absurd and unreasonable to
us. (Thackeray to Jane Octavia Brookfield: Ray, ii. 438.)

§ 1

We have seen that Thackeray spent a great part of the
years 1832–7 in Paris. During the next three years his
headquarters were in London, but he made several visits to
Paris, partly because his mother and stepfather had settled
there after the failure of the *Constitutional,*[1] and partly
because he planned to make a book about the French.

This book, *The Paris Sketch Book,* appeared in July
1840. It is a strange medley, and much of it is ephemeral.
All the same, it is not difficult to discover from the medley
what he thought of France and the French at the time of
writing; and the views he held then did not change very
much in the next three and twenty years.

He loved Paris. That is certain. From the time of his
first visit as an undergraduate (when he gambled and lost
money at Frascati's) to the time, in the sixties, when *The
Cornhill Magazine* was bringing in so much money that he
did not know how to spend it, he never missed a chance of
darting over to Paris, strolling along the boulevards and
the Champs-Élysées, gormandizing and cracking a bottle
in a favourite café, gazing at paintings in the Louvre and

the artists' studios, and surrendering to the delights of the French playhouse, even when he admitted that he ought, on the ground of morals, to condemn the entertainment there provided. But although he loved Paris, yet, until his dying day, he remained little better than an English tourist.

French he spoke fluently, and with a good accent. Of this, to be sure, he appears to have been rather vain. In a letter to his wife, written at Boulogne on 5 March 1838, he professes to find a certain Frenchwoman a humbug because she remarked, in a loud whisper, that he spoke French almost better than a Frenchman.[2] We need not take the profession very seriously.[3] All his heroes—even the Warrington twins, who were born and brought up in Virginia—had the same accomplishment, and aired it. What is more, he now and then falls into Gallicisms in his writing;[4] and only too often, in order to give a French colouring to some passage, he will knowingly impose a French idiom on the English prose.[5]

His knowledge of French literature was patchy, but by no means superficial, and his judgements on it showed independence, if not always great understanding. The extravagance of the Romantics repelled him; he called it 'mental intoxication'. But the 'undertaker wit' of Racine pleased him no better. If only he could have forgotten that Voltaire, Helvétius, and the Encyclopaedists in general had been anti-Christian, he would probably have found his account in their writings, more than in any other products of the French genius. But when his head approved of them, his heart, untutored and in some degree dissociated, violently rebelled.

Though he found it very pleasant to sojourn among the French, he remained a stranger, a foreigner. He once confessed to an American friend that he had 'never in his life been intimate in a single French family'.[6] Everything he wrote proves it. He praises the French painters, whom he thinks incomparably superior to the English as draughtsmen;[7] he praises the French people for respecting the arts and showing a far finer taste than his own middle-class countrymen;[8] and he is forced to admit that the French have the best of reasons for disliking these Philistine English—'brutal, ignorant, peevish bullies'—who elbow their way across the Continent, understanding little and condemning everything.[9] As a gentleman and a guest, Thackeray behaves in France with the good manners that a gentleman and a guest ought to show, and is properly indignant with compatriots who don't. Yet, in his heart, he is a party to the characteristic English prejudices. He is not even sure, being himself punctilious in the social graces, whether the 'boasted amenity and politeness' of the Champs-Élysées is not, in fact, inferior to the true, though less demonstrative, 'politeness of Wapping'.[10] Behind all his animadversions on French politics, the French habit of rattling sabres, the French legal system, and above all, French social and ethical conventions, there lies the tacit assumption that these, being un-English, must be wrong or worthless. He is honest enough, at least once, to come pretty near admitting this monstrous misconception.

> About the British Snob . . . there is commonly no noise, no bluster, but the calmness of profound conviction. We are better than all the world: we don't question the opinion at all: it's an axiom. . . . My dear brother reader, say, as a man of honour, if you are not of this opinion. Do you think a Frenchman your equal? You don't—you gallant British Snob—you know you don't: no more, perhaps, does the Snob your humble servant, brother.[11]

Whibley accuses Thackeray of an 'inborn Philistinism'.[12] This is misleading, and, if taken literally, ridiculous. Even if it means that Thackeray's Philistinism was absorbed unconsciously from the English society he was familiar with, we must enter a demurrer. Thackeray wore his Philistinism with a difference. Much of it was due, consciously or unconsciously, to the continuous influence of his mother.

The principal reason for his condemnation of the French was very similar to that for his condemnation of the upper middle-class English: they had a wholly wrong attitude to sex and marriage. Of course he is indecisive, often too vehement, and by no means consistent. That is Thackeray. On the whole, however, it is what he believes to be the sexual laxity of the French that angers him; for such an attitude (he would maintain) has this in common with the lordolatry and Mammon-worship of Victorian society—it makes love and marriage 'impure', mercenary, mere 'fortune-hunting'.

To quote at length from his writings would be tedious, but anyone who wishes to verify this contention may refer to 'Some Fashionable Novels' and 'Mme Sand and the New Apocalypse' in *The Paris Sketch Book*. These should be compared, first with 'Mr. and Mrs. Berry', a story in the *Fitz-Boodle Papers*, and then with *The Newcomes*. In all these, Thackeray rages at the French marriage-system. He does not argue the case against it. That is not his way. He does not even imply that something may be said for it. Enough for him that the system conflicts with certain deeply rooted prejudices of his own, the origin of which he does not fully realize and the strength of which he does not pause to test. For him, sexual laxity comprehends all vices, and his obsession with it blinded him to a host of French virtues.

It will not do to plead, as Saintsbury does, that Thackeray's attitude to things French is one of humour, that he merely saw incongruities in the customs of a people whom he none the less liked very well.[13] Balance is implicit in humour; and balance is conspicuously lacking in the articles in *The Paris Sketch Book*. Nor are his French characters in fiction—of which the best known are Mirobolant, the chef in *Pendennis*, and M. de Florac, the husband of Miss Higgs of Manchester, in *The Newcomes*—so remarkable as a number of his English readers thought. Mirobolant is a caricature, and M. de Florac is two-dimensional. It is not surprising that de Wyzewa should insist that his own countrymen in France were all the time conscious of antipathy, unreasoning and ineradicable, in the mind of Thackeray towards the whole French people.[14]

§ 2

Many of the Irish have accused Thackeray of a similar antipathy towards the Irish people—a similar blind, insolent, and uncomprehending John-Bullishness. The wilder and less responsible believed that in *Catherine*—the heroine's surname was Hayes—and again in a casual reference in *Pendennis*, afterwards deleted, he had intended a deliberate insult to a living Irish actress, Catherine Hayes, and so to the nation she belonged to; and one infuriated young man named Briggs warned Thackeray that he would soon dust his coat for him.

The story of Mr. Briggs is familiar to students of life in nineteenth-century London, but will bear repeating. Incensed at Thackeray, Briggs came to London, took lodgings in a house opposite Thackeray's, and there lay in wait. Thackeray's reply to this threat was typical enough. He first strengthened his defences by installing a detective in his house; then he took the fire-eating Briggs off his guard, marched in upon him unattended, and demanded explanations. This worked. He was able to persuade Briggs that the Catherine Hayes he had written about had been hanged at Tyburn for the best of reasons more than a century before. Neither Briggs nor his friends had been studying the *Newgate Calendar*, or had ever heard of this criminal Catherine. They professed themselves satisfied. Thereupon Thackeray, to celebrate the peace, bought a Chippendale chair from Briggs's landlady, carried it home in triumph, and dismissed the detective.[15]

Certain more responsible Irishmen could not be so easily satisfied about Thackeray and his attitude towards the Irish people. Major Dwyer, who contributed an appendix to Fitzpatrick's *Life of Charles Lever*, makes illuminating comments on the English journalist when he came to Ireland:

[Thackeray] abhorred boasting and exaggeration to such an extent as to be frequently tempted to disbelieve the naked truth. . . . This tendency to doubt, disbelieve or attenuate every positive statement of fact, was particularly conspicuous in his judgement of Irish people and Irish affairs; he distrusted everything he heard, and a great deal of what he saw, in Ireland.

Hence, Dwyer continues, Thackeray was able to combine theoretical vindication of Irish Catholics with 'contempt for the Irish themselves', and seemed 'always to wish to betray every Irishman he met into boasting'.[16]

§ 3

The Irish Sketch Book, which appeared in 1843, was received in Ireland with varying degrees of resentment. Charles Lever, to whom Thackeray dedicated it in a friendly letter, found the dedication disconcerting; and when *Barry Lyndon* appeared shortly afterwards, flew into a patriotic rage, and wrote to Harrison Ainsworth to complain of Thackeray's 'rascality'.[17]

If we take *The Irish Sketch Book* by itself, this resentment by the Irish does not appear very reasonable; for the work differed radically from *The Paris Sketch Book* not only in form but in tone. All serious-minded Englishmen in the hungry forties were concerned over Ireland, and with reason; and in the spring of 1842, when Thackeray suggested to Chapman and Hall that he should tour the island and produce a book about it, they accepted the suggestion very readily. He landed at Kingstown in the summer, and before returning to England, travelled widely and saw much. He made an honest attempt to understand and sympathize with the Irish. Throughout the book there is little of the John-Bullishness that disfigures many of his writings on the French. Nor is there much aggressive Protestantism. All his life Thackeray showed a hearty dislike of asceticism, and in his condemnations of it in this book he is quite impartial as between Catholics and Protestants. To the Irish people as a whole he gives warm and repeated praise for kindliness of heart and hospitality to strangers; when he discovers a landlord who is doing what he can for a group of wretched tenants, he commends him; when he

finds the clergy of the two faiths at loggerheads, he bestows
caustic blame impartially; and throughout, though he
evidently thinks the Irish 'peevishly suspicious of the
English',[18] he nowhere suggests that the English are without fault. As for Irish women, he has nothing but the best
to say about them: they are gracious, gay, and the chastest
of their sex in Europe.[19]

Doubtless the total effect of *The Irish Sketch Book* was
a little patronizing, but the Irish might have pardoned
that in an author so inveterately English. Scotsmen would
have proved more tolerant. Conscious of their superiority
to the English, they would probably have taken up the
attitude: 'Poor fellow, he's an Englishman, and can't
help it.'

§ 4

The effect of other books of Thackeray's is less amiable.
He boasted to David Masson that whereas he could never
invent a Scotsman—James Binnie in *The Newcomes* being
'a mere facsimile' of a man he knew—he 'could describe
an Irishman perfectly'. 'I'm quite at home with the Irish
character', he said complacently[20]—as if Irishmen were
all the same. And he seemed to believe they were. For one
thing, he thought of them as 'foreign'. It was after spend-
ing an evening in the company of Sheil and Fonblanque
that he wrote the comment on the Irish quoted at the
opening of this chapter.

If we examine the Irish characters dispersed through
his books, of whom the most conspicuous are Captain
Costigan, Captain Shandon, and Mrs. O'Dowd, it becomes
obvious that he thought of them as fantastic, usually
boastful, and often untrustworthy. It was not Thackeray
who invented the stage Irishman, but Thackeray's Irish
in novels nearly all come from the same mould: they are
nearly all braggarts, spongers, shiftless, and more or less
farcical. Remembering his boast that he knew the Irish
perfectly, we may think it a little remarkable that the
Irish as he presents them to us in his fiction should

resemble one another so closely; and we may also see good reasons for the charge levelled at him—that he held the Irish people in contempt.

Casual references and *obiter dicta* reinforce this impression. A good many people in Thackeray's books have 'Hibernian relatives' who plague them. 'I think', he says in *The Book of Snobs*, 'the shams of Ireland are more outrageous than those of any country.' Then he adds: 'O Ireland! O my country! (for I make little doubt that I am descended from Brian Boroo too) when will you acknowledge that two and two make four, and call a pikestaff a pikestaff?'[21] In *The Virginians* the Negro Gumbo boasts in the servants' hall of his descent from African kings, and this prompts Thackeray to the pungent comment: 'In Caffraria, Connaught, and other places now inhabited by hereditary bondsmen, there must have been vast numbers of these potent sovereigns in former times, to judge from their descendants now extant.'[22]

Occasional gibes of this sort are common enough from the mouths or pens of the English in most centuries; but they are much too frequent from Thackeray to be labelled 'occasional'. It is not surprising, therefore, to learn that an Irish groom of Trollope's once remarked to Thackeray: 'I hear you have written a book upon Ireland, and are always making fun of the Irish. You don't like us.' Nor is Thackeray's alleged reply improbable: 'God help me! all that I have loved best in the world is Irish.'[23]

This reply, if it were ever made, reminds us once again of the personal and accidental way in which Thackeray arrived at many of his opinions, attitudes, and *idées fixes*. His antipathy to the French may be linked with devotion to his mother; his varying attitudes to the Irish—sometimes hostile, sometimes sentimentally affectionate or patronizing, but in the main contemptuous—depended in great measure on which of his various memories happened to be active at the time of writing. Hostility derives, it would seem, partly from Irish journalists that he worked with in London, notably Maginn, but far more from 'Hibernian relatives', the Shawe group; whereas affection, which was much less frequent, has the origin that he suggested—the Irish girl that he had married. As, with the passage of time, affectionate memories of Isabella Shawe tended to fade, and even to give place to an ill-defined feeling that his wife had been hardly worthy of him (see *The Newcomes* and *Lovel the Widower*), the kindliness that he had shown to her fellow countrymen in the years 1842–3 gave place to other feelings: he became more prone to think of all Irishmen as Maginns, and of all Irishwomen as Mrs. Shawes.

VIII. PAINTING

To be a painter, and to have your hand in perfect command, I hold
to be one of life's *summa bona*. (*Philip*, p. 159.)

§ 1

T HE remark in *Philip* just quoted was no casual judgement of Thackeray's, but expressed a firm conviction.
Even after thirty years' practice in the art of letters, he
still turned with relief to the sister art, in which he had no
more skill than a gifted amateur; he had to force himself
to write, and found the occupation less irksome in clubs,
taverns, *pensions* abroad, anywhere except at home,
whereas he would look forward all the week to a quiet
Sunday morning in his study with a drawing-board. Thus
equipped, and with his two daughters as companions and
assistants and excited commentators, he would entertain
himself for hours very peacefully. Drawing, said the elder
daughter, always 'rested him when he was tired'.[1]

Whether Thackeray would have been happier and better
integrated as a professional painter than he proved to be
as novelist, essayist, and poet is an idle speculation. For
he lacked the gifts. George Cruikshank, who claimed to
have taught him to etch, said that he 'had not the patience
to be an artist with pencil or brush', adding: 'I used to
tell him that to be an artist was to burrow along like a
mole, heaving up a little mound here and there for a long
distance.'[2] Thackeray was the last man in the world to
content himself with the slow, subterranean existence of
a mole; he was quick, dashing, and erratic. Not only did
he never learn to paint, he never even learnt to draw. The

sketches of people and incidents with which he embellished his private letters are often enchanting as improvisations, dashed off with the pen that he had taken in hand for a different purpose; and among the best of them are his pleasantly satirical self-portraits. As an illustrator of his own books, however, he is quite incalculable. Sometimes the illustration is meaningless; sometimes it is startling in direct revelation of a trait of character. Most of his attempts at representational drawing or the serious portrait are depressing failures. When, for example, he tried to portray the lovely Jane Brookfield, the result was scarcely better than the product of a girl's 'accomplishment'. Jane Brookfield herself, having been duly taught to draw in the nursery by governesses, could have done it better.

All the same, he looked back upon his desultory years in painters' studios and in art schools, mainly of course in Paris, as the most continuously happy of his whole life. In essays and novels, and especially in *The Newcomes*, the scenes in which young painters, 'those scowling whiskerandos', play their parts are infused with the warmth of a long-cherished memory.

§ 2

It was not the least of Thackeray's qualifications as a free-lance journalist that he could write with knowledge and assurance on the art of painting; and between 1838 and 1846 he wrote more than twenty articles on this topic, most of them for *Fraser's*, the *Pictorial Times*, and *Punch*. They reveal him as more 'literary' in his judgements than we might have looked for in a would-be painter. What he seeks in a picture is precisely what he seeks in a novel or a drama—story and sentiment.

This is evident in his first notable review, 'Strictures on Pictures' (June 1838), and in 'A Pictorial Rhapsody' two years later. In the first, after disapproving of a painting by Etty—'a sleepy nymph, most richly painted; but tipsy-looking, coarse, and so naked as to be unfit for appearance among respectable people at an exhibition'—he passes on to 'a far nobler painting—the Prodigal kneeling down lonely in the stormy evening, and praying to heaven for pardon'.[3] This gives him the chance to elaborate on the story, but without reference to the picture. He brings the story of the Prodigal up to date. Strange to say, it is not improved by his tinkering.

Thackeray's aesthetic creed is plainly stated in 'A Pictorial Rhapsody':

> And if I might be allowed to give a hint to amateurs concerning pictures and their merit, I would say look to have your *heart* touched by them. The best paintings address themselves to the best feelings of it; and a great many very clever pictures do not touch it at all. Skill and handling are great parts of a painter's trade, but heart is the first; this is God's direct gift to him, and cannot be got in any academy, or under any master. Look about, therefore, for pictures, be they large or small, finished well or ill . . . that contain sentiment and great ideas. He who possesses these will be sure to express them, more or less well. Never mind about the manner. He who possesses them not may draw and colour to perfection, and yet be no artist.[4]

These principles—which to most of us now seem so silly that we need not waste time discussing them—he proceeds to apply to a picture of Eastlake's entitled 'The Salutation of the Aged Friar'. He calls it 'as pure as a Sabbath-hymn sung by the voices of children'—note the *pure* and the strongly emotive reference to children's voices, which sometimes had so strong an effect on Thackeray as to cause him to break down and weep in public. He then admits that he might very easily discover faults in the mere painting; does, in fact, discover some, such as excessive whiteness in the linen, excessive redness in the shadows, and repetition in the faces; but concludes that the merits of the performance far outweigh the faults, the merits being 'of the purely sentimental and intellectual kind'.[5]

§ 3

The notion that a great heart is the first quality in a painter remains singularly constant in the mind of Thackeray, giving to his criticism of the fine arts more consistency than we find either in his criticism of literature or in his own fiction. That it suited the Victorians is apparent from the pictures they delighted in; that it exactly suited the Thackeray who whimpered over Helen Pendennis, despised the French, denigrated Swift, and admired Irish women for their grace, kindly hearts, and chastity, is apparent, too. It was a thoroughly 'sentimental' notion.

In some moods, Thackeray would have taken this adjective as complimentary. He was gratified, in 1848, that those admirers of his in Edinburgh who presented him with a silver statuette of Punch had been sharp enough to discover 'that under the mask satirical there walks about a sentimental gentleman, who means not unkindly to any mortal person';[6] and a little later, writing to Mrs. Brookfield about his mother, for whom he had just hit upon the name *Mater Dolorosa*, he said: 'Is not that a pretty phrase? I wrote it yesterday in a book, whilst I was thinking about her—and have no shame somehow now in writing thus sentimentally to all the public.'[7]

In other moods, however, the word *sentimental* becomes a derogatory adjective in his writing. He is given to equating it with the 'namby-pamby', the 'spoony', and 'a propensity to small sentiment',[8] and twice at least, in a phrase he was proud of having coined, he speaks of the sentimental as the 'milk-and-water of human kindness'.[9] He derides others for what he is himself prone to. John Bull is laughed at for his 'simple admiration of the namby-pamby', and the painters, for encouraging John Bull in this 'regular babyhood of taste'.[10]

To define sentimentalism as a 'propensity to small sentiment' will scarcely do. Sentimentalism implies excess rather than deficiency of feeling—an excessive response of the so-called tender emotions, love and pity, in their various combinations. But to determine whether a response is excessive, adequate, or deficient, there is only one thing to do, and that is the thing which Thackeray, when speaking of painting, begged us not to do—to bring 'criticism and calculation' to bear.[11] It is the head that keeps proportionate the discordant heart.

§ 4

Except when one of his prejudices or obsessions interfered, Thackeray was as well aware as anybody, and better aware than most, of the importance of the cool, critical, and calculating head. He can and does admire men like Pope, Fielding, Hume, and Voltaire. Unfortunately, his prejudices and obsessions interfered pretty often. Present him with any of the situations 'Mother and Child', 'Marriage and Chastity', 'Jesus and Children', or with any other situation linked with these in his past experience— and coolness and balance disappear, leaving him almost as sentimental as the annuals or as muddily transcendental as the French Romantics he condemns.

His attitude to nudes has provoked harsh judgements, not without cause. Whibley accused him of 'prudishness reduced to the absurd',[12] and Mr. Sadleir offers, as one of the clearest proofs of his 'moral inconsistency', that 'nudes are sniggered over, but declared an offence to the purity of British womanhood'.[13]

A snigger is the sign of some conflict in the mind. This was evident enough in Thackeray when confronted with a nude. Having been trained in artists' studios, he knew as well as anyone that sex and morals have but little to do with the painting of nudes; and indeed, when 'the highest quarter' (Queen Victoria) showed her disapproval of the custom, he did not hesitate to call this squeamishness and to applaud Etty for ignoring royal wishes: let the painter go his own way, he said, and despise 'nec dulces amores nec choreas'.[14] But the Latin tag gave him away. Given his adolescent preoccupation with chastity and the mysterious sacredness of women, he could not in his heart concede to artists this privilege denied to other men—of looking without shame or desire at the naked female body. Thus in all his comments on nudes he wobbles. He can see the

artist's point of view, and would willingly adopt it if he
could; but his nurture, outside the studios, interferes.

Thackeray's judgements on painting vary from trucu-
lence to timidity. He calls himself an 'anti-humbuggist',
and detects humbug both in the fashionable Christian art
of France and in the straining after the sublime that the
Royal Academy in England was encouraging. He will do
his best to pull down 'the bloated, unnatural, stilted,
spouting, sham sublime, that our teachers have believed
and tried to pass off as real'.[15] His recurring demand is
therefore for 'simple smiling beauty and nature'[16]—whatever that may mean. And once, in a burst of candour, he
confessed to being 'fonder of pretty third-rate pictures
than of your great thundering first-rates'.[17] This, at least,
was consistent with the aesthetic creed that he professed;
but for a professional critic of painting, it ought to have
been damning enough.

IX. THE SOCIAL CRITIC

No doubt a man may be an earl of eleven descents, and yet be a pitifully mean creature. All the same for that, I am of opinion that it takes three generations to make a gentleman. (Thackeray in conversation, as reported by Jeaffreson, i. 250.)

§ 1

IT sounds like Thackeray, though Cordy Jeaffreson is not to be wholly trusted in these matters. Thackeray would never have doubted his own right to the title of 'gentleman'; nor, it would seem, did anybody else in his time challenge him on the point. The Victorians recognized a gentleman when they saw one—or at least thought they did. They perfectly understood Thackeray when, in describing poor half-imbecile Plantagenet Gaunt Gaunt, he remarked: 'And yet you see somehow that he is a gentleman.'[1] They also understood when Thackeray commented on Bloundell, the card-sharper, that he had been a gentleman once, and still retained 'some faint odours of that time of bloom'.[2]

None the less, there are signs in Thackeray's works that he is not quite so sure about the 'gentleman' as he sounds.

§ 2

'The Snobs of England', afterwards republished as *The Book of Snobs*, appeared weekly in *Punch* from 28 February 1846 to 27 February 1847. Considered as a piece of literature, the book is rather tiresome. Though sometimes entertaining, it is much too long, too full of repetitions; its humour is often forced, and its wit flat. Considered as a fact in the life of Thackeray, however, it is most important. For one thing, the astonishing success of the weekly papers gave him confidence in himself, which he had previously lacked. He now knew that, at last, he 'had taken the great stupid public by the ears';[3] among the *Punch* men, he had now taken his place alongside, and perhaps a little ahead of, Douglas Jerrold. He had still an immense distance to travel before he could catch up with Charles Dickens. That, he would have admitted readily enough. Nevertheless, he was now moving steadily in the right direction.

The 'Snob' papers may also be regarded as a sort of catchment-area in the development of Thackeray as a writer. Turbulent streams from a great many of his earlier works flow into them, settle, then pour out again, purified, less turbulent, and less turbid, into later novels. After this series in *Punch* it is always the mature Thackeray that we encounter in print. For better, for worse, he is what he is. Though he may still develop and improve his technical skills, yet the substance of his work, his prevailing interests, themes, types of character, and opinions on life—these will change very little in the seventeen years still remaining to him. His mind and habits of thinking were formed by the time he completed 'The Snobs of England'.

How casual, accidental, and imprecise his mind and habits of thinking were may be shown by the use he made of the very word *snob*. It was a Cambridge word; and he had been familiar with it since his days as an undergraduate. Originally meaning only 'townsman', as opposed to 'gownsman', it had soon been turned by members of the University into a term of abuse roughly equivalent to 'low fellow, cad, or bounder'. Thackeray now and then makes use of it in this sense in his earlier writings, and even continues to do so after *The Book of Snobs* has established it in general slang with the more restricted meaning, 'person with an exaggerated respect for wealth or social position'. The truth is that although Thackeray himself must be held chiefly responsible for giving the word this special twist of meaning, he did not set out with this intention; nor did he realize at any stage of composition exactly what he had done. He had no clear notion what the word meant to him or to anybody else. His chief need was for a short explosive term which he could fling like a hand grenade at the people he disliked. The term *snob* seemed to him as good a projectile as any other. It exploded prettily—though it often missed the target.

His famous definition of a snob as one 'who meanly admires mean things',[4] though it may sound excogitated, was in fact casual, irrelevant, and at once forgotten by Thackeray himself. In any event, it was far too comprehensive. A little later, while blundering round a meaning, he equated snobbishness, first with worldliness, then with humbug, then with 'an unhappy passion for peacock's feathers'.[5] Then he admitted nonchalantly: 'We can't say what it is, any more than we can define wit, humour, or humbug; but we *know* what it is'—[6] a statement to which his own 'Snob' papers give the lie.

No student of Victorian England in the forties will dispute that snobbishness (in the modern, restricted sense of 'exaggerated respect for wealth or social position') needed scourging. The comparatively stable society of the previous century had been thrown off balance. The Industrial Revolution had produced, and the Reform Bill of 1832 had enfranchised, a vast body of manufacturers, tradesmen, merchants large and small, apothecaries, surgeons, physicians, lawyers, and speculators who were elbowing their way up the crowded steps of the social pyramid, aping the manners of the older landed gentry, but without knowing very clearly what they wanted. It is always in these conditions, when the climbers feel uncertain of their footing, that the attitude of mind which we call snobbishness, and the actions which we call snobbery, prevail; and we do not need Thackeray's exposures to convince us that the people we call snobs were ubiquitous in the England of which he was writing. But the trouble with him was that he had no relatively firm social theory to control his pen. He had no standards, except the vague ones of a 'gentleman', by

which he could measure social aberrations. Like many
another social physician, he could only name the disease,
and attack its symptoms. To get down to ultimate causes
would have needed more systematic thinking than his un-
trained and inconstant mind was capable of undertaking.

No doubt he made many of his victims uneasily conscious of their symptoms. Berdmore believes that during
the vogue of the 'Snob' papers many hosts stopped drib-
bling their sherry, and many hostesses stopped boasting of
their titled relatives.[7] London clubmen, too, grew a little
nervous of Thackeray when he dined at the same table
with them, or stationed himself in his lordly manner with
his back to the fire-place in the same smoking-room. To
the bulk of them, perhaps, this *Punch* was a ribald rag; but
they read it; and this Thackeray was a dangerous Radical;
but they thought it safer to admire his wit. So the sales of
the rag and the fame of the Radical increased.

Beyond this, he did little to reform those he pilloried.
He had no effective cure for the 'sickness of an acquisitive
society'. He delivered his blows so impulsively and indis-
criminately that they fell almost as often on the innocent
as on the guilty. His values were confused and variable;
and the final impression after a reading of *The Book
of Snobs* is one of exasperation. If everybody is a snob
(including Mr. Snob, the author), and if nearly every
human action is an example of snobbery, both terms are
meaningless.

§ 3

Perhaps the nearest that Thackeray ever got to a general
principle of social conduct was the maxim, 'We must live
according to our degree.'[8] This meant, not only that no one
must act as if he were wealthier or better born than the
facts warranted, but also that no one must act as if he
were poorer or worse born. When the amiable but sententious Mr. Brown, whose 'Letters to his Nephew' ran in
Punch from March to August 1849, and who may be taken
for a much cooler and less vituperative critic of society

than the earlier Mr. Snob, rebukes his nephew for becoming rather too familiar with 'an uncommonly good-looking parlourmaid', we assume him to be speaking with the voice of Thackeray: 'The butcher-boy who brings the leg of mutton to Molly, may converse with her over the area railings; or the youthful grocer may exchange a few jocular remarks with Betty at the door as he hands in to her the tea and sugar; but not you.'[9] This is also the burden of the *Roundabout* (April 1861) in which Thackeray discourses lightly on domestic servants.

Between me and those fellow-creatures of mine who are sitting in the room below, how strange and wonderful is the partition! . . . If I met Hannah in the street with a bonnet on, I doubt whether I should know her. And all these good people with whom I may live for years and years, have cares, interests, dear friends and relatives, mayhap schemes, passions, longing hopes, tragedies of their own, from which a carpet and a few planks and beams utterly separate me.[10]

This is the 'gentleman' speaking; kindly, of course, as a gentleman should be; but perfectly sure of his own superiority. The gentleman has always been privileged; for his rank cuts diagonally across others, as Broadway cuts across the avenues of Manhattan. A gentleman can associate on equal terms with all other gentlemen, whether they are peers or commoners, rich or poor, merchants or professional men. It does not hurt him in the least to be 'utterly separated' from the people who are not gentlemen —the butcher-boy, the youthful grocer, John and Molly in the servants' hall, his tailor, and all members of what used to be called 'the labouring classes' or 'the lower orders'. The rank of Gentleman, in fact, is a typically English institution, ill defined, far from rigid, mitigating the rigours of social stratification, and enabling individuals in a lower group, in special circumstances, and as it were inadvertently, to escape into a higher without seriously disordering the social scheme.

Unfortunately there is apt to be disagreement as to who is, or is not, a gentleman. Thackeray himself would pass, no doubt, but some of those he rejected would be passed by others. For the chastiser of snobs, so indeterminate a principle as 'We must live according to our degree' seemed scarcely adequate: it laid him open to the charge of snobbishness himself. And the case against him was strengthened by his own Mr. Brown, who also laid it down as a maxim that 'It is good for a man to live where he can meet his betters, intellectual and social'.[11] This is possible, no doubt, for the gentleman. Even he, however, if he gratifies the ambition too freely, may be called a 'tuft-hunter'.

Thackeray had a bitter tongue for the tuft-hunter. When Harrison Ainsworth bought the *New Monthly Magazine*, and advertised that he had secured for it 'writers eminent not only for talent but for high rank', Thackeray pounced on him.

A literary gentleman who respects his calling doesn't surely mean to propitiate the public by saying, 'I am going to write for you, and—and Lord Fitzdiddle is going to write too.' Hang it, man, *let* him write—write and be—successful, or write and be—unsuccessful, according to his merits. But don't let us talk about high rank in the republic of letters—let us keep *that* place clear.[12]

This is excellent—or it would have been, if Thackeray had not at the same time been engaged in a private quarrel with Ainsworth on another matter. The previous owner of the *New Monthly Magazine* had been guilty of a piece of sharp practice towards Thackeray; Thackeray had protested sharply to Ainsworth, and had received no reply; and had there and then written 'Immense Opportunity' (from which the quotation above is taken) for *Punch*. Ainsworth's apology arrived after the article had gone to press, and there is something a little disturbing in Thackeray's hasty counter-apology. Although, he says, he would always think this advertisement of Ainsworth's 'very objectionable', yet he would not have raised his hand to smite his friend if the explanation, not of the advertisement, but of the sharp practice, had arrived in time.[13]

§ 4

Far too many of Thackeray's salvos against snobs leave us with the uncomfortable feeling that he is not quite disinterested. Whibley does not exaggerate when he says that the author of *The Book of Snobs* 'seems to be haunted by a species of self-consciousness; he is surprised that he is where he is; he knows that somebody is above or below him; but he cannot take his place in the world (or anybody else's place) for granted'.[14]

Once again it is a case of egocentricity and wavering. In a conversation in America, as reported by Thomas W. Parsons, Thackeray admitted this wavering, but assigned the blame for it to England.

> There is one thing in this country [i.e. America] which astonishes me [he is reported as saying]. You have a capacity for culture which contradicts all my experience. There are —— (mentioning two or three names well known in New York) who I know have risen from nothing, yet they are fit for any society in the world. . . . Now, in England, a man who has made his way up, as they have, doesn't seem to feel his social dignity. A little bit of the flunkey sticks in him somewhere. I am, perhaps, as independent in this respect as anyone I know, yet I'm not entirely sure of myself.[15]

The last sentence does not ring true, and for my own part I doubt if Thackeray ever uttered it in the form reported. He always considered himself a gentleman by birth and breeding, and it is highly improbable that he would speak of himself as one who had 'made his way up' socially. The rest of the alleged statement, however, is extremely Thackerayan.

He may have been right about England. A century has passed since 'The Snobs of England' appeared in *Punch*, and the country has undergone enormous changes; but no impartial observer of the English will deny that flunkeydom and snobbishness still flourish among them. It is probable enough, also, that Thackeray casually admitted 'a little bit of the flunkey' in himself, though without suggesting that he had brought it up with him from a lower position in society. To be honest, he had more than a little bit.

After *Vanity Fair* took the public's fancy, Thackeray became an eminent novelist; he was 'courted by dukes and duchesses, and wits of both sexes'. At least, so his friend Fitzgerald said.[16] And Thackeray's letters confirm it. One evening he is to dine with the Dowager Duchess of Bedford, and to go on afterwards to two parties, one at Mrs. Procter's and the other at Lady Granville's;[17] then he has to attend 'a grand dinner in Jewry';[18] and in the spring of 1850 he has 'an awful week of festivities':

> To day Shakespeare's birthday at the Garrick Club, dinner and speech—lunch Madame Lionel Rothschild   ball Lady Waldegrave   She gives the finest balls in London & I've never seen one yet—tomorrow of 5 invitations to dinner the first is Mr. Marshall—the D of Devonshire's Hevening party Lady Emily Dundas's ditto—Thursday Sir Anthony Rothschild —Friday the domestic affections, Saturday Sir Robert Peel, Sunday Lord Lansdowne—

And so on it went, for years, in both London and Paris.

Thackeray liked being lionized by dukes and countesses, Presidents of France and of the United States, princes of banking and their ladies. It is beyond question that he liked it, because he continued to accept invitations long after he knew that grand dinners and lunches were ruining his health. Nor is it difficult to forgive him for letting his head be turned at first. After some ten years of struggle and comparative poverty in Grub Street, it was pleasant to be taken up by peers and prime ministers. And when he wrote, to Jane Brookfield or some other kind female correspondentess, about the grand dinners and balls to which he had been invited, it was always jokingly, as if he knew how little it all amounted to. For example, in continuation of the passage just quoted, he remarks to Mrs. Brookfield:

> Isn't it curious to think (it was striking my great mind yesterday as Anny was sorting the cards in the chimney glass) that there are people who would give their ears or half their income

to go to these fine places. I was riding with an old Bailey
Barrister yesterday in the park and his pretty wife (On les aime
jolies Madame)—he apologized for knowing people who lived
in Brunswick Square, and thought to prove his gentility by
calling it 'that demmed place'.[19]

But all this was precisely what we should expect from
the equivocal Thackeray. He has an eye for a snob because
he is himself 'Mr. Snob'; he knows how to reveal the
flunkey because there is something of the flunkey in his
own character.

Later, he thought up an excellent excuse for his alleged
tuft-hunting. 'If', he said, 'I don't go out and mingle in
society, I can't write.'[20] Later still, he revised this statement in a review of John Leech's *Pictures of Life and
Character*: 'A social painter', he said, 'must be of the
world he depicts, and native to the manners he portrays.'[21]

Perhaps it is the final phrase that is most significant.
After all, although Thackeray might profess republican
and anti-aristocratical views, might abuse Society for its
'lordolatry' and 'mammoniacal superstitions', and might
often, immediately after some grand dinner or ball in
Mayfair, be found in Evans's Supper Rooms in the company of true Bohemians, he could not, even if he would,
cancel the effects of his own birth and breeding. He had
been born a gentleman, and brought up by one whom he
thought and spoke of as one of the finest ladies in the land.
He was 'native to the manners he portrayed'.

At the same time, as I have tried to show again and
again, he never felt secure. All snobbery has its origin in
a feeling of insecurity. It is little wonder, then, that this
historian and satirist of snobs should have suffered from
the very ailment that he diagnosed in others. It would
seem that you cannot have a 'gentleman' of the Thackeray
sort, without some traces of the 'gentleman's gentleman'.

§ 5

Thackeray 'appealed to the middle classes'.[22] Most of
the Victorian novelists did, but only Thackeray affirmed

it quite so openly. One result of this is to-day so obvious that it needs no elaboration: the calculated omission from Victorian novels of such vast and capital experiences as religion, speculation on Man's place in Nature and his relation to the supernatural, and the passionate loyalties and destructive infamies of sex. These may be hinted at in Thackeray, but all too discreetly.

It is more important to underline the courage than the timidity of the greater Victorians—a point made with force by Mr. G. M. Young:

> The world desired to be instructed: it was given Grote and Thirlwall, Milman and Macaulay, Lyell's *Principles of Geology*, Mill's *Logic*, Mill's *Political Economy*; to be elevated: it had *Past and Present*, *Modern Painters*, and *In Memoriam*; it asked for theology and got Newman, for education and got Arnold. Out of the Minerva Press came Disraeli, out of the horseplay of sentimental Cockneys, Dickens.[23]

One is tempted to add that it asked for frank comments on its social system and got *Vanity Fair*, *Pendennis*, and *The Newcomes*.

But this addition would be hardly legitimate. Few Victorians of the forties and fifties seem to have asked at all persistently for a frank comment on their social system. Those who might have done so, having most to gain, were of 'the lower orders' and, as yet, mainly inarticulate. 'The higher orders' took the social system very much for granted. For this reason we may say that *Yellowplush*, *Jeames's Diary*, *The Book of Snobs*, and *Vanity Fair* were not so much supplying a demand as creating one. They were forcing some of the more obvious imperfections of society upon their readers' notice; and therefore, and to this extent only, we may class the author with the early Socialists. A dangerous Radical he was not—whatever London clubmen may have thought. But he was so far Radical, that he helped to undermine what had once seemed firm and unshakable.

He was dimly aware of this himself. Writing to his mother on 26 March 1851 he said:

The present politics are behind the world: and not fit for the intelligence of the nation. The great revolution's a coming a coming: and the man not here who's to head it.—I wonder whether he's born and where he lives?—The present writers are all employed as by instinct in unscrewing the old framework of society, and get it ready for the Smash. I take a sort of pleasure in my little part in the business and in saying destructive things in a good humoured jolly way.[24]

Nearly all Victorians were individualists to a degree now possible only in Americans. At a time when the family and the churches—perhaps the only social institutions that were well enough organized to count—pressed more heavily upon the individual than at any time for two centuries, men continued to pretend that the individual had the fullest liberty to go to hell or heaven in the way that seemed good to him; they remained curiously unconscious of the influence that society was exerting on them, in their offices, their drawing-rooms, their clubs, even in their double beds; and they felt not a little shocked when a member of their community began telling them about it in his sub-acid way. This, to be sure, proved more irritating and less effectual than the frontal attacks launched by Dickens on the private schools, Bumbledom, debtors' prisons, the Circumlocution Office, and the Court of Chancery. Dickens was, in their view, an honest fellow, bluff and hearty, coming himself from 'the lower orders'. He was privileged; he could make them laugh abundantly; he could also make them cry. But this Thackeray! He was a gentleman. He was an ironist. Instead of attacking this or that abuse, he was undermining the entire Code from within. It made them uncomfortable. They decided that he sneered.

And of course he did. He sneered and withdrew. Lacking a coherent, integrated social theory, he grew timid and unsure, like a sniper who decamps when the battle grows warm. His avowed doctrine, 'Fun is good, truth better, love best of all', though it sounded well, did not seem to bear directly on his practice as novelist or critic. He lacked

the jaunty optimism of Dickens, which most of the other
Victorians both understood and approved, being jaunty
optimists themselves. Dickens's work was buoyed up by
his genuine belief in the goodness of man, and in the power
of charity to reform the world. That was excellent; it was
individualism moralized and justified. Thackeray, on the
contrary, presented human society as Vanity Fair—'not
a moral place certainly; nor a merry one, though very
noisy'.[25] He informed his readers that his 'amiable object'
was to walk with them through the Fair; and he advised
them that after their walk they 'should all come home . . .
and be perfectly miserable in private'.[26] Nor could he find
any more comfortable words with which to end his first
full-length novel than: 'Ah! *Vanitas Vanitatum!* which of
us is happy in this world? Which of us has his desire? or,
having it, is satisfied?—Come, children let us shut up the
box and the puppets, for our play is played out.'

To appeal to the Victorian middle classes in a tone so
morne was extraordinary, irritating, and in the end in-
effectual. Had they taken it for the genuine expression of
a whole man—whole though splenetic and probably mistaken, like the Sage of Chelsea—they would probably have
listened, even when they disagreed. For the Victorians
on the whole were not petty: they recognized and respected
conviction. But the Sage of Chelsea spoke for the majority
of his contemporaries when he called Thackeray 'very uncertain and chaotic'. Dickens with his gusto, and despite
much cheap jollity and still cheaper pathos, did more to
shake the Victorians' complacency than his saturnine, disjointed rival. Dickens hung together. Thackeray did not.

X. 'VANITY FAIR'

I think I could be a good woman if I had five thousand a year.
(Becky Sharp in *Vanity Fair*, p. 407.)

§ 1

An attentive reading of *Vanity Fair* when the story
reaches Pumpernickel brings out two trifling oddities—
trifling, at any rate, for every purpose but a study of the
Thackerayan method of composition. Suddenly, in Chapter
LXII, the author introduces 'the right line I', which he
has been careful to avoid up to then. 'It was [he says] at
the comfortable little ducal town of Pumpernickel that I
first saw Colonel Dobbin and his party.' Then, in Chapter LXVI, comes an unexpected statement: 'Tapeworm,
Secretary of Legation, poured out into the astonished
Major's ears such a history about Becky and her husband
as astonished the querist, and supplied all the points of
this narrative, for it was at that very table years ago that
the present writer had the pleasure of hearing the tale.'

There is no reason to doubt the literal truth of the last
part of this statement, since Thackeray in *Vanity Fair* is
not working through an imaginary narrator like Arthur
Pendennis (as he is in *The Newcomes* and *Philip*). No one
doubts that Pumpernickel stands for Weimar, where the
young Thackeray spent about a year on being removed
from Cambridge; and no one need have any hesitation
in identifying Tapeworm in the novel with Thackeray's
friend Lettsom, whom he had met first at Cambridge and
whom he met again at Weimar, where Lettsom was studying German in preparation for the diplomatic service. The

question to which only a conjectural answer may be given is, Whom did young Thackeray hear the tale about?

Mr. A. Lionel Stevenson supplied the most likely answer when he suggested the name of Lady Morgan.[1]

Sidney Owenson, afterwards Lady Morgan, whose private life excited the interest of the *Quarterly*, *Blackwood's*, and *Fraser's*, wrote novels in the first half of the nineteenth century, the very titles of which have been generally forgotten. It is not these novels but the outline of her life that matters. She was the daughter of a happy-go-lucky Irish actor. As her mother died while the child was still very young, Sidney spent much of her early life back-stage, where she acquired not a little skill as an entertainer. Then she became a governess, rising later to be companion to the Marchioness of Abercorn. Small, not very pretty, but vivacious, she caught the eye of my Lord Marquis, whose attentions to her did not pass unnoticed; but, like Becky Sharp, she could play a weak hand skilfully, and at last agreed to compound the threatened scandal by a marriage with Dr. Morgan, the family physician. But she laid down conditions. The chief was that her husband must be knighted. This the Marquis contrived for her; and Sidney Owenson, penniless adventuress and fashionable novelist, ended up as Lady Morgan.

Like Becky, too, she could make a little money go a long way. It was very easy if you never paid debts. After the Battle of Waterloo she and her husband led a gay, easygoing, but expensive life in Paris till the city grew too hot for them. Then they travelled round the Continent; turned back to Dublin; and in 1838 cast their anchor where they started from, in London.

The parallels between this biography and the career of Thackeray's green-eyed, artful, and vivacious heroine are, I would say, too close to be mere coincidence. I believe Lettsom's story in Weimar, in the year 1830 or the year 1831, was about Lady Morgan. Further evidence for the belief is that George Fitz-Boodle mentions her in conversation with Dorothea von Speck at Kalbsbraten-Pumpernickel; and no one doubts that in writing of Fitz-Boodle's adventures there, Thackeray was drawing on his own at Weimar.[2]

There are sufficient references in Thackeray's letters to show that he knew Lady Morgan in London in the thirties and forties, and found her something of a joke.[3] But there is nothing to prove that she was the woman referred to in a well-known anecdote by Lady Ritchie:

> One morning a hansom drove up to the door, and out of it emerged a most charming, dazzling little lady dressed in black, who greeted my father with great affection and brilliancy, and who, departing presently, gave him a large bunch of fresh violets. This was the only time I ever saw the fascinating little person who was by many supposed to be the original of Becky; my father only laughed when people asked him, but he never quite owned to it.[4]

I would suggest that Thackeray 'never quite owned to it' for the very good reason that Becky was *not* drawn from a single original. It is extremely likely that Thackeray used some of the reported episodes from Lady Morgan's early life as hints to start his invention off; it is possible that he used some traits of her character to bestow on Becky; and, consciously or unconsciously, he may have given Becky something of Lady Morgan's appearance as he fancied it must have been many years before. None of which matters much. Other claimants for the honour of being the original of Becky are Valérie Marneffe in Balzac's *La cousine Bette* (sponsored, apparently, by Mr. Ray[5]) and Theresa Reviss, an illegitimate daughter of Charles Buller, whose mother adopted her.[6] There may well have been many more.

The point to be emphasized is that whether Thackeray had one model or several models for his Becky Sharp, he did not allow the model or models to dictate to him, and the higher level reached in *Vanity Fair* than in any of his other novels (with the possible exception of *Esmond*) is in the main due to this independence in the author. Had he attained to the same independence and 'anonymity' in his handling of Amelia Sedley, *Vanity Fair* might have been one of the first half-dozen novels in European literature.

§ 2

The book, in the form in which most of us know it, has a sub-title, *A Novel without a Hero*. This was added only when Bradbury and Evans published the novel as a whole. The serial publication had another sub-title: *Pen and Pencil Sketches of English Society*, a relic, apparently, of earlier and unsuccessful drafts of the story.

Thackeray might have done better to describe the book as *A Novel with two Heroines*. This, at any rate, is how he thought of it as soon as he gave up the idea of a series of articles like the 'Snob' papers, and began shaping it as a novel. The principle he worked on was a good one—contrast. Becky Sharp and Amelia Sedley were to balance one another; the first being plain in appearance, but clever, witty, resourceful, unscrupulous, dangerous to her associates, and, for a time at least, successful in life, and the second being pretty, simple-minded, gullible, charming in an unobtrusive way, 'pure', of course, tender-hearted, and, for a time at least, unsuccessful in life. They were also to be linked very closely through a plot. Amelia's task was to give Becky her start in life through the homely society of Russell Square, and Becky's was to destroy Amelia's happiness by stealing her first husband, and then, if the novel could be made to end happily, to restore it with casual generosity by presenting her with a second. As the outline of a plot, this was excellent. Fielding could have woven it into a complex and enthralling pattern. Thackeray tried to. He knew, admired, and often imitated his Fielding, from whom, depend upon it, he had learned the importance of the principle of contrast.

Elaborating as he went along, he continued to apply this principle. Round the pair of heroines he grouped other pairs of characters, each member of the pair balancing the other: George Osborne and Rawdon Crawley, old Osborne and old Sedley, old Sir Pitt Crawley and the Marquis of

Steyne (both would-be lovers of the naughty heroine),
Miss Crawley, with her Regency outlook, and the Evangelical Lady Southdown. But for fear that the pattern
should become too formal, he devised cross-groupings:
George Osborne and William Dobbin, Rawdon Crawley
and his elder brother, Miss Crawley and the covetous Mrs.
Bute Crawley, Becky and her sister-in-law (*née* Sheepshanks). Actions, too, he balanced and contrasted: Becky's
marriage of convenience with Amelia's marriage for love;
Becky's rise to social eminence with Amelia's descent into
poverty; Amelia's final complacent and respectable happiness with Becky's restless and disreputable life at foreign
spas.

But this, to be sure, is plotting, and although Thackeray
could work out a plot in outline, he lacked Fielding's gift
of working it out even to its smallest details. Besides, he
was tied to serial composition, and being by habit indolent
and dilatory, he soon found himself writing hurriedly,
trusting very largely to the inspiration of the moment, in
order to get his next number delivered to the printers in
time. *Vanity Fair* is unified and shapely up to and including the episodes of Brussels and the Battle of Waterloo:
for although it contains two heroines, the adventures and
sufferings of the one are causally related to the adventures
and sufferings of the other. It becomes unified and shapely
again after Chapter XLIII (Pumpernickel), and for the
same reason. But in between—roughly 300 pages—the
plot of the first and last sections of the book is suspended,
and the unity of the novel disappears. Two stories now
occupy the author's attention alternately. One is centred
in Becky, the other in Amelia. They are still built on the
principle of contrast, undoubtedly, for Becky's fortunes
are steadily rising until the crisis, and Amelia's just as
steadily sinking until the return of Dobbin from India; but
there is no causal relation between them, and each might
very well have been the basis of a separate novel.

Nothing quite like this occurs in any other book of
Thackeray's. The nearest approach to it is to be found in

The Virginians, where, instead of having two heroines, he
has two heroes. In this novel, however, he has never devised any obvious plot to unite the heroes, and so the
reader is not conscious of a break in it. *Barry Lyndon,
Pendennis, Philip,* and (as far as it went) *Denis Duval* are
built upon a much simpler plan, the 'life and adventures'
of a single hero; and they contain not so much a single
plot as a succession of minor plots, loosely strung together
on the thread of the central figure. *Esmond* follows the
same plan, though it achieves a greater unity, partly
through making play with the mystery of Harry's parent-
age, and partly through making him in love with a mother
and a daughter simultaneously. *The Newcomes* is built
round a theme, namely, 'Marriages entered into for the
wrong reasons lead to disaster', and its various plots,
though at first glance they may seem disconnected, all
illustrate this central theme. As for *Lovel the Widower*, it is
little better than a jumble; the reader is never quite sure
whose story he is listening to—Lovel's, Batchelor's,
Elizabeth's, or even Bedford's.

§ 3

I can only conclude that when Thackeray began upon
Vanity Fair he intended that Amelia should be entangled
all along in the meshes of the Becky story, but that after
the scenes in Brussels and the death of George Osborne at
Waterloo he discovered that he could not keep it up. It
was Amelia herself who destroyed the plan. She had gone
limp upon his hands. This was something he had not foreseen when he started, because, apparently, it had not
occurred to him that the original of Amelia, his own 'poor
little wife',[7] had not enough in her to support the role of
a major character. And being emotionally tied by his
memories of Isabella, he did not know what to do. His first
intention, clearly, had been to make Amelia what Mrs.
Procter, after reading only seven numbers of the serial,
blandly told Abraham Hayward, the *Edinburgh* reviewer,
that she was: 'Charming . . . not an angel, only a good,

true, kind-hearted girl.'[8] But something had gone wrong. Although Thackeray may well have believed that it was only kindly memories of the 'poor little woman' that he was using for the novel, yet in fact, not being able to stand back and reshape 'emotion recollected in tranquillity', he was mingling these memories with others not so kindly; and, to make matters worse, he was trying to give solidity to the character by importing certain traits from two other women to whom he was emotionally in bondage, his mother and Jane Brookfield. It was all very well to draw on several originals for Becky. His own relationship to these originals was cool, intellectual, properly 'distanced'; and so he could reshape what he borrowed into a coherent and living personality. But the same method would not work when he was borrowing from Isabella, Jane, and his mother, since from none of these could he withdraw to the proper 'distance' for artistic creation. The result was that Amelia became one thing one moment and another another, according to his mood and the real woman he was thinking of. It was well-intentioned nonsense on the part of Mrs. Procter to compare her with Wordsworth's 'Phantom of Delight'—

> A creature not too bright and good
> For human nature's daily food,
> For transient sorrows, simple wiles,
> Praise, blame, love, kisses, tears and smiles—

and laziness or critical incompetence in Hayward to repeat this comparison in the *Edinburgh*.[9]

When Thackeray surrendered to the excitement of creation, his unconscious mind often took control. He once told Whitwell Elwin: 'I have no idea where it all comes from. . . . I am often astonished myself to read it after I have got it on paper.'[10] This is as it should be; at any rate, as it seems to be with most of the greater artists, whether men of letters, painters, sculptors, or musicians: they draw from a well that is deeper than conscious memory. Unfortunately, the waters beneath the level of Thackeray's conscious memory were often troubled, and on the present

occasion he was troubling them still more by interference
at the fully conscious level.

At all events, Thackeray had to make the best of a
failure. Prompted by Hayward's article, perhaps, and
certainly by what both Mrs. Carmichael-Smyth and Jane
Brookfield had to say about Amelia (which was not much
more encouraging than Hayward's attack), he recognized
that she would not serve his purpose in the way that he had
planned. The trouble was, he could not drop her. At the
beginning of the novel he had warned his readers in his
customary half-serious, half-joking tone to accept Amelia
and not Becky as the heroine.[11] Now, he had to gloss this
over. After admitting in Chapter XXX, still in the same
tone, that the indomitable Becky had become the heroine,
he surrendered more and more to the joys of writing about
her, with the result that he tended more and more to follow
the lead given him by his mother and Jane Brookfield, and
depreciate Amelia. Whibley exaggerates when he says that
Amelia 'is drawn with a cold contempt'.[12] It was not so bad
as that. But contempt became an ever stronger element in
Thackeray's attitude as the book progressed. The 'poor
panting little soul', 'poor tender heart' of the days before
Waterloo turned into 'a namby-pamby milk-and-water
affected creature';[13] at any rate, he allowed Dobbin's
sisters to call her that, and did not take any very active
steps to prove that they were wrong. Speaking of her letters
to Dobbin himself, he admits that they are 'cold, kind,
hopeless and selfish',[14] and when he quotes one for the
reader's benefit, he makes it about as simpering and facti-
tious as it is possible for a letter to be.

Even when he repents of his harshness to this silly but
forlorn creature, and does his best to prove sympathetic,
he betrays himself by fustian ('a sainted agony of tears'[15]),
or by that tell-tale repetition of the adjective ('an humble
humble heart'[16]) which is nearly always the symptom of an
unresolved conflict in his mind. Most significant of all, he
completely changes his attitude towards another character, whom he had first presented as a little ridiculous—

Lady Jane Sheepshanks. The name he had given her had to stand. Possibly he regretted that now. But, Amelia having failed, he now used Lady Jane as a foil to Becky.

It is easy, therefore, to believe an anecdote related in the biography of Dean Liddell. When Mrs. Liddell, an excited reader of *Vanity Fair* as a serial, exclaimed, 'O Mr. Thackeray, you must let Dobbin marry Amelia', he is said to have answered: 'Well, he shall, and when he has got her, he will not find her worth having.'[17]

Life influences fiction, obviously. But fiction also influences life. One wonders whether in the course of writing *Vanity Fair* Thackeray had come round to the same conclusion about himself and Isabella Shawe as he now allowed himself to express about Dobbin and Amelia. There can be no doubt but that he had reached that conclusion by the time he put the futile Rosey Mackenzie into *The Newcomes*.

§ 4

In the middle portion of *Vanity Fair* (Brussels to Pumpernickel) Thackeray devotes rather more than a third of the space to Amelia and rather less than two-thirds to Becky. The style in the different sections often turns out very different. Writing of Becky and the Crawleys, his pen moves easily and swiftly, with vigour and felicity of phrase; writing of Amelia and her family, or of Dobbin and his stupid infatuation, it is apt to flag. But it does not always flag. His account of the decay, moral as well as financial, of the Sedleys is in his best sober-sympathetic manner—gentle, unforced, yet concise and penetrating. He portrays the deterioration in Mrs. Sedley relentlessly—it is one of his proper themes—but without the suggestion of personal animus that we are conscious of in his treatment of Mrs. Prior in *Lovel the Widower*; and though he moralizes on the death of Mr. Sedley, he resists the temptation to become sentimental about it.

As for 'the famous little Becky puppet', Thackeray boasts in 'Before the Curtain' that she 'has been pronounced to be uncommonly flexible in the joints, and lively on the wire'. No one will deny it. Puppet none the less she must often be called. Readers can watch the author's supple fingers as he pulls the wires; they can listen to his voice, ventriloquizing. He has manufactured her. Sometimes we can see the tool marks. Becky, though a masterpiece of skill, has not been quite 'assembled'.

The usual impression that we get of her is of selfish good-nature. She is too self-possessed to be quick-tempered. She is also greedy for admiration. Why then should she box the ears of her child, young Rawdon, when he listens to her singing? It is not in character. The sudden unfair blow is Thackeray's, not hers. He has jerked the wrong wire. He has remembered with a start (for he secretly admires Becky very deeply) that he ought to make her odious, that the book in which she is disporting herself so gaily ought, like the earlier *Catherine*, to be followed 'to edification'; and being always sentimental when it comes to a 'Mother and Child', he brutally ascribes to her an act which is not credible. And he does something similar twice again. When Lord Steyne discovers that his protégée has not paid Briggs with the money he gave her for that purpose, and accuses her good-humouredly of sharp practice, Thackeray again jerks the wrong wire. Becky, he says, was not disconcerted for long; which is right. Then she made up 'another neat plausible circumstantial story':

'It was my husband, by threats and the most savage treatment, forced me to ask for that sum about which I deceived you. . . . He took the money. He told me he had paid Miss Briggs; I did not want, I did not dare to doubt him. Pardon the wrong which a desperate man is forced to commit, and pity a miserable miserable woman.' She burst into tears as she spoke. Persecuted virtue never looked more bewitchingly wretched.[18]

This is not Becky, the resourceful, brazen Becky we have learnt to know. It is a new, melodramatic Becky from the Lyceum Theatre. Fortunately the shocking impersonation is but temporary.

All the same, we can guess at Thackeray's motive here.

He is getting very near the crisis in the Becky plot. When the crisis comes, Becky is to behave with unpardonable callousness towards her blundering but affectionate husband. This behaviour must be led up to; otherwise the reader who has watched and delighted in her triumphs at Gaunt House will receive too great a shock when he finds her mean and treacherous.

And yet, puppet though she is, we believe in her. Here is the most infuriating paradox of all in the novelist Thackeray. He can put men and women on their legs and endow them with vitality; and this, after all, is the one essential gift for the novelist. Other powers, as of humour, satire, a comprehensive knowledge of human nature, skill in the handling of words, may be added to him, but without the essential gift he is nothing. And Thackeray was so perverse that he did not seem to value what the gods in their magnanimity had bestowed on him. The miracle of creation once performed, he would set about spoiling it. He had little reverence for his own creations; he would treat them either as a manufactured article, or, when the fancy took him, as a moral emblem. Unlike other gifted novelists, he is not content that the readers shall 'know' his characters; he must be fussing over them, in the hope that they shall 'know about' them.

How miraculous are his opening scenes! How immediate is the 'knowledge' that the reader gains of Becky at Miss Pinkerton's Academy, of Major Pendennis as he breakfasts at his club, of the boy Esmond as he waits in the empty house at Castlewood for the new Viscount, of Colonel Newcome as he listens with increasing anger to the ribald song of Costigan! And how often afterwards is this immediate 'knowledge' blurred and confused by the author's 'knowingness about'!

Whenever, in *Vanity Fair*, Thackeray will trust Becky, she will be herself, unerringly, miraculously vital. It is this vital Becky who puts the puppy George Osborne in his place when he tries to patronize her in Miss Crawley's drawing-room,[19] who takes her revenge on

112

Lady Bareacres,[20] and who exploits her triumphs in
the drawing-rooms at Gaunt House.[21]

'How cool that woman is!' said one; 'what airs of independence she assumes, where she ought to sit still and be thankful
if anybody speaks to her!' 'What an honest and good-natured
soul she is!' said another. 'What an artful little minx!' said a
third. They were all right very likely; but Becky went her own
way. . . .[22]

They *were* right, all of them. Becky, in contrast to every
other woman who appeared in a Thackeray novel (not
excluding Beatrix in *Esmond*, who comes nearest to her),
shows 'infinite variety'. And yet the essential Becky
emerges in a single statement: 'I think I could be a good
woman if I had five thousand a year.'[23]

She went her own way, says Thackeray. Would that he
had always allowed her to! He cannot leave well alone. As
soon as she has made her statement about five thousand a
year, he comments on it:

And who knows but Rebecca was right in her speculations—
and that it was only a question of money and fortune which
made the difference between her and an honest woman? If you
take temptations into account, who is to say that he is better
than his neighbour? A comfortable career of prosperity, if it
does not make people honest, at least keeps them so. An alder-
man coming from a turtle feast. . . .

and so on. Thackeray would not trust his daemon.

§ 5

For comments that, in their context in a novel, are
shallow, irrelevant, cheap, untrue, turbid, or pretentious,
there can be no excuse; and *Vanity Fair* has some of each
of these kinds. Thackeray will now and then write like a
novice in a school magazine;[24] he can be arch and cheap,
when Becky is attempting to entrap Jos;[25] he can sink
almost to the level of Mr. Chadband, when he is moralizing
on the illness of Miss Crawley: 'Picture to yourself, O fair
young reader, a worldly, selfish, graceless, thankless,
religionless old woman, writhing in pain and fear, and

without her wig. Picture her to yourself and ere you be old, learn to love and pray.'[26] Fortunately, exhortations like these are less common than in later works.

Against them, it is true, must be set other comments more mature and in better taste. Thackeray can be admirably caustic, as in the following comment on the younger Sir Pitt Crawley:

> But though he had a fine flux of words, and delivered his little voice with great pomposity and pleasure to himself, and never advanced any sentiment or opinion which was not perfectly trite and stale, and supported by a Latin quotation; yet he failed somehow, in spite of a mediocrity which ought to have ensured any man a success.[27]

This is what might be called an 'embodied' comment; since it appears to be dealing only with a single case, but implies a judgement on the world. The good 'detached' comment is not so common in *Vanity Fair*, though examples of it can be found.[28]

Readers who complain that a Thackeray novel contains too much commentary cannot be gainsaid. The amount increased as he grew older: he provided more in *The Newcomes* and *The Virginians* than in *Vanity Fair* and *Pendennis*, and so grievously overloaded *Philip* with it that in many parts this novel is unreadable. More important than the fact, however, is the reason for it, which is the increased self-confidence of Thackeray. (The growing sententiousness and smugness of the age may have had something to do with it also, but less than one might think.) Once Thackeray had succeeded in taking the public by the ears, he could afford to write in the way that he had always wished to. We might almost say of him that he became a novelist by accident. What he wished to be was a social commentator and a lay preacher. To him Vanity Fair was a panorama, best seen from a little distance off, as a man surveys a street from a balcony above it. People and things might emerge from the passing show and remain arrested for a moment in the field of vision. But they faded again. Others took their place, only to fade in their turn

and be lost in the moving mass. It was the background
that continued, ever changing, yet in some subtle way the
same. Thackeray's concern was less with unique persons
and unique events than with what was general and typical.
Indeed, unique persons and unique events had a way of
frightening him. He would have liked to be a 'mass
observationist'.

His casual admission in *Vanity Fair* that 'sick-bed
homilies and pious reflections are, to be sure, out of place
in mere story-books, and we are not going (after the fashion
of some novelists of the present day) to cajole the public
into a sermon, when it is only a comedy that the reader
pays his money to witness',[29] is only casual, the sign,
perhaps, of a momentary irritation with another homiletic
novelist. How far it is from representing his usual practice
and usual way of thinking may be seen from the remainder
of the paragraph: 'But, without preaching, the truth may
surely be borne in mind, that the bustle, and triumph, and
laughter, and gaiety which Vanity Fair exhibits in public,
do not always pursue the performer into private life, and
that the most dreary depression of spirits and dismal
repentance sometimes overcome him. . .' and so on and
so on till he comes to the statement of his 'amiable object'
in writing the book, namely, 'to walk through the Fair'.
This, to be sure, is precisely what he would have liked to
do all the time—to walk unhurrying through the Fair,
observing, commenting, but avoiding too intimate an
acquaintance with the passers-by. Not for nothing did he
avow his kinship with Addison, the 'Spectator'. 'Com-
mend me', he says, 'to this dear preacher without orders—
this parson in the tie-wig.'[30]

In any case, the public did not need to be 'cajoled' into
a sermon. The Victorians had been fed on sermons from
their infancy, and most of them seem to have preferred the
diet they were used to.

A young man brought up in a careful home [says Mr. G. M.
Young] might have heard, whether delivered or read aloud,
a thousand sermons. . . . If we consider the effect, beginning in

childhood, of all the preachers on all the congregations, of men
loud or unctuous, authoritative or persuasive, speaking out of
a body of acknowledged truth to the respectful audience below
them, we shall see why the homiletic cadence, more briefly
Cant, is so persistent in Victorian oratory and literature.[31]

When Thackeray sermonized, he was in the fashion. 'He
looked upon himself', says his daughter, 'as a lay preacher
even more than as a maker of stories.'[32]

§ 6

'Discursive' is the epithet that he applies to his Muse.
It is aptly chosen. What he enjoys doing and can do extremely well is panoramic narrative. Chapter XXXVIII
of *Vanity Fair* offers a good example. He entitles it 'A
Family in a very small Way', and uses it to give a summary
account, unhurried but economical, of the Sedleys after
their downfall. An even better example is the long discursive tale of Becky's social ascent, leading up to the
triumphs at Gaunt House, and so to the crisis in her life.
Nothing finer of its kind is to be found in Thackeray, and,
indeed, not many passages of sustained narrative in the
whole range of English literature surpass it. Thereafter the
tempo quickens in the chapter 'In which we enjoy three
Courses and a Dessert', recounting Becky's first dinner-
party at Lord Steyne's; and, after a brief interlude with
Amelia, quickens still more in the chapter 'In which a
Charade is acted which may or may not puzzle the Reader'
—perhaps the most skilfully written chapter in the whole
body of Thackeray's work. This is followed by a chapter
(LII) which is chronologically misplaced, and was probably an afterthought; it nevertheless gets its effect by
lowering the tension just before the crisis. When the crisis
does come, Thackeray handles it deftly and with most
remarkable economy.

As a 'dramatic' writer, presenting what Henry James
calls 'the discriminated occasion', Thackeray varies in
power. He lacked the dramatic gift of sustaining an occasion at a high pitch, and when he tried to do this, often

tumbled into melodrama, fustian, or cant. On the other hand, when he kept the occasion brief, he could often make it memorable. In *Vanity Fair* Becky is concerned in all the best of the discriminated occasions, and, apart from the crisis, Thackeray has pitched every one of them on the level of high comedy.[33] As for the crisis itself—when Rawdon returns from the spunging-house and finds Becky alone with Lord Steyne—this is one of Thackeray's undoubted triumphs. Bulwer, Ainsworth, or Dickens would almost certainly have presented the scene in the big-bow-wow manner, and have prolonged it. Thackeray knew better. He is not entirely free from the influence of these and similar writers, and he strikes two false notes—one when he bestows a 'horrid' smile on Becky, and one when he allows the noble marquis to 'grind' his teeth. Otherwise the performance, quick and sure-fingered, is without a flaw.

But, this discriminated occasion over, in sidles Thackeray the preacher to exploit it: 'What *had* happened? Was she guilty or not? She said not; but who could tell what was truth which came from those lips; or if that corrupt heart was in this case pure? All her lies and her schemes, all her selfishness and her wiles, all her wit and genius had come to this bankruptcy.'[34] For the reader of to-day there is no need to comment on this comment.

To the reader of to-day, also, Thackeray's question, 'Was she guilty?', is astounding. Even more so is his care not to answer it. It is true that he was thinking of his prudish readers, but this is not the whole truth. He was squeamish himself. Sex to him was a dangerous volcano, and now, as always, he refused to approach too near. He could only skirt round and round the crater with his nerves a-jangle.

XI. 'PENDENNIS'

Even the gentlemen of our age—this is an attempt to describe one of them, no better nor worse than most educated men—even these we cannot show as they are, with the notorious foibles and selfishness of their lives and their education. Since the author of *Tom Jones* was buried, no writer of fiction among us has been permitted to depict to his utmost a MAN. We must drape him, and give him a certain conventional simper. Society will not tolerate the Natural in our Art. (Preface to *Pendennis*.)

§ 1

Perhaps it was this passage that Saintsbury had in mind when he remarked, a little unexpectedly, that Arthur Pendennis was *l'homme sensuel moyen*.[1] Despite Thackeray's outburst, neither of the French epithets seems altogether congruous with the so-called hero of the novel; for, whatever other characteristics he may have, he is obviously cleverer than the average man, and, at least in relation to the other sex, too conspicuously virtuous. But during most of the book we remain mighty indifferent to the hero. Whether he is this or that or an undecided mixture of the two does not seem to matter much. Other people seem more important, or at any rate they provide better entertainment; and the farther the book advances the greater our temptation to ignore Pen altogether. In so far as he is somebody, however, and not just a name, a voice (somewhat given to prating), or a centre from which fortunes and misfortunes radiate, he is Thackeray himself. His good nature, generosity, selfishness, coxcombry, vanity, touchiness, priggishness, superciliousness, vacillation, habits of a young aristocrat, brilliance, and (despite his many tire-

118

some faults) likeableness, are all very Thackeray. 'A
literary hack, naturally fast in pace and brilliant in action'[2]
—this was the young journalistic Thackeray precisely.

§ 2

If *Pendennis* is taken piece by piece (for a whole the
novel is not), it will be found to contain a greater propor-
tion of Thackeray's best writing than any other book. The
first section of it, from the memorable opening with the
Major at breakfast in his club to the conversation, so
quiet, quintessential, and perfect in tone, between Pen and
Bows on the bridge at Chatteris, is as good as anything else
of its kind in the whole range of English fiction: it is
virtually a long-short story, complete in itself, beautifully
balanced, continuously interesting, remarkably free from
digressions and almost entirely free from sermons, and
written throughout in Thackeray's current, sinewy, well-
bred prose—prose which Hannay said reminded him of the
legs of a racehorse.[3] The second section—Pen at Oxbridge
—has already been referred to. It is nearly equal to the
first. Then the trouble starts: the novel begins to vary in
quality from the very good to the very bad. Thackeray can
still write with something like the brilliance he maintained
throughout the first section; but only for a chapter or two
at a time; and there is no telling when he will. He has
become erratic and uncertain. Strange to say, he has also
lost his skill in the art of panoramic narrative, the very art
in which he excelled in *Vanity Fair*, and in which, happily,
he was to excel again in later novels. Except for the quiet
study of Pen's half-innocent pursuit of Fanny Bolton,
there is no long passage composed of narrative which we
can properly call excellent after the Oxbridge chapters.

What the critical reader recalls from this novel, when he
looks back upon it, is a quite unusual number of discriminated occasions, some short, some long, some very
good, some very bad. It is almost as if Thackeray, in his
now conscious rivalry with Dickens, had resolved to
surpass Dickens in his own field—the dramatic. He could,

so long as he kept within the bounds of high comedy. The tense scene, the pathetic scene, were for the present beyond him. And so, when the critical reader picks up *Pendennis* after an interval of time, he returns to the Fotheringay episode and the three Oxbridge chapters with delight. Then he starts skipping. He will remember and return with pleasure to the episode of the Baymouth Ball, to Pen's first visit to the Back Kitchen, to the scene with Shandon in the Fleet Prison, to the dinner-party at Bungay's, to the defeat of Morgan by the intrepid Major, and to several of the scenes in which Pen plays *to* Blanche Amory and Blanche Amory plays *with* Pen; but if he remembers, he will take care to skip Pen's quarrel with his mother and Laura over Fanny Bolton, and the painfully overwritten reconciliation scene just before Helen's death.

Structurally, there is little good to be said of *Pendennis*. As I have already pointed out, it tends to fall into sections, related to one another only by the presence of the hero and perhaps a few other characters; and although, as in his previous novel, Thackeray ultimately works in both a love-story and a plot of intrigue, neither is of much account, since, Laura Bell being what she is, no reader is prepared to worry very much about her difficulty in finding a suitable husband, and the Altamont–Clavering–Blanche plot of intrigue resembles a patch of gaudy cloth clumsily stitched into a garment that it does not tone with. Thackeray had little aptitude for the sort of plotting that includes blackmail, mysteries, shady schemes to preserve an inheritance, ex-convicts, bigamy, and the rest of it. This was not his *métier*, as, long afterwards in a *Roundabout*, he willingly admitted.[4]

It is pretty clear that when Thackeray began to think about the novel in preparation for the writing of it he had only a general notion to work on: he would use his own life. Pen would live in Devonshire, go to the Charterhouse and Cambridge, drift to London and become a journalist, write a novel, then marry. He had almost certainly fixed upon the girl: she was to be founded on early memories of his cousin, Mary Graham, his mother's ward. This must have seemed good enough to start with, and he started. But the thing did not please him.

Then he paid a visit to Brighton, where he met the daughters of Horace Smith, famous as one of the authors of *Rejected Addresses*. As his habit was, when he fell in with sympathetic women, he told them all about his work in progress and his disappointment with it; and, in return, one of them told him a story out of real life which resembled the episode of Pen and the Fotheringay. This seemed to him the very thing for his novel. He discarded the first opening, and began again.[5]

Now that readers have the whole novel before them, it is hard to believe that only an accidental conversation in Brighton gave us the Fotheringay, and saved us from an opening with a sixteen-year-old Laura Bell making stilted speeches to her guardian. By substituting an opening on the note of high comedy for one on a note of highfalutin sentiment (which it might well have been), Thackeray was enabled to introduce immediately one of his masterpieces in characterization, Major Pendennis.

And so the novel started merrily enough. It was even brilliant. Alfred Tennyson discovered this. Sitting over the fire with Fitzgerald in the spring of 1849, and discussing old college friends, he spread his great hand in a favourite gesture and pronounced judgement on the new serial by 'Thack': 'Delicious . . . so mature.'[6]

§ 3

I have already discussed Helen Pendennis, and her derivation from Mrs. Carmichael-Smyth, which Thackeray always freely admitted; and I shall say no more on that topic. It is Laura Bell and Blanche Amory who call for comment, the more so because, incredible though it may sound, Thackeray seems to have borrowed traits for both from the same original, his cousin, Mary Graham (afterwards Carmichael). Laura at Fairoaks is a portrait, and a pretty faithful one, of Mary Graham at Larkbeare, when

121

she and Thackeray were young; whereas Blanche Amory, authoress of *Mes Larmes*, certainly owed a good deal to the same Mary, after she had married Major Carmichael-Smyth's brother.[7] It would be foolish to maintain that Thackeray used nobody but Mary Carmichael for Blanche. Like Becky, Blanche must have been a composite portrait; and Jane Welsh Carlyle was probably right when she saw a powerful resemblance between Blanche and the same Theresa Reviss on whom Thackeray is said to have drawn for the character of Becky.[8] But, to adopt a saying of Thackeray's in another connexion, we may say that Mary Carmichael *y était pour beaucoup*.

It astonished Thackeray that Mary (or Polly, as she was just as often called in the family) should have been brought up by his mother and yet have developed into a queer, artificial, even dangerous woman afterwards.[9] Until she married in 1841, at the age of twenty-six, Lieut.-Col. Charles Montauban Carmichael-Smyth, C.B.—he dropped the 'Smyth' soon afterwards—who was twenty-five years older than herself, she seems to have remained on affectionate terms with her former guardian, Thackeray's mother, and with Thackeray himself. They thought of themselves as brother and sister. Thackeray told Mrs. Brookfield later that he supposed he had never fallen in love with her because they had been brought up together, adding: 'She was a very simple generous creature then.'[10] When his second child was born in 1838, Mary was living at Great Coram Street, and Isabella told her mother that she had been 'to me every thing the most affectionate sister could have been'.[11] Moreover, in 1841, when Thackeray's purse was empty, Mary and her husband lent him £500. This debt sat very heavily on his conscience later, when the quarrels between the Carmichaels and Mrs. Carmichael-Smyth began.

The causes of these quarrels do not matter at the moment. It is enough to note that Mary was estranged from both Thackeray and his mother for a number of years after 1841 or 1842. Her husband's income did not go as far as they had hoped, and about 1848 he returned to India to repair his finances, leaving her in Paris. Thackeray met her again there at the beginning of February 1849.

This was not long after one of the early upheavals in the Brookfield household, owing to Thackeray's having been seeing too much of the mistress of it; and I strongly suspect that he had run away to Paris in the hope of discovering what effect absence would have on their feelings for each other. But he could not, or at least would not, stop writing her long letters. Extracts from these letters tell the story of his reconciliation with his cousin.

He met her a few days after his arrival in Paris.

We had a long talk [he says]: in wh. she showed me her interior and I inspected it and left it in a state of wonderment wh. I can't describe. . . . She is kind frank open-handed not very refined: with a warm outpouring of language—and thinks herself the most feeling creature in the world. The way in wh. she fascinates some people is quite extraordinary. . . . Her husband adores her—He is an old Cavalry Colonel of 60 and the poor fellow away now in India and yearning after her writes her yards & yards of the most tender submissive frantic letters— Five or six other men are crazy about her. She trotted them all out one after another before me last night. . . . Friends lovers husband she coaxes them all and no more cares for them than worthy Miss Fotheringay did. O Becky is a trifle to her: and I am sure I might draw her picture and she never wd. know in the least that it was herself.[12]

The next day he met her again, and reports to Jane Brookfield:

I drove about with my cousin and wondered at her more and more. She is come to my dearest William now: though she doesn't care a phig for me: she told me astonishing things showed me a letter in wh. every word was true and wh. was a fib from beginning to end—a miracle of deception—flattered fondled coaxed—O she was worth coming to Paris for.[13]

Whether by this time Thackeray had already thought of introducing some woman into *Pendennis* who could act as a foil to Laura, I do not know. He was still engaged on the Oxbridge chapters, and immediately on his return to

London he and Brookfield paid a hurried visit to Cambridge, no doubt in order that Thackeray might refresh his memory about the university. Blanche made her appearance in the novel in No. VII, which contained Chapters XXI–XXIII, and which was published at the end of April.

§ 4

It is in Chapter XXI, also, that Thackeray offers his first full description of Laura, his heroine. And a poor job he makes of it. He opens his paragraph by disclaiming any skill at the description of female beauty; then he proves the truth of this by some twenty lines, simpering and wordy. I suspect that the meeting with Mary in Paris had put him off. With his new knowledge of her as she was now, a highly sophisticated woman of thirty-four, he could no longer reconstruct the picture of her as she had been some sixteen or seventeen years before; nor could he quite decide what he wished to make of her, in the capacity of heroine. At no point in the book did he ever 'live' Laura, as he had lived Becky, as he was beginning to live Blanche, and as, later, he would live Beatrix in *Esmond* and, off and on, Ethel in *The Newcomes*. The reader cannot get on terms with Laura. Whibley calls both her and Helen 'bottles of tears, reverberating phonographs of sobs'.[14] This is witty, but not discriminating enough. Laura sobs when it suits the author, and remains hard and dry-eyed when you might expect tears. She is alternately gushing and prim, forgiving and intolerably self-righteous, childish and mature, strong-willed and feeble. She is not even, as Whibley would have us think, a stock character from the fiction of the day.[15] Stock characters are predictable, being stereotypes. Laura is not. Characters in fiction, like people in real life, may be inconsistent and yet convincing. Laura is just inconsistent.

The meeting with Mary Carmichael in Paris seems to have ruined the character of Laura. In compensation, it made the character of Blanche Amory. We 'know' Blanche instantly, when she opens her mouth for the first time in

Chapter XXII, just as we 'know' Becky when we first meet her at Miss Pinkerton's Academy for Young Ladies.

'Sir Francis is a very judicious parent', Miss Amory whispered. 'Don't you think so, Miss Bell? I shan't call you Miss Bell—I shall call you Laura. I admired you so at church. Your robe was not well made, nor your bonnet very fresh. But you have such beautiful grey eyes, and such a lovely tint. . . .

'Your cousin is handsome, and thinks so. He is uneasy *de sa personne*. He has not seen the world yet. Has he genius? Has he suffered? A lady, a little woman in a rumpled satin and velvet shoes—a Miss Pybus—came here, and said he has suffered. I, too, have suffered—and you, Laura, has your heart ever been touched?'

This, and the rest of the conversation, too, are perfect. Even if Thackeray got only a little of it from his cousin in Paris about whom five or six men were crazy, his reconciliation with her had been well worth while.

But what a topsy-turvy affair it is! Mary Graham talking to Mary Graham!

§ 5

But by this time the finest part of the novel had been written. The remaining 500 pages are very uneven, and not a few of them are just dull. What keeps them from the oblivion that has overtaken *Philip* is the remarkable variety of living characters they present. Despite its faults (which are grievous), *Pendennis* comes nearest of all Thackeray's books to revealing the essential novelist—if by this is meant a writer who can present his readers with immediately 'knowable' human beings. Of the principals in *Pendennis*, only Laura is an out-and-out failure. Pen will serve; he is better, at all events, than the bulk of so-called heroes. The treatment of Helen is infuriating; but if we prune away all the sentimentalizing, agonizing, and sermonizing with which Thackeray tries to choke the life out of her, we discover, a little to our surprise, that she is not only central to the book, but also credible and veracious to the last detail. Blanche and the Major are the greatest triumphs.

Of characters in the second rank—the Fotheringay, Captain Costigan, little Bows, Harry Foker, the Begum, Sir Francis Clavering, Colonel Altamont, the Chevalier Strong, Morgan, Fanny Bolton, and George Warrington— all except Altamont are adequate to the parts assigned to them, and at least three—Costigan, Foker, and the Begum —are among the best of Thackeray's eccentrics. It is known that some of these were drawn from life, but as none of them (except perhaps Warrington) touched Thackeray's emotions, the dictation of fact had no very harmful effect on him.

For a study of Thackeray's methods, however, the most interesting characters in this novel are the Fotheringay and George Warrington. The first is a remarkable achievement; one of the most remarkable in English fiction. For she is a character without a character—a Galatea. She is little more than a statue which has been trained to declaim speeches. Yet somehow the statue lives. The reader believes in her, 'knows' her, though the amount that he can 'know about' her is negligible. Anyone can fill a void with something tangible; but to leave a void empty, and yet compel the reader to a sense of some living presence there, is something of a triumph in the art of the novelist.

George Warrington is composite, and not quite there. One is apt to think he is there, but in this one is deceived. He can talk well. Nevertheless the voice is nine parts Thackeray's. Warrington, indeed, during most of the book, is a second incarnation of the author—Thackeray some ten years older, wiser, less romantic and impulsive than the young Pendennis. This becomes a trick of Thackeray's: he repeated it in *The Newcomes* and *Philip*, though in these novels it is Pendennis who is the older incarnation, and Clive and Philip the younger ones. In *Esmond* he achieves something like the same effect by turning the book into memoirs, the memoirs of a mature Harry looking back upon his younger self; and part of his dissatisfaction with *The Virginians* was very likely due to his not being able to do the same sort of thing there. Even in that novel, however, he gropes after it. Although the heroes are twins, George Warrington is shown throughout as a good deal more mature than Harry, the 'Fortunate Youth'. Harry in many ways resembles the improvident and gullible Thackeray of the thirties; George, the Thackeray of the forties, when misfortunes have sobered and aged him.

But the George Warrington of *Pendennis* is not merely the mature commentator looking back with amused tolerance at his younger self. For reasons in the plot, he has to be given another role. Pen having wandered from his duty and amused himself with Fanny Bolton, Laura in her turn must be allowed a diversion, and is therefore made to fall decorously in love with George. George is safe, being already married; he has had his Fanny Bolton, and is now rueing it. This, too, is without doubt an oblique presentation of the maturer Thackeray, with a wife who was no wife, but who nevertheless prevented him from marrying again.[16]

It is not only characters of the first or second rank who will come vividly alive at a touch in *Pendennis*. Thackeray can perform the same miracle with his 'supers'. Lady Agnes Foker has a very small part to play, but the author is generous and gives her lines to speak which would make any character: with very few changes, her foolish babbling about her son might have been recorded by Jane Austen. And with what a lavish hand he bestows character and circumstance on mere names! When Pen falls ill, and Helen and Laura hurry up to London, Laura must be found a room to sleep in. Happily, Mr. Percy Sibwright and Mr. Bangham had chambers on the second floor of Pen's staircase in Lamb Court, and were conveniently out of town; so Laura was provided for. Most novelists would have let it go at that. But not Thackeray in his then state of prodigal creativeness. He devoted a paragraph and a half to Sibwright and Bangham, bringing them alive off-stage, for all the world as if his store of unique persons was completely inexhaustible.

'One of Dickens's immense superiorities over me',

Thackeray told his mother in 1853, 'is the great fecundity of his imagination.'[17] Perhaps that was true by the time the letter was written. In the years 1848–50 the superiority of Dickens was far less marked.

§ 6

One section of *Pendennis* gave offence to old friends; and that was the section recounting Pen's adventures as a London journalist. It was evident that the Thackeray who had once depended for a living on the *Constitutional*, *Fraser's*, the *Examiner*, and the *Morning Chronicle* had now given himself airs. The tone in which he wrote about his old occupation and companions was offensive. Arthur Pendennis (an obvious self-portrait) was a supercilious puppy, and Shandon, Bacon, Bungay, Wenham, Wagg, Archer, and others of the scribbling or publishing community, were all very easily identified with real people. Thackeray had not handled the men of Fleet Street and Paternoster Row with gloves on, and since he had only just escaped from this milieu, and was now being courted by Belgravia, many of his older friends might be pardoned for accusing him of snobbery and bad taste. They were right—at all events about the bad taste. A novelist more detached, less egocentric, would at least have waited for a few years. Even then he would not have written so contemptuously about the rock out of which he had been hewn.

Both the *Examiner* and the *Morning Chronicle*, which had befriended him in his days of need, now attacked him. The *Examiner* accused him of caricaturing his literary fellow labourers 'in order to pay court to the non-literary class', and the *Morning Chronicle*, 'of fostering a baneful prejudice against literary men'.

Thackeray replied in an article entitled 'The Dignity of Literature', which the *Morning Chronicle* published.[27] Admirably written, this article seems to dispose of the overt charges. As usual, Thackeray takes the high moral line. Literary men, he insists, must be judged by the same standards as the rest of mankind; roguery must be exposed and humbug ridiculed in men of letters as in men of other callings; and to do so is not necessarily to vilify the profession as a whole.

If there are no spendthrifts or parasites among us, the satire becomes unjust; but if such exist, or have existed, they are as good subjects for comedy as men of other callings. . . . Are we to be passed over because we are faultless, or because we cannot afford to be laughed at? And if every character in a story is to represent a class, not an individual—if every bad figure is to have its obliged contrast a good one, and a balance of vice and virtue is to be struck—novels, I think, would become impossible, as they would be intolerably stupid and unnatural; and there would be a lamentable end of writers and readers of such compositions.

All this is well enough. One may endorse, too, his dislike of the cant about poor, down-trodden, unrecognized men of letters which had become current in his day and remained current for a long time after. It was one of his firmest convictions that men of letters as a rule got the recognition they deserved. And perhaps he was right.

Thackeray also turned the tables neatly on his accusers:

If I sit at your table, I suppose I am my neighbour's equal, and that he is mine. If I begin straightway with a protest of 'Sir, I am a literary man, but I would have you to know that I am as good as you', which of us is it that questions the dignity of the literary profession—my neighbour who would like to eat his soup in quiet, or the man of letters who commences the argument?[18]

Nevertheless, Thackeray in his article had evaded the issue. Charlotte Brontë remarked upon this as a habit of his; for, when asked by her publisher if she objected to Thackeray's being shown certain criticisms she had passed on *Esmond*, she replied that she did not, but added:

What is said in that note I would, if I had nerve, and could speak without hesitating and looking like an idiot, say to himself, face to face, prepared, of course, for any amount of sarcasm in reply, prepared, too, for those misconstructions which are the least flattering to human pride, and which we see and take in and smile at quietly and put by sadly; little ingenuities in which, if I mistake not, Mr. Thackeray, with all his greatness, excels.[19]

She did not mistake. The 'little ingenuities' are evident in Thackeray's article on 'The Dignity of Literature'. Since, in *Pendennis*, which was the only book brought in question at the time, nearly all the frequenters of Fleet Street and Paternoster Row had been shown as disreputable—through drunkenness, extravagance, venality, non-payment of debts, snobbishness, humbug, or positive illiteracy—there could be little doubt what *general* impression of men of letters Thackeray had conveyed to the non-literary public. It might be true, as he claimed, that no author was obliged to balance a bad character with a good one; but the contrast pointed in the book had not been between one member of a group and another, but between the group itself and other, non-literary groups; worse still, the young hero manifestly felt himself superior to his fellow journalists. In these circumstances, all the author's 'little ingenuities' were of no avail. His former colleagues on the *Examiner* and the *Morning Chronicle* were as clear-eyed as Charlotte Brontë: they could see, take in, smile quietly, and put by.

It was very like Thackeray, too, never to forget or forgive this attack on him. Later in *Pendennis* he threw out a passing gibe at his critics;[20] and even after ten years had passed the affair was still rankling in his mind. Speaking of a journalist who lodged with Mrs. Prior in *Lovel the Widower*, he said: 'But regarding Mr S——'s valuable biography, let us speak very gently. You see it is "an insult to literature" to say that there are disreputable and dishonest persons who write in newspapers.'[21]

XII. THE LECTURES

It is incident to this kind of literary entertainment that much should be sacrificed to effect. (John Forster on Thackeray's lecture on Swift, *Examiner*, 24 May 1851.)

§ 1

SPEAKING of his finances in April 1849, Thackeray told the Brookfields that although he had a balance of only £120 in his current account, and had just received a demand for £112, being unpaid capital invested in some 'abominable Irish railway', yet, all things considered, his position wasn't so bad.[1] No doubt this was true. He must have had all he needed for the day-to-day expenses of himself and his daughters, and it seems that he had cleared off all, or nearly all, his own and his stepfather's debts.

Still, having lost one fortune in the thirties, he was now determined to amass another—not for himself (as he went on repeating rather tiresomely), but for his daughters and their unfortunate mother. This became an obsession with him in the years between 1849 and 1863. To correspondent after correspondent he glories in the amount of money he is earning, or is just about to earn. An experienced reader of his letters soon learns to keep an eye open for the £ or $ sign, and then to skip what follows. All Thackeray's gloating over earnings becomes wearisome, even nauseating.

Having finished *Pendennis*, he began to cast about for another way of making money, and through keeping one eye on Dickens, by this time his only formidable rival in the art of fiction, he got an idea. Dickens had been giving dramatic readings from his own works, and had done extremely well financially. But then Dickens was a born actor, and his stories were dramatic. Thackeray had no gifts as an actor, found the making of public speeches almost as painful an ordeal as visits to his dentist, and had very few long dramatic scenes in his novels. So he had to modify the Dickens plan. He decided he would lecture, reading from a manuscript; first in London, then in provincial cities, and perhaps afterwards in the United States. He disliked the thought of 'this quackery',[2] and disliked the performance even more when he found himself engaged in it. Friends also told him he was lowering his dignity. But he needed money, and resolved to go through with it.

What with all the reading he had been forced to do both as a reviewer and in preparation for *The Memoirs of Barry Lyndon,* he now had a good knowledge of the eighteenth century and its writers; and so, almost inevitably, he chose the English humorists from Swift to Goldsmith as the topic of his lectures. He set to work on them. At the same time he roughed out plans for another novel, which he had determined should be nothing less than a masterpiece, the setting for which was to be the late seventeenth and early eighteenth centuries, and the necessary reading for which could be combined with his reading for the lectures. All this occupied him during the months January–April 1851.

§ 2

The first lecture on 'The English Humourists of the Eighteenth Century' was delivered at Willis's Rooms in London for the first time on 22 May 1851, and the remainder had been completed by 3 July. During the rest of 1851 and the first half of 1852 Thackeray went round repeating them in various provincial cities in England, and in Edinburgh and Glasgow. At the end of October he took them to America, where he delivered them in many cities.

His declared object was 'rather to describe the men than their works; or to deal with the latter only in as far as they seem to illustrate the character of their writers'.[3] No one will now deny that the writing was generally graceful, often remarkably felicitous in phrasing, and at times epigrammatic. On the other hand, it has to be confessed that the lectures often wilfully distorted facts, and again and again revealed an unpleasant smugness in the author. Whibley describes them as 'the worst blot upon Thackeray's literary reputation',[4] and I for one must agree with him. Thackeray did more than anyone else to give the man in the street false opinions concerning Swift, Fielding, and Sterne.

It is not enough to say that he looked back upon the humorists of the previous century with the eyes of a man of 1850.[5] Had he done nothing but act as the mouthpiece of his own age, he would probably have chosen other topics; at any rate, he would have left out Congreve, Fielding, and Sterne. One ought to remember that it needed courage, in the year 1851, for a man of his standing in the world of letters to discourse publicly on such wicked writers. To Anthony Trollope the comic dramatists of 1660–1700 were not only shameless but dull: 'Congreve's muse', he says, 'was about as bad as any muse that ever misbehaved herself—and, I think, as little amusing.'[6] As for Sterne, says Trollope virtuously, the less often his works are taken from the shelves the better.[7] It was profoundly shocking to Charlotte Brontë that Thackeray should appear to worship 'his Baal—Bel—Bülzebub (they are all one), his false god of a Fielding';[8] and she wrote to W. S. Williams: 'I was present at the Fielding lecture; the hour spent in listening to it was a painful hour. . . . I do most deeply grieve that it never entered into his heart sadly and nearly to feel the peril of such a career.'[9] Moreover, when the lectures were taken to America, some of them (at least so Arthur Hugh Clough is reported to have said) were 'thought dangerous in their tendencies for the moralities of the young Yankee men'.[10]

What spoiled Thackeray's judgements on the English humorists was not echoes of the conventional judgements of his day but his own obsessions, timidities, and inhibitions. Each writer was brought to the bar and sentenced in accordance with a private law, which was not codified, was often inconsistent, and was carried only in the judge's head. That is why the lectures provide a more important document for the study of the judge than for a study of the prisoners at the bar.

§ 3

Thackeray's omissions from the lectures are significant. To him, humour meant 'love plus wit', with the emphasis upon the first.[11] 'The humourous writer professes to awaken and direct your love, your pity, your kindness—your scorn for untruth, pretention, imposture—your tenderness for the weak, the poor, the oppressed, the unhappy. . . . He takes upon himself to be the week-day preacher.'[12] Given a definition so comprehensive, why did the lecturer omit the two Samuels, Johnson and Richardson, from his survey of the humorists? The former he regarded with great but somewhat distant respect. The solidity and forthrightness of Johnson frightened him a little. It was typical of him, when he had to write a paragraph about Johnson in the second series of lectures (on *The Four Georges*), to sentimentalize the picture in a manner quite disgusting to Johnsonians, by talking about Johnson behind the scenes at Garrick's theatre, with the actresses dropping him a curtsey as they passed to the stage—'youth, folly, gaiety, tenderly surveyed by wisdom's merciful, pure eyes'.[13] On the other hand, the 'sentimental twaddle' of Richardson arouses Thackeray's contempt. He feels nothing but sympathy for Fielding when Fielding vents his scorn upon 'the puny Cockney bookseller'.[14] The truth (extraordinary though it sounds) seems to be that Thackeray had not read Richardson's novels, not even *Clarissa*, when he dismissed them, and that his judgements were mainly, and perhaps even completely, based on hearsay.[15] Himself, he stood midway between the pharasaic sentimentalism of Richardson and the downright good sense of Johnson. Both repelled him, as both Bulwer and Swift repelled him, because he had so strong a tendency to be himself like Richardson, and, try as he might, could not reach the stability and the more manly virtues of Johnson.

The distribution of emphasis in the lectures is significant also. Swift has a lecture to himself, and so has Steele, whereas Addison must share one with Congreve. Even more unexpectedly, Pope ('the greatest name on our list')[16] must share a lecture with Gay and Prior, and Fielding, despite Thackeray's great admiration for him, has to share one with Hogarth and Smollett. Steele, in short, is allowed too much space, Addison, Pope, and Fielding too little.

The man Steele had taken Thackeray's fancy, and his portrait had to be elaborated, not only in the lectures themselves, but also in *Esmond*. Despite this elaboration, the portrait did not give the real Steele; it gave a highly romanticized version of him, a version attractive to the lecturer because, while Steele was not big enough to be frightening, he seemed to possess the same amiable virtues and many of the same amiable weaknesses as the lecturer himself.

I referred at some length in an earlier chapter to the injustice of the portrait of Swift, and do not propose to say more about it here. A word or two must be given to the portraits of Fielding and Sterne.

The portrait of Fielding is overcharged in some respects and undercharged in others. Thackeray says that he can neither offer nor hope to make a hero out of Henry Fielding. There are heroes and heroes, however. In avoiding 'the marble toga' and 'heroic attitude', it was not necessary to make a disproportionate display of the 'inked ruffles' and the 'claret stains' on the 'tarnished lace coat',[17] or to suggest that it was Fielding's nightly habit to reel home to his chambers on the shoulders of the watchman.[18] A man so like Sydney Carton could not have done all the things that Fielding did. What Thackeray missed in both Samuel Johnson and Henry Fielding was their stature. Physically big though he was himself, he was always somewhat afraid of the mentally big in others—just as he preferred third-rate sentimental paintings to 'your great thundering first-rates'.[19]

All the same, he can talk well on Fielding the writer, as he can on Swift the writer.

As a picture of manners, the novel of *Tom Jones* is indeed exquisite: as a work of construction, quite a wonder: the by-play of wisdom; the power of observation; the multiplied felicitous turns and thoughts; the varied character of the great Comic Epic: keep the reader in a perpetual admiration and curiosity.[20]

He protests only against Fielding's asking us to accept Tom as a hero: 'A hero with a flawed reputation; a hero sponging for a guinea; a hero who can't pay his landlady, and is obliged to let his honour out to hire, is absurd, and his claim to heroic rank untenable.'[21] With some boldness, he does not protest against the inclusion of such a character; Tom may be allowed as an 'ordinary young fellow, ruddy-cheeked, broad-shouldered, and fond of wine and pleasure'; but he holds that 'Fielding's evident liking and admiration for Mr. Jones shows that the great humourist's moral sense was blunted by his life'.[22]

This is evidence of a strange blindness—one is tempted to say, a wilful blindness. It is not to be believed that Thackeray had read and re-read *Tom Jones* without being aware that Fielding was embodying in it a moral theory, a coherent and, in a philosophical sense, a sentimental moral theory, namely, that a good heart will redeem all sins. Let us refute the theory if we wish to; the task is not very difficult. But do not let us pretend, in the face of Fielding's repeated disquisitions, that it was not a conscious and deliberate theory at all, but merely a 'blunted moral sense'. Thackeray's knowledge of philosophy was superficial; it is doubtful if, despite his predilection for the eighteenth century, he had any acquaintance at all with the British moralists. And so he took the easy path, and it led him away from an understanding of Fielding. The least he could have done, in justice to his author, was to call attention to the theory that lies behind *Tom Jones*; since the theory is fundamental. Instead, he was content to remind his hearers of what he had previously enlarged upon, Fielding's wild life, and then, with a kind of smirk, to suggest to them that his own plan in fiction—not to have a hero at all—was a good deal sounder, for all that it had told against him when he tried to sell his novels.

For Sterne the man Thackeray had a greater liking than he was ready to admit in these lectures. In *The English Humourists* he puts on an air of severity. Sterne is a quack, who 'exercised the lucrative gift of weeping', 'a great jester, not a great humourist', a mountebank, incapable of genuine feeling. He even makes the outrageous statement that 'there is not a page of Sterne's writing but has something that were better away, a latent corruption— a hint, as of an impure presence'.[23] And yet, self-conscious and self-doubting craftsman that he is, he cannot help thinking: 'Am I like that, too? Isn't there a great deal of Sterne in me?' Then he expresses this disquiet:

A perilous trade, indeed, is that of a man who has to bring his tears and laughter, his recollections, his personal griefs and joys, his private thoughts and feelings to market, to write them on paper, and sell them for money. . . . How much of the paint and emphasis is necessary for the fair business of the stage, and how much of the rant and rouge is put on for the vanity of the actor? His audience trusts him: can he trust himself?[24]

A pertinent question. Had Thackeray asked it of himself oftener, he might, and probably would, have become a better novelist. Had he tried to see through the paint with which Sterne—there is no denying it—daubed his face, he would certainly have proved a better critic.

§ 4

The 'quackery' was repeated in a second series, with the general title of *The Four Georges*—a strange medley of history, gossip, and homily, which Thackeray began writing in September 1855 and took with him for delivery in America not many weeks later.

To prepare these lectures did not cost him much labour.

He had done most of the necessary reading before. He could now claim to be well acquainted with the eighteenth century, and, undoubtedly, liked it better than the fashion of his time approved. Whether he understood it better than some twenty years before may be questioned. The Victorian Code had been pressing on him steadily and more effectually, perhaps, than he would have openly admitted. It was hostile to the spirit of the mid and later eighteenth century, and was all the while whispering in his ear that to show admiration for the Humes and Gibbons, Horace Walpoles, Henry Fieldings, George Selwyns, and Lord Chesterfields who had graced England during the Enlightenment was a little unbecoming in a family novelist of an age so respectable and earnest as Victoria's. Nor was he sure enough within his own mind to repel these suggestions. For a number of reasons (popular success being only one of them), he was losing that clarity of vision, that detached, ironical tolerance, that independent judgement on men and affairs, which he had learnt from the men of the eighteenth century and had never quite lost (save when under the domination of an obsession of some kind) in the years up to 1852. When acquaintances of his—Whitwell Elwin, for example—who were far more Victorian in outlook than himself, and of whom, in the middle and late fifties, he saw more than of older, less respectable acquaintances, told him that the prevailing attitude of his eighteenth-century favourites was deplorably Sadducean, he was half persuaded to believe it. It was all most disturbing to a writer and historian of his vacillating and uncertain temper. It confirmed those Victorian or mother-determined scrupulosities which had been evident from time to time even in the earliest of his work.

Moreover, he required audiences. Audiences brought him the large sums of money that he craved—for his daughters, of course, for his daughters. It was whiskered and complacent fathers of families, strait-laced mothers of families, who were buying his novels and the tickets for his lectures. They desired to be edified; they resented being shocked.

We should do Thackeray a wrong if we said that he was thinking only of his pocket. He did think of his pocket; he thought too much of it. But it was not thoughts of his pocket which solely determined his conduct. There was much in his own character that concurred with Victorian demands and Victorian scruples. The result was that he yielded more and more to the ethos of his world, and, between 1855 and 1863, allowed sentiment and sanctimony, together with repeated illness, gradually to erode what had never been a well-compacted and robust mind.

The erosion becomes egregious for the first time in *The Four Georges.*

Towards George I and George II, who had both been a long time dead, he is not unduly savage: and the 'Sketches of Manners, Morals, Court and Town Life' between 1700 and 1760 he often turns prettily enough even when he fails to suggest depth and solidity. It is very like him, at one time to cry out against the 'flaunting vice and levity' of the Court of George II,[25] and not long afterwards to deplore the passing of the 'merrier England' of our ancestors.[26] He grossly sentimentalizes George III, extolling him for his domestic virtues and then, absurdly, comparing him with Lear at the conclusion of the tragedy.

There is no excuse for his lecture on the last of the Georges. After all, George IV, so-called First Gentleman of Europe, was to Thackeray an old familiar topic. Even in Thackeray's younger days, when over-righteousness could hardly be laid at his door, he had shown more than a casual antipathy to George IV; he had trounced him several times, in fiction and reviews;[27] he had never been ready to admit any virtues in 'the great simulacrum'. To Thackeray—and he had lain in the garden of Great-Grandmamma Becher's house at Fareham and listened to the bells ringing for George IV's coronation[28]—this king had always been a faithless and debauched dandy— nothing more. Now, in 1855, with the added influence of the Victorian Code at work within him, he set out to overwhelm the 'royal old mummy' with what Elton prettily called 'a cascade of pulpit eloquence'.[29]

The lecture on George IV is not history; it is not even clever and amusing satire; it is sanctimonious and stupid. Thackeray overreached himself, and in spite of continual hammering on the moral note, failed to convince even audiences who were predisposed to be edified. His audiences, on both sides of the Atlantic, felt uncomfortable. Often enough, they did not know just why, and, groping after reasons, concluded that the lecturer must be anti-royalist, and that anti-royalism, though it might be permissible and even laudable in an American citizen, was to be resented in a British subject. The English clergyman who, after listening to this lecture, dubbed Thackeray an 'elderly infidel buffoon',[30] showed not only his irritation but his muddle-headedness. Republicanism did not go very deep in Thackeray. The truth was that in abusing George IV to the extent that he did, he out-Victoria'd the Victorians. In this priggish lecturer they dimly saw themselves, but in a caricature. Little wonder they were discomposed.

XIII. MRS. BROOKFIELD

God bless her. For all the pain and grief to both of us: I would not
have *not* had her love for anything in the world. It's apart from
desire, or jealousy of anyone else, that I think of her and shall
always. There is nothing I know or have ever read or thought of so
lovely as her nature is. (Thackeray to the Perry sisters, 3 March 1853:
Ray, iii. 221.)

§ 1

THE story of Thackeray's infatuation with Jane Octavia
Brookfield is relevant to the present book in two ways: it
confirms the general impression we get of him as a man
lacking in decision of character and easily enfeebled in will
by an emotional dependence on women; and it affected his
fiction both directly and indirectly. If only for these
reasons, it is worth telling at some length.

§ 2

The most likely date for his first meeting with her is
November 1841, when she came to London as a bride. She
was then twenty years of age, the daughter of Sir Charles
Elton, Bart., of Clevedon Court, Somerset. She had just
married the Rev. William Brookfield, a man who had been
a fellow student of Thackeray's at Trinity College, and
who, as curate of St. James's Church, Piccadilly, was
already making a name for himself as a popular preacher
in the West End.

Many years later, Thackeray told her that he could not
live 'without the tenderness of some woman'.[1] It is not
probable that he told her anything like this in 1841, when
it might have startled her; but the statement would have

been as true then as at any other time. His mother had accustomed him to such tenderness from his earliest years, and his wife, foolish and empty-headed, perhaps, but affectionate, had confirmed him in the need for it. Separated now from both, living in clubs and taverns and sparely furnished lodgings, he turned almost instinctively to Jane Brookfield. She was beautiful, gentle, still very young, and ready enough to accept him as her husband's best friend; and that, we may be certain, was the most that Thackeray expected from her in the early forties. If they drifted into another relationship later, it was very gradually, almost insensibly. Years had to pass before either would admit, even privately, that another relationship was conceivable.

Meanwhile, Jane Brookfield had the gift of listening. She needed it, with a witty and linguacious fellow for a husband, and a boisterous, satiric visitor who, when he was not stretching out his long legs towards the fire in her drawing-room, was composing entertaining letters to her. Brookfield, who should have been an actor, and could play any part from buffoon to hero (tragic), gave Thackeray all the verbal stimulus he needed. It was Jane's business to be audience. That part she played very well. Before very long Thackeray had learnt to depend on her as someone whom he could talk to about almost anything that occupied his mind.

She was flattered; even then she was flattered. Thackeray, although still nothing but a hard-working journalist, who, for all his airs and bustle, had in ten years made less impression on his fellow Londoners than her husband had been able to produce in a few months with his wit, good talk, and inspiring sermons, was a big man in appearance, fluent and exuberant; and he easily persuaded her that to him (as to her husband) she was indispensable. She became his friend and counsellor. He consulted her about his daughters,[2] and about his 'poor little wife'; about his most affectionate but 'imperial' and obstinate mother, who alarmed her;[3] about where he ought to live; and about his work—most flattering of all.

Till the year 1851 Thackeray continued on the best of terms with her husband. They had amiable nicknames for each other—'Vieux', 'Mr. Williams', 'His Reverence', 'Little Frank Whitestock' for the parson, and 'Thack', 'Thackwack', and 'Tackeridge' for the journalist. Jane spoke of them, with perhaps a touch of jealousy, as 'very hand in glove'. They would go for long rambles over London, and come back to dine at Thackeray's favourite club, the Garrick, or to sup and smoke and have 'goes' of something strong at a Bohemian haunt like the Back Kitchen, where Brookfield had to keep his priestly conscience in subjection—not a very difficult performance. It seems that Jane now and then felt a little doubtful, on the score of propriety. It shocked her to learn that 'Father Prout', who had been a crony of Maginn's, and whom someone had called 'the most delightful unbeliever', sometimes made a third in these escapades. For Thackeray to be intimate with Father Prout might be well enough; but for her husband, curate at St. James's and a preacher with a growing reputation, it was scarcely fitting. For, after all, Father Prout had been a priest once, and the rumour went that he had been unfrocked, or, at best, had unfrocked himself.

But the Rev. William reassured her with a lie: Father Prout was by no means indecorous. Whether she believed this or not, we have no means of telling.

All the same, she was right in her fears. Brookfield as a preacher continued to draw large crowds, but, having gained the reputation of laxity, if not in morals, at least in his social behaviour, he received no promotion in the Church, and began to grow peevish and unreasonable. Early in 1848, however, he was appointed an inspector of schools, and his clerical superiors were much relieved.

But it does not seem that he was equally relieved. He had hoped for a bishopric. Failure in his chosen profession, together with a natural vanity which his congregation at St. James's had continued to feed by their admiration of his melting eye, fine head of hair, and delightful, witty sermons, had increased his peevishness. Besides, though he said little, he was not quite easy in his mind over Jane and his old friend Thackeray.

He had cause. Once, when oppressed by his blue devils, Thackeray wrote to her: 'Je fais de la littérature ma parole d'honneur—du style—du Sterne tout pur.'[4] It was true. He had begun to play Sterne to the Eliza of Jane Brookfield.

The Brookfields had begun to suffer from 'matrimonial irritations' as early as 1845. In 1847 they went visiting to Southampton, whither Thackeray followed them; and while there, Thackeray expressed publicly, and too warmly, something of the admiration he had long felt for the lovely Jane. It was too much. The Rev. William flared up.

Thackeray bethought himself, and on the way back to London, 'under the confessional seal in the railway', he wrote to Brookfield:

Her innocence, looks, angelical sweetness and kindness charm and ravish me in the highest degree; and every now and then in contemplating them I burst out into uncouth raptures. They are not the least dangerous—it is a sort of artistical delight (a spiritual sensuality so to speak)—other beautiful objects in Nature so affect me. . . . My dear old fellow, you and God Almighty may know all my thoughts about your wife. . . . If I had envy, or what you call passion, or a wicked thought . . . I should have cut you long ago.[5]

Whatever Brookfield may have thought of this strange epistle, he endorsed and kept it; then, for the next three or four years, he behaved to Thackeray as if the incident in Southampton had been forgotten. As for Thackeray, he seems to have thought that a protest of his unimpeachable intentions was sufficient; and he now felt even freer to indulge himself in 'spiritual sensuality'. For the next two years or thereabouts 'il faisait du Sterne tout pur'.

Of the two, he was the more deceived; for women have a way of seeing through 'uncouth raptures' and 'artistical delight'. In his letters he is guarded but equivocal. He insists on calling her his 'dear lady' and his 'dear sister'—

self-deceptions that remind us of a boy of seventeen when he first falls in love with an older woman. For the rest, much of his phrasing can be taken innocently or not, as the recipient of the letters chooses.

Some of the 'uncouth raptures', nevertheless, are extremely uncouth. Here is one on the theme of death:

> We will love each other while we may here and afterwards: if you go first you will kneel for me in Heaven and bring me there; if I, I swear the best thought I have is to remember that I shall have your love surviving me and with a constant tenderness blessing my memory. I can't all perish living in your heart. . . . It seems to me that Love proves God. By Love I believe and am saved.[6]

To such shifts had his perplexities and the Victorian Code reduced Thackeray!

The clouds blew up again at the beginning of January 1849, when Jane's uncle, Henry Hallam the historian, seems to have told Thackeray that he was seeing too much of her. Thackeray wrote to her the same night, asking her to tell her uncle that he claimed 'to be as one of your brothers'.

> As for William [he goes on], I am bound to him by benefits by the most generous confidence and repeated proofs of friendship; and to you dear lady by an affection wh. I hope wont finish with my life of wh. you have formed for a long time past one of the greatest and I hope the purest pleasures. If I had a bad thought towards you I think I could not look my friend or you in the face, and I see no shame in owning that I love you.[7]

All the same, this episode seems to have forced Thackeray to take stock of the situation as it was slowly developing. He must have now admitted to himself that his feelings for Mrs. Brookfield were no longer merely 'spiritual' or 'artistical'. And so, like his own Harry Esmond, he tried absence.

The whole of *Esmond* is steeped in recollections of the Brookfield entanglement. Here is one example:

> Doth any young gentleman of my progeny, who may read his old grandfather's papers, chance to be presently suffering under the passion of Love? There is a humiliating cure, but one

that is easy and almost specific for the malady—which is, to try an alibi. Esmond went away from his mistress and was cured half-a-dozen times; he came back to her side, and instantly fell ill again of the fever. He vowed that he could leave her and think no more of her, and so he could pretty well, at least, succeed in quelling that rage and longing he had whenever he was with her; but as soon as he returned he was as bad as ever again.[8]

Harry found his cure for the time being, and perhaps so did Thackeray. He spent the first fortnight of February 1849 in Paris, and that was when he renewed acquaintance with his cousin, Mary Carmichael. Though he wrote long letters to Jane Brookfield, there is nothing in them to suggest that he was missing her very badly. Indeed, he was having a fairly lively time without her.

§ 3

Matters were allowed to drift for the next two years. There was no longer much love between Brookfield and his wife. He was short-tempered with her, and apparently contemptuous; and her attitude to him was that of the dutiful Victorian wife who had made her bed and must lie on it. But they kept up appearances. Thackeray knew that things had gone wrong between them, but what could he do? Being victims of the Victorian Code, he and she seem to have remained technically virtuous, eating out their hearts in submission to it. At least, that is what Thackeray did. As for Jane Brookfield, it is doubtful if she had much heart to eat. Though she certainly looked angelical, she was cold, timid, and calculating by nature.

Nevertheless, in February 1850, to the surprise of most people and the half-acknowledged distress of Thackeray, she presented her husband with a daughter, after eight years of marriage. The child was christened Magdalene. The name startled many of the parents' friends and relations. Old Mr. Brookfield, up in Yorkshire, had to search the works of the Christian Fathers in order to prove that *the* Magdalene had been something much better than a harlot. It was all very disconcerting.

But the infant grew, quite unconscious of the minor scandal that her name had caused. Very soon she became a special favourite of Thackeray's daughters; and in August it was arranged that these girls, with their governess, should share a house in Southampton with the Brookfields. Brookfield himself, one gathers, did not welcome the plan, though he did not actively oppose it. In any case, during most of the month he was moving back and forward between Southampton and London. As for Thackeray, he now had a very good excuse for renewing his acquaintance with Southampton. To be near his daughters he booked rooms at the Dolphin, and when not at work there went visiting with Jane in the Isle of Wight. He returned to London on 20 August and wrote to her the next day:

I wonder whether ever again I shall have such a happy peaceful fortnight as that last! How sunshiny the landscape remains in my mind, I hope for always; and the smiles of dear children and the aspect of the kindest and tenderest face in the world to me. God bless you, God bless you my sister. I know what you'll do when you read this—well, so am I. I can hardly see as I write for the eye-water, but it isn't with grief, but for the natural pathos of the thing. How happy your dear regard makes me! How it takes off the solitude and eases it. . . . O Love and Duty—I hope you'll never leave us quite.[9]

The appeal to Love and Duty is the more significant, because, long afterwards, Thackeray confessed that he and Mrs. Brookfield had been restrained from taking the final step towards which they had been heading for years—going off to live together somewhere on the Continent—mainly by the thought of the children—Anny, Minny, and now Magdalene. After all, Thackeray must have known something about what happened to the children in such cases, since his maternal grandmother had eloped with Colonel Butler while his mother was very young.

Again matters were allowed to drift till the spring of 1851. Then it was discovered that William Brookfield's lungs were in poor shape. He had to stay away from London for weeks at a time, and even crossed to France in search of a cure. Somehow one gets the impression that he was not so ill as he pretended, and that his wife knew it. At all events he missed the excitement of the Great Exhibition and of Thackeray's lectures on the humorists, stories of which his wife passed on to him in letters. As for her, she was enjoying herself very well in London, and becoming quite a personage. Thackeray was able to call on her nearly every day.

By 10 July the 'quackery' was over for the time being, and he and his daughters left for a tour of the Rhine, Switzerland, and Italy. During the first part of the tour he went on prattling to Jane in letters, mostly about incidents of travel; only once or twice did he fall back into the affectionate, caressing tone that we find in earlier letters. Writing from Switzerland on 17 July, he calls her the 'one good thing' in London.[10] He is daily expecting letters from her.

None came. Then, abruptly, his own letters cease. None that he may have written to her between 21 July 1851 and October 1852 have been printed anywhere. Our knowledge of what occurred during this period is incomplete.

It seems, however, that William Brookfield timed his return to London so that he just missed Thackeray. During July and August he had his wife to himself, and what evidence there is goes to show that he made life anything but pleasant for her. There was no meeting with Thackeray until September. Then there was a stormy one. It is not clear whether Jane Brookfield was present or not, but there is no doubt that high words were spoken on both sides, and that Thackeray denounced the husband as a selfish, valetudinarian bully and egoist, incapable of valuing a wife far too good for him. They parted in anger. It was understood that Thackeray was not to see Mrs. Brookfield again. 'The affair', Thackeray wrote to Kate Perry, one of his and Jane's most sympathetic friends, 'is at an end and the rupture complete.'[11]

London became unbearable to Thackeray. He hurried

away into Derbyshire, settled himself at an inn, and tried
to forget his pain in writing. 'I wrote a bit yesterday that
was quite Satanic,' he told Kate Perry, 'and raged about
with a dreadful gaiety.'[12]

Meanwhile Jane Brookfield was showing her distress
also. She wrote a letter to her friend, Mrs. Fanshawe of
Southampton, which was both about and directed at
Thackeray; and Mrs. Fanshawe did as she was meant to,
and passed the letter on to him. On the spur of the moment
he wrote back, asking Mrs. Fanshawe 'to inform her
principal that even this roundabout correspondence
oughtn't to be'; Brookfield, he said somewhat oddly, was
acting 'nobly and gently' and must be nobly and gently
used.[13]

But to keep so heroically aloof was beyond Thackeray.
Two days later he found himself writing a letter that was
meant for Jane herself:

> The fact of your position makes it impossible to write almost
> —I am not to show that I feel you are miserable. I am not to show
> that I think your husband is wicked and cruel to you. I am not
> to show that I think you know you are unhappy, and are
> treated with the most cruel tyranny—Nobody is to know any-
> thing of your misery. We are to go on grinning as if we were
> happy, because William's cough is certainly very bad, and he
> should not be disturbed in exercising his temper.[14]

He did not send this letter—at least, not direct to Jane.
He enclosed it in another to Kate Perry, to whom he exploded: 'What hasn't she given up for that man? Youth
and happiness and now her dearest friend—what a friend
—and to what a man—a fellow that says to her face that
he ought to have married a cook, and treats her like one.
He'll do better now after this great shock, and shows a
great generosity on a great occasion.' At the end he added:
'After his letter by which I saw how much the poor soul
had given me up, I . . . checked all correspondence through
that dear good Mrs. F. There can be no harm in a message
between friends now and then.'[15]

What Brookfield's great generosity consisted of we do

not know. It is not to be understood as forgiveness of his
wife for actual adultery with Thackeray; for that, I am
convinced, never took place at any time. The distressing
story of Lady Clara in *The Newcomes* is Thackeray's
imaginative working out of what *might* have happened in
the lives of Jane and himself if they had been able to overcome their scruples. He shows sympathy for Lady Clara,
and permits even the self-righteous Laura Pendennis to
show sympathy too—so long as Lady Clara is only
tempted and remains formally virtuous. After she runs
away from the odious Barnes Newcome, her husband, and
elopes with Jack Belsize, he paints in drab colours the
misery of her outcast life; though sorry for her, he nowhere
suggests that Society's condemnation of the two sinners
is unjust; he contents himself with railing in his usual
manner at the snobbishness and mammoniacal supersti-
tion which had driven her into marriage with such a blackguard as Barnes to begin with. She was 'sold' to Barnes as
a virgin. That is what infuriates him. But apparently she
had no right to break the iniquitous contract after she had
once been forced into it.

It is probable, too, that Thackeray was thinking of his
own case when he delivered his tiresome exhortation to
Philip Firmin and Charlotte Baynes (in *Philip*) at the time
of their marriage: 'Husband, father, whatsoever your lot,
be your heart pure, your life honest. For the sake of those
who bear your name, let no bad action sully it. . . .'[16]

Brookfield's 'great shock' must have been realization
that his wife had no longer either affection or respect for
him. This would be shock enough for a man of his character, accustomed to admiration and devotion from the
women in his churches and schools.

Thackeray, brooding over events for another week after
his message to Jane through Kate Perry, began to think of
Jane, too, with resentment. He wrote again to their
common friend:

I don't see how any woman should not love a man who had
loved her as I did J.; I don't see how any man should not love

150

a woman so beautiful, so unhappy, so tender; I don't see how any husband, however he might have treated her, should be indifferent at the idea of losing it. . . . I'm sure that one or the other on their side were wrong in not dismissing me. . . . I wish that I had never loved her. I have been played with by a woman, and flung over at a beck from the lord and master—that's what I feel. . . . I was packing away yesterday the letters of years. These didn't make me cry. They made me laugh as I knew they would. It was for this that I gave my heart away. It was 'When are you coming dear Mr. Thackeray,' and 'William will be so happy,' and 'I thought after you had gone away how I had forgot etc.', and at a word from Brookfield afterwards it is—'I reverence and admire and love him with not merely a dutiful but a genuine love'—Amen. The thought that I have been made a fool of is the bitterest of all, perhaps.[17]

We could delete the final *perhaps*. Thackeray being the sort of man he was, the thought that he had been made a fool of *must* have been the bitterest of all to him. But this letter of his is ungenerous, even if Jane Brookfield merited his condemnation, which is probable enough. A man may think such thoughts; he may even express them to the offender; but he deserves no respect if he expresses them, so soon after the event, to a third party.

A second meeting between Thackeray and Brookfield was arranged in October 1851 by Lady Ashburton. It took place at her country house, the Grange. They were formally polite, shook hands, and parted. 'I'm very thankful [Thackeray wrote to Kate Perry] that her dear little heart is made tranquil on the source of our enmity at least. Friends of course we're not; but bear each other, and in six months things may be better.'[18] Not that Brookfield had made the occasion easy: 'He is full of queer ceremonies, punctilios unheard of amongst men of a franker sort. He clings to the fancy that nobody knows anything about his interior; and I shall of course hold my wagging tongue and speak of his affairs as little as possible.'[19]

The same month Thackeray reported to Dr. John Brown of Edinburgh, to whom he had previously confided his secret: 'The wound's healed, but the weakness is not over quite.'[20]

§ 4

It never was over quite. After his return from America Thackeray began to meet the Brookfields again in London, but not, of course, on the old footing. His attitude towards them varied with his mood. For Brookfield he seems to have felt more contempt than ever, and this found indirect expression in the characters of the Rev. Charles Honeyman in *The Newcomes* and Parson Sampson in *The Virginians*, both popular preachers whose cadences must, one feels sure, have contained many echoes of Brookfield's. To Jane he sometimes professed to be wholly indifferent, but if this mood was genuine it was always short-lived. In December 1853 he was suffering from something very like the old 'rage and longing', and, being the man he was, must needs unpack his heart to Kate Perry:

I admire human nature in thinking of her. I think I am nearer to her when away than when sitting by her, talking of things we don't feel—with poor Tomkin's restless eye ever and again trying not to look at us. It's happier that we should love each other in the grave, as it were, than that we should meet by sham-chance, and that there should be secrets or deceit. When you see her preach this to her again and again. Many and many a time a friend of mine whispers me (he is represented in pictures with horns and a tail), 'My good friend *a quoi bon* all this longing and yearning and disappointment; yonder gnawing grief and daily nightly brooding? A couple of lies and the whole thing might be remedied. Do you suppose other folks are so particular?' Behold there are 4 children put their innocent figures between the devil and me; and the wretched old fiend shirks off with his tail between his hoofs. Go and wipe away her tears, you dear kind sisters of charity. My girls I suppose see all about it; but they love her all the same.[21]

Increasingly, however, resentment gained on him. Jane Brookfield had no heart, had never had any heart, and had made a fool of him—these were the thoughts uppermost in his mind.

It was like him, too, not to be able to 'hold his wagging

tongue'. As soon as Thackeray got a new 'love' (his own word) he could not resist talking to her about his 'ex-loves' (his own word again). It was no doubt another expression of vanity, but seems to have been very little restrained by the male code of honour, 'Kiss if you like, but do not kiss and tell'. It is clear that when he began to take more than a passing interest in Sally Baxter in America in the winter of 1852–3, he told her a good deal about the Brookfield affair; writing to her afterwards from Europe he refers to Jane Brookfield as *l'autre* or 'the frying pan'. This rather cheap jocularity might be forgiven him if the *affaires de cœur* had been superficial and harmless; but the affair with Jane Brookfield at any rate was serious.

Moreover, he nearly reproduced it in a novel. The Rev. Whitwell Elwin met him in Piccadilly on an autumn day of 1856, reminded him of the half-promise at the end of *The Newcomes* to make J. J. Ridley the hero of a later novel, and inquired if the novel had been started yet. Thackeray hedged a little, and the parson, a true mid-Victorian, urged him to describe 'a domestic family, enjoying the genuine blessings of calm, domestic felicity, put in contrast with the vexations and hollowness of fashionable life'. This fatuous suggestion Thackeray brushed aside. How could he describe what he had never seen? Besides, such a story 'must of necessity want movement.'

Then he outlined the novel he had planned and started: 'I intended to show J. J. married, and exhibit him with the trials of a wife and children. I meant to make him in love with another man's wife, and recover him through his attachment for the little ones.'[22]

The horrified Elwin protested; but whether only on the general ground that a theme like this was improper for a novel, or because he knew enough about the Brookfield affair to be shocked at the parallel, we cannot tell. Nor can we tell whether it was this protest or a sudden access of good sense and good taste in himself that induced Thackeray to discard his plan. But discard it he did.

XIV. 'ESMOND'

Here is the very best I can do, and I am carrying it to Prescott as a reward of merit for having given me my first dinner in America. I stand by this book, and am willing to leave it where I go as my card. (Thackeray in conversation, as reported by Wilson, *Thackeray in the United States*, i. 17.)

§ 1

THACKERAY wrote *Esmond* during the second half of 1851 and the first half of 1852. It was the only one of his novels which did not first appear in serial form. The printing was somewhat delayed, owing to a shortage of the special type used for it, but a few advance copies were handed to him at the dockside in Liverpool, only an hour or two before he sailed for America on 30 October 1852. It was probably one of these copies that he gave to Prescott the historian.

Owing to the Brookfield imbroglio, the whole period of the writing was one of 'grief and pain so severe' that the author did not care to recall it afterwards.[1] The book itself is accordingly grave and sad. He spoke of it at one point as being marked by 'cutthroat melancholy'.[2] Even so, he was probably right in thinking it his best achievement in fiction.

Esmond is more steadfast and inexorable than any of his other works. Many good judges have disliked it, but few who have been willing to surrender themselves to it have failed to get the sense of its inevitability. All the events recorded *must* have happened just so; the characters are not puppets being manipulated by the author's supple fingers and discoursed upon in weekday sermons; like the sun shining on their heads and the waters of the Thames flowing past their homes, they appear actual, inerrably known. They are lived.

On visiting Bavaria in August 1852, after the book was finished, Thackeray told his daughters:

What I was pleased with was to find that Blenheim was just exactly the place I had figured to myself except that the village is larger, but I fancy I had actually been there—so like the aspect of it was to what I looked for. . . . I saw the brook wh. H. Esmond crossed, and almost the spot where he fell wounded and walked down to the Danube and mused mighty thoughts over it.[3]

For this and similar reasons the book has been called 'picturesque'. The adjective needs qualification. *Esmond* is full of what seem like pictures, sharply visualized and beautifully composed; it is fuller of these, undoubtedly, than the other novels. The discriminated occasions that we recall from *Esmond* are more often immobile or 'posed' than the ones that we recall from *Vanity Fair* or *Pendennis*; they are tableaux rather than scenes of action. At all events, they appear so, till we turn back and look more closely. We recall the lonely and forgotten little boy in the great Yellow Gallery at Castlewood, when he first meets his *Dea certe* and her daughter, Beatrix; the departure of the sinister Lord Mohun from Castlewood, when Rachel watches from the drawing-room window and Lord Castlewood stands in the courtyard gazing into the basin of the fountain; the dimly lit duel by night in Leicester Fields, with the chairmen peering in through the railings; Esmond's discharge from Newgate and slow journey by boat up the sunshiny bustling river to Chelsey; Esmond's visit to Winchester Cathedral and his watching of Lady Castlewood and Frank during the evening service; Beatrix posed on the stairs at Walcote House, showing her scarlet stockings; Esmond at his mother's grave in Flanders; the Duke of Hamilton bowing to the Marquis of Esmond after the spirited dialogue about the diamonds. These are like tableaux and might be called picturesque. But let us be careful what we mean by the word. None of the tableaux are detachable from the narrative; and they are all seen through the eyes and grasped by the mind of the memoirist, Harry Esmond. What we receive on each occasion is not so much a picture presented and valued for its own sake as the effect of the picture on the man.

Take the description of the journey from Newgate Prison to Chelsey:

> The fellow in the orange-tawny livery with blue lace and facings was in waiting when Esmond came out of prison, and, taking the young gentleman's slender baggage, led the way out of that odious Newgate, and by Fleet Conduit, down to the Thames, where a pair of oars was called, and they went up the river to Chelsey. Esmond thought the sun had never shone so bright; nor the air felt so fresh and exhilarating. Temple Garden, as they rowed by, looked like the Garden of Eden to him, and the aspect of the quays, wharves, and buildings by the river, Somerset House, and Westminster (where the splendid new bridge was just beginning), Lambeth tower and palace, and that busy shining scene of the Thames swarming with boats and barges, filled his heart with pleasure and cheerfulness.[4]

This is no moving-picture of the river; it is a recording of human experience, of what Esmond thought and felt, of what 'filled his heart'.

It is the same in Winchester Cathedral. The picture is built up only as it is necessary to account for what is passing in the minds of Harry, Rachel Castlewood, and young Frank. Indeed, it is some time after the party has left the cathedral when we learn that the gold sun had shone round Harry's head when Rachel first looked up and saw him. The gold sun was not important in itself; it was important only in the experiencing of it by Rachel.

Not that all the discriminated occasions in the book are mainly pictorial in this way; it is only that there are a greater number of pictorial occasions than in the other novels. Many contain dialogue and action as well. As in the other novels, the best are short; indeed, there is only one

long one—the last in the book. But they differ from the
occasions in the other novels in another way too: the
best, instead of being scenes of high comedy, are extremely
serious, even tense; they are the kind of scenes that we
expect in tragedy.

In *Esmond*, too, Thackeray wrote one perfect speech
that is both serious and long—the speech in which Beatrix
takes leave of Harry when he is setting out to fetch the
Prince to England.[5] Not a word of its five or six hundred
could be bettered.

§ 2

One discriminated occasion in *Esmond* Thackeray
spoiled, as he did the scene of the crisis in the life of Becky
Sharp, by interpolating a paragraph of comment. This is
when Esmond returns from Vigo, goes to Walcote House,
and is reconciled with his friends there. Rachel Castlewood
takes one of her 'wild' fits, falls laughing and sobbing on
the young man's heart, and cries: 'Bringing your sheaves
with you—your sheaves with you.' It is the climax, the
climax to which Thackeray has been skilfully working up
for pages; and he should have stopped his chapter there.
But he cannot. He must needs add a strident, theatrical
paragraph, which reminds us unpleasantly of Helen and
Arthur Pendennis. Once again it is primarily a case of
mother and son, for Rachel has stood in the place of a
mother to Harry. The mature Thackeray loses grip—all
the more so because there is now a sharp conflict between
his conscious mind, which is building Rachel mainly on
Jane Brookfield, and his unconscious or half-conscious
mind, which is mixing her up with his own mother. Hence
the adolescent or pre-adolescent fustian.

His grip relaxes again for a page or thereabouts when
he brings Esmond to tell Beatrix that the Duke of Hamilton has been killed. It is an unaccountable failure. The
preparations for the episode were excellent; the setting
was well contrived; nothing, indeed, could have pointed

the irony better than that Esmond should find Beatrix
chaffering with tradesmen in anticipation of her marriage
with the now-murdered Duke. But the dialogue went false.
Then, as if to emphasize its falsity by contrast, Thackeray
added as wonderful a paragraph of quiet, dignified, and
shapely prose as he ever wrote:

As Esmond and the Dean walked away from Kensington
discoursing of this tragedy, and how fatal it was to the cause
which they both had at heart, the street-criers were already out
with their broadsides, shouting through the town the full, true,
and horrible account of the death of Lord Mohun and Duke
Hamilton in a duel. A fellow had got to Kensington and was
crying it in the square there at very early morning, when Mr.
Esmond happened to pass by. He drove the man from under
Beatrix's very window, whereof the casement had been set
open. The sun was shining though 'twas November: he had
seen the market-carts rolling into London, the guard relieved
at the Palace, the labourers trudging to their work in the
gardens between Kensington and the City—the wandering
merchants and hawkers filling the air with their cries. The
world was going to its business again, although dukes lay dead
and ladies mourned for them; and kings, very likely, lost their
chances. So night and day pass away, and to-morrow comes,
and our place knows us not. Esmond thought of the courier,
now galloping on the North Road to inform him, who was Earl
of Arran yesterday, that he was Duke of Hamilton to-day, and
of a thousand great schemes, hopes, ambitions, that were alive
in the gallant heart, beating a few hours since, and now in a
little dust quiescent.[6]

§ 3

In spite of occasional lapses into theatricality and rant,
to which Thackeray was always liable, *Esmond* reaches
and sustains a level of style unique in his work. For one
thing, he was not all the while writing against time, with
the printer's devil sitting in the hall, waiting for copy to
fill the next instalment; he could revise and polish. Apart
from that, however, he was cultivating a style, a special
style. As the book purported to be the memoirs of a man
born in the late seventeenth century, and living as the

familiar of the Augustan wits, a man who drank with Steele, discoursed of state business with Swift, and wrote a *Spectator* paper for the great Addison, it was necessary that his style should correspond. But to say that Thackeray imitated or affected the Augustans is to suggest that the style of *Esmond* is unnatural—a collection of antiques out of Wardour Street. It is not. The marvel of it is that it always reads like Thackeray, and yet, simultaneously, like someone who had died a century before him—not Steele or Addison or Swift or Pope or Bolingbroke, but someone unidentified who *might* have been a close friend and admirer of all of them. Very rarely do we catch the author at his tricks.[7] He has not only assimilated the political and social history of the time but also acquired the very tone of voice of a man who lived then.

To do all this cost him an immense labour. Writing to his mother from Glasgow in April 1852, he says that *Esmond* 'takes as much trouble as Macaulays History almost', and regrets that he lacks this historian's prodigious powers of memory. Given another six months, he might make the book into a 'durable history, complete in it's parts and its whole'.[8]

§ 4

This prompts the question, What was Thackeray's aim in *Esmond*? To write a novel, or to write a 'durable history'?

Charlotte Brontë, after reading only the first two volumes (in manuscript), thought the book overloaded with history, and wished the author could be told not to trouble himself so deeply over the political and religious intrigues of the day, since what he could do far better was 'to show us human nature at home, as he himself daily sees it'.[9] Other readers have agreed with her.

Had Charlotte Brontë's opinion been based on the whole novel, instead of only the first two volumes, she might have been less certain that the history overloaded the fiction. Vol. iii contains the story of an abortive Jacobite plot, which depends on the likeness between the Prince (the Old

Pretender) and Frank Castlewood. No adequate preparations for the plot have been made earlier in the book, all that the reader has been told being that the Prince and Frank are of an age.[10] Apart from this hint, given twice, there is nothing in the first 300-odd pages to make the Jacobite plot in the remaining 70 or 80 inevitable. It is rather an episode within the story than essential to it. For the main plot of the novel is entirely independent of history. It turns on the love of Harry Esmond for Rachel, Lady Castlewood, and hers for him—love that begins as filial on the one side and maternal on the other, and is gradually transformed into sexual on both. *Esmond*, in fact, is not an historical novel with a love-story thrown in; it is a love-story of a peculiar kind cast into an historical setting.

As soon as we realize this, as soon, that is to say, as we realize that the warp of the novel is the love-story of Harry and Rachel, not the attempt to set James III on the throne, or the infatuation of Harry with Beatrix, or the mere 'life and adventures' of a boy supposed illegitimate who turns out to be 'the true heir', many things become clear that were dark before. We see that Thackeray has planned his book pretty carefully, and, apart from certain digressions which he could not resist (e.g. the Webb–Marlborough quarrel), and a tendency to load the first and second volumes with history, has kept the plan steadily in view. Some history was essential, first because the Esmonds had a tradition of loyalty to the Stuarts and could not be kept from meddling in affairs of state, and secondly because the historical setting gave the book a massiveness, dignity, and 'distance' that no domestic setting (Charlotte Brontë's 'human nature at home') could have built up so easily. On the whole, history served Thackeray very well in *Esmond*. It did much to push the events and characters in the book away from him. Had he used the period 1851–2 to compose a novel like *Pendennis*, his then obsession with Jane Brookfield would pretty certainly have ruined it. Jane Brookfield did influence *Esmond* considerably, but what might have been ill effects were counteracted or diminished by historical 'distance'.

Moreover, if we are to see the novel in its right proportions, we must think of Beatrix as secondary, not as the heroine. Her role, as Thackeray first conceived it, was similar to that of Blanche Amory in the story of Pen and Laura, and not altogether dissimilar from that of Becky Sharp when she interposed herself between George Osborne and Amelia. Beatrix was a third party in the love-story, not a second. It is true, of course, that she did her best to seduce Thackeray from his first intentions. But though he wavered from time to time, he was able in the end to resist her blandishments.

Hasty readers of *Esmond* (like Mrs. Jameson) are liable to overlook Thackeray's intention to show Rachel Castlewood as falling in love with Harry Esmond long before she knew what was happening to her, before the death of her first husband, and before Harry himself got an inkling of it. There are hints enough, however, in the first two volumes. When Lord Mohun, whose Christian name is also Harry, is thrown out of his chaise and knocked insensible, and Lord Castlewood announces to his wife, 'Here's poor Harry killed, my dear', she screams and falls in a faint; and when the right Harry arrives home safe and sound, she greets him 'with one of her shining looks, and a voice of tender welcome', as well as a kiss—''twas the second time she had so honoured him'.[11] Thackeray does not mean his readers to make too much of this hint, but he does not mean them to ignore it either; for in the next chapter he underlines it in the dialogue between Esmond and Lord Castlewood. Soon afterwards Lord Mohun kills · Lord Castlewood in the duel in Leicester Fields, and this marks the beginning of the long misunderstanding between Harry and Rachel. She visits him in prison, behaves 'wildly', reproaches him with allowing her 'dear lord' to die, and goads him into saying that he wishes he were dead too. At the same time she gives him a glance 'that was at once so fond and so sad' that he is half-distracted.[12] Despite this fond glance, she continues to behave outrageously. She sends him a message by her chaplain that she wishes to see him no more in this world, and when Steele intervenes on Esmond's behalf:

'The lady shook her head', continued my kind scholar. '"The hearts of young men, Mr. Steele, are not so made", she said. "Mr. Esmond will find other—other friends. The mistress of this house [i.e. the elder Dowager Lady Castlewood] has relented very much towards the late lord's son", she added with a blush, "and has promised me—that is, has promised that she will care for his fortune. Whilst I live in it, after the horrid, horrid deed which has passed, Castlewood must never be a home to him—never. Nor would I have him write to me— except—no—I would have him never write to me, nor see him more. Give him, if you will, my parting—Hush! not a word of this before my daughter." '13

This is clumsy, being a report at two removes. But there are two things to be said about it. First, the motives and feelings behind Rachel's hesitant severity are clear: her cruelty to Esmond is cruelty to herself; it is herself she is punishing for having been unfaithful in will, though not in deed, to her murdered husband. Secondly, the whole episode, and this passage in particular, is full of memories (perhaps all conscious ones, perhaps not) of Jane Brookfield and her behaviour in 1851. Like Rachel, Jane wanted it both ways: she wanted to punish herself but to throw the blame on Thackeray; she wanted Thackeray to continue writing to her, and probably even to come secretly and see her; but she told him not to.

When it comes to the 'sheaves' scene at Walcote House, all disguises are removed. This is a love scene, no more and no less. Esmond, discovering how matters stand with his 'dearest mistress', there and then proposes to her that they should leave England together and begin a new life in Virginia. She refuses, urging duties to her children and her father, and when Esmond becomes more ardent and insistent, hushes him with a sudden return to the maternal. The chapter ends with an embrace—'as a brother folds a sister to his heart; and as a mother cleaves to her son's breast'.[14] The way Thackeray's ill-regulated fancy tends to mix, without properly fusing, the tutelary spirit of his childhood (Mrs. Carmichael-Smyth), the 'dear sister' that he tried to pretend Jane Brookfield had been in the years 1848–51, and the lover that he half-heartedly wished her to be at the same time, would repay the study of a clinical psychologist.

This scene takes place just short of the middle of the book. Thereafter the story may wander, but it always returns to the main track, which is the gradual transformation of Esmond's dutiful but indeterminate affection for Rachel into love of the same kind, though perhaps never of the same intensity, as hers for him.

Thackeray plans boldly, and takes risks. The echo of Harry's proposal to Rachel has scarcely died away when Beatrix makes her triumphal descent of the stairs at Walcote House. This is enough. Harry at once forgets Rachel, being 'rapt in admiration of the *filia pulchrior*'.[15]

§ 5

George Eliot found *Esmond* 'the most uncomfortable book you can imagine';[16] Mary Russell Mitford described it as 'painful, and unpleasant, and false';[17] Charlotte Brontë was angered by Thackeray's usual injustice to women, saying that there was scarcely any punishment he did not deserve for making Lady Castlewood 'jealous of a boy and a milkmaid';[18] Lord Rosebery thought the plot of the novel 'simply repulsive';[19] and Mrs. Jameson railed at its author in a loud voice:

And then Lady Castlewood—so evidently a favourite of the author, what shall we say of her? The virtuous woman, *par excellence*, who 'never sins and never forgives'; who never resents, nor relents, nor repents; the mother who is the rival of her daughter; the mother, who for years is the confidante of a man's delirious passion for her own child, and then consoles him by marrying him herself! O Mr. Thackeray! this will never do! Such women may exist, but to hold them up as examples of excellence, and fit objects of our best sympathies, is a fault, and proves a low standard in ethics and in art.[20]

Another contemporary reader remonstrated with Thackeray face to face for having made Esmond 'marry his mother-in-law'—an accusation that must have startled the man who had the strongest of feelings against mothers-in-law. 'I didn't make him do it,' Thackeray is said to have answered; 'they did it themselves.'[21]

George Eliot's word is right. For all its admirable qualities, *Esmond* is uncomfortable. It was disingenuous in Thackeray to suggest that his characters, Harry and Rachel at any rate, had run away with him, since he had obviously planned from the beginning how the book should end. But how far his choice of this plan was determined for him by something of which he was not fully conscious, is another question. Once before, in dealing with Helen and Arthur Pendennis, he had touched lightly on the relation between maternal and sexual love,[22] and it would seem that he had now deliberately chosen this as a central theme for *Esmond*, setting himself the delicate task of working out the transformation of what was predominantly maternal or filial to begin with, into what was predominantly sexual to end with. This was bound to disturb many readers. It conflicted with established sentiments. Worse still, he introduced the further complication that infuriated Mrs. Jameson—the rivalry of mother and daughter. Two interlocking themes, each highly unpopular with romantic readers, made the book almost insupportable.

No one wishes Beatrix away. She is one of Thackeray's triumphs. (And so is the Baroness Bernstein into whom she grew for *The Virginians*.) But it would have been simpler if he had made her the daughter of some other Esmond. As a niece or distant cousin of Rachel's, Beatrix would have been just as effective; and half the discomfort caused by the plot of the novel would have been removed.

Yet, when all is said, Thackeray spoke truth when he admitted the compulsion exerted upon him by his hero and

heroine. Harry and Rachel were projections from his own
private life. Harry is a self-portrait in a strange frame,
and Rachel is a portrait, sometimes idealized, sometimes
vitiated, of Jane Octavia Brookfield. They had to marry
in the end, for the story was a working out to a propitious
conclusion in fiction of contingencies which had worked
out wrong in life.

The resemblance between Harry Esmond and William
Thackeray is so marked that it has become a commonplace
of criticism. Writing to his mother, Thackeray calls
Esmond 'a handsome likeness of an ugly son of yours'.[23]
That is open confession. Whibley finds the likeness over
close,[24] and Saintsbury neatly disarms objections by
speaking of the 'triplicity' of the novel: 'Thus [he says]
Henry Esmond, who is on the whole, I should say, the
most like him of all his characters (though of course,
"romanced" a little), is himself and "the other fellow", and
also, as it were, human criticism of both.'[25]

It is also undisputed (though this is but a trifle) that in
Castlewood, the country house, Thackeray reproduced
Clevedon Court, Mrs. Brookfield's home during her child-
hood, doing no more to it than shift its location from
Somerset to Hampshire.

As for Rachel, Lady Castlewood, she is gracious, affectionate, tender, and, until she caught the small-pox, very
beautiful; apparently self-sacrificing, and sometimes really
so; but unjust and petty, too; pious, and for her day, too
prim; as a rule dignified, but apt in her 'wild' moments to
lose control and become hysterically calumnious, lachrymose, or tremulous; a foolishly fond mother to her son
Frank;[26] and alternately fond and jealous of her daughter.
In a moment of exasperation her husband damns her for
a woman who will not go astray because she has not
passion enough. She 'neither sins nor forgives', he says.
It is an acute judgement.[27]

Mutatis mutandis, all this might be said of the 'dear
lady' who is mirrored in Thackeray's letters to Jane
Brookfield, and in hers to him.

Beatrix, too, derives from Jane Brookfield, though less obviously. To Thackeray she represents the Jane Brookfield who is not so much his 'dear lady' or 'dear sister' as a galling infatuation, a disease in the blood, which is temporarily cured by absence. He gave Beatrix more attributes of Jane than we might imagine—physical coldness, social ambition, waywardness, to say nothing of her dazzling beauty.

For the most part, however, he trusted his daemon to vivify Beatrix. And he trusted not in vain.[28]

XV. 'THE NEWCOMES'

So they have found out that there's no story have they? There is
one coming: and I think it will be a very good one. No. IX wh. I have
done is a stunning number for incident and there's plenty of action
& passion too from that stage of the story to the end of the XXV
numbers. . . . In VIII. the Colonel goes back to India. The story
seems to breathe freely after the departure of the dear old boy—
Tell B & E [Bradbury & Evans] not to lose heart about it I know if
I live it will be a very good one. It has a slow beginning to be sure.
But just wait. In IX & X [Chapters XXVII to XXXII] the people
are all moving very friskily and in Vol. II. there will be some lively
business. Let 'em talk. I'm not afraid. (Thackeray to Percival Leigh,
25 February 1854: Ray, iii. 349 f.)

§ 1

THE endless round of breakfasts, luncheons, dinners,
suppers, and balls during Thackeray's first tour of the
United States in 1852–3 made it 'one unbroken indiges-
tion'. Or so he said.[1] Like other European visitors to
America before and since, he often longed to be left alone,
or, failing that, to be allowed to spend a few hours with
friends who were not for ever 'going places'.

The Baxters, who lived at the Brown House, Second
Avenue, New York City, were friends of that sort, and
when he could, he escaped to them. They consisted of a
father and mother; Sarah (or Sally), a débutante; Lucy,
aged seventeen; a son still younger; and a niece about
Lucy's age named Libby. On first meeting Sally, Thackeray was astonished at her resemblance to his imaginary
Beatrix. 'I have found Beatrix Esmond', he told both
Mrs. Procter and Mrs. Brookfield in letters. To the former

167

he added 'and [have] lost my heart to her';[2] but to the
latter he said: '. . . but Ah, me! I don't care for her, and
shall hear of her marrying a New York buck with a feeling
of perfect pleasure.'[3] Then he hastened to add that he
thought he liked her mother best of all—'a sweet lady',
but upwards of fifty-five.

This was no doubt a politic statement to make to Jane
Brookfield; but it was not true. Even then he did care a
good deal for Sally Baxter, a young woman alternately
gay and melancholy, childish and worldly, charming and
petulant; and as time went on he became more and more
attracted by her. It is hard to say just how deep this affair
went. Evidently he began by being arch and avuncular.
He referred to himself as 'an elderly Cupid'.[4] He had not
known Sally very long when, somewhat to his own surprise,
he kissed both her and Lucy on taking his departure for
Boston. This, after all, was a trifling episode, though
possibly less so in the year 1852 than it would be to-day.
But what is significant is that he made a great bobbery
about it. He hoped the girls had taken no offence, he
apologized to the parents, he assured them that he had
meant no harm, and he promised Mr. Baxter the privilege
of kissing his own daughters when the opportunity came.
All this underlined the incident in a way that, if the
Baxters were acute, may have set them wondering. Then
he sent Sally a pearl ring as a New Year present, once
again hoping that the gesture would offend no member of
the family.

It is chiefly, however, from the letters that he wrote to
the Baxters after his return to Europe that we gain the
impression that he had been 'caught on the rebound' from
Jane Brookfield. He seems to have found it difficult to get
the right 'tone' into his letters to Sally herself. Some were
too full of 'jibes and scorn', and he tore them up.[5]

I shall never fall in love any more [he tells her in June 1853].
There's a pretty girl with whom I could do it though: there was
a little talk about her coming with my girls as their governess
and dame de compagnie—But says I 'No my dear you are a

great deal too good looking. Knowing the susceptibility of this aged heart I'm determined to put it to no more temptation than I can help. . . .'[6]

News that Sally might be going to marry a 'New York buck' merely because he was 'a good parti' irritated him, leading him to compose tirades on the 'godless respectable thing', Society, which made such an event possible. The shorter of these tirades he put into his letters, the longer into *The Newcomes*.

Sally Baxter, in fact, is all mixed up with *The Newcomes*, which he is trying hard to plan before he begins to write it. He is haunted by ghosts, and cannot make a satisfactory start on the story.

It torments me incessantly [he tells her in a letter of 4 July 1853], and I wander about with it in my interior, lonely & gloomy as if a secret remorse was haunting me. I saw a pretty American girl in a carriage in the Rue Vivienne today. She was like you, she had your colour &c—a great gush of feelings came tumbling out of this bussam at the sight. . . . O ye old ghosts! I declare I saw nothing of the crowded city for a minute or two so completely did the *revenans* hem me in—Nothing is forgotten. We bury 'em but they pop out of their graves now and again and say Here we are Master. . . . We shall say Do you remember S. S. B. do you remember her eyes? Do you think she had 2 dimples in her cheeks and don't you recollect this was the note of her laugh, that used to be quite affected at times but you know the music of it, you poor old rogue? . . . I wonder whether all literary men are humbugs and have no hearts. I know one who has none. Why you may marry anybody you please & I don't care: I dare say there is some young fellow at Newport or Saratoga at this very minute—and I'm amused I give you my honour I'm amused. *L'autre* and her lord & master are reconciled and I'm not in the least annoyed: and one of my loves being here the other day with two babies I nursed the youngest with a graceful affection that the father himself couldn't have equalled.[7]

A more Thackerayan letter it would be difficult to find. What effect it produced on Sally we have no means of knowing. At a guess, it left her puzzled and uneasy. Thackeray was a few thousand miles away, certainly. But he still seemed to be holding her, to demand her allegiance, to insist on the right to direct her life.

Later, when *The Newcomes* began to arrive in its monthly parts, she was probably more disturbed; for the young Clive was beyond question the young Thackeray, and the young Ethel was unmistakably herself.[8] It was very flattering, perhaps, but disturbing all the same.

Sally Baxter married a Southerner named Hampton in December 1855. Thackeray was on his second visit to America at the time, and was invited to the wedding. But he declined, making thin excuses. Later, he admitted to Sally's father that he would as soon have gone to a dentist's and watched one of his own daughters having a tooth extracted as come to see Sally married off.[9]

She died seven years later; and for a little while all the old ghosts haunted Thackeray again. It was hard to write a letter of condolence to her parents. He delayed, then forced himself to do it.[10] She had become one of his 'Yesterdays'. But he still sharply recalled 'that first look of her, with the red ribbon in her hair'.[11]

Sally Baxter still lives vicariously, however, in Ethel Newcome.

§ 2

While still engaged on *Esmond*, Thackeray began turning over in his mind plans for another novel, which he meant to base, like *Pendennis*, on his own early life. Such information as we have about it while it was still in embryo is provided by Lady Ritchie.[12] It was to open, she says, 'with something like Fareham and the old people there'. And the hero was to resemble the author in at least one respect —birth in India.[13]

But he made no serious start on it before June 1853, when he signed a contract with Bradbury and Evans for *The Newcomes: Memoirs of a Most Respectable Family*, to be published in twenty-four monthly parts. He wrote the first page or two at Baden on 9 July; by the end of the month he had finished two monthly numbers, and by

the middle of August a third; though all this while he and
his daughters were travelling about from place to place on
the Continent as the fancy took them. The final pages
were written in Paris, under considerable pressure, in the
summer of 1855.

§ 3

It was the beginning that gave him most trouble; for
when he sat down in Baden to compose what he called the
preface he had still only a hazy notion of the course that
the novel was to take. By the preface we may understand
the opening fable of the birds and animals. This, though
competently done, has no greater relevance to *The Newcomes* than to any other book of Thackeray's. It is a fable
of Vanity Fair, that is all; and the story he now promised—

in which jackdaws will wear peacocks' feathers, and awaken
the just ridicule of the peacocks; in which, while every justice
will be done to the peacocks themselves . . . exception will be
taken to the absurdity of their rickety strut, and the foolish
discord of their pert squeaking; in which lions in love will have
their claws pared by virgins; in which rogues will sometimes
triumph, and honest folks, let us hope, come by their own—

was in no way distinctive. He had been writing such stories
since the days of *Catherine*. Prefacing like this is equivalent
to marking time, and he was forced to mark time, because
he did not yet know his destination.

Three days later he recorded in his diary: 'Wonderful
scene in the Café between Maynard? and Dillon.'[14] No
details are available. This is a pity, because I suspect that
the scene gave just the fillip needed to the novelist's
imagination. Out of it, and out of an earlier incident when
he and Brookfield had met an incarnation of Captain
Costigan in a London tavern,[15] he now built up a wonderful
opening scene, set in the Cave of Harmony, with Colonel
Newcome, the boy Clive, Arthur Pendennis, and the ribald
Costigan. It is one of the best of his discriminated occasions, admirable as an introduction of the *preux chevalier*
who was to prove the most memorable figure in the

171

book. Significantly enough, he was engaged at the time
in re-reading *Don Quixote*.[16]

Even after composing this wonderful opening scene, he
continued to have difficulty. It seemed to him that his
powers of 'invention' were on the wane. Comparing himself with Bulwer and Dickens, he admitted to his mother
that he fell short of both in 'fecundity of imagination'.[17]
To the Baxters also he grumbled: 'I'm in low spirits about
the Newcomes. It's not good. . . It haunts me like a great
stupid ghost. I think it says why do you go on writing this
rubbish? You are old, you have no more invention, etc.
Write sober books, books of history leave novels to younger
folks.'[18]

We, with the whole book before us, can see how freely
he drew upon his own past life when he wrote it. Fareham
and Great-Grandmamma Becher he dropped; nor did he
pick them up again for use in literature until he came to
write the *Roundabouts* in the early sixties. Great-Aunt
Becher he retained as Martha Honeyman, though he
moved her house from Fareham to Brighton and imposed
on her the indignity of letting lodgings, which she bore very
well. The Rev. William Brookfield easily turned into the
Rev. Charles Honeyman, that egregious humbug. Clive,
the nominal hero of the novel, whom Whibley rather unkindly dismissed as 'a barber's block',[19] so far conformed
to the original plan, made in 1851–2, and to the author's
own early history, as to be born in India, and to be
mothered from time to time by the kindly Aunt Becher-
Honeyman. If, in that tentative plan, there had been no
more parallels between Clive and Thackeray, more now
appeared in the book itself: Clive was sent to Grey Friars
School (the Charterhouse); tried, not very successfully, to
learn the art of painting at Gandish's Academy (otherwise
Hatherley's, where Thackeray had studied for a short
time); had to marry Rosey Mackenzie, who is all too
obviously modelled on the ill-starred Isabella Shawe;
and thereafter underwent not only the same kind of *res
angusta domi* as the newly married Thackeray, but also the

intolerable persecutions of the Campaigner, known to the real world as Mrs. Shawe. The Evangelicals of Clapham, who are economically and not very viciously handled in the early pages of the book, must derive in part from the Evangelical pastors and masters much affected by Mrs. Carmichael-Smyth; and the gentleness with which he handled them must have been due to a reluctance to distress his mother. James Binnie was admittedly a portrait, though we do not know of whom.[20] Most important of all, Colonel Newcome, however much he may have owed to the Don Quixote of fiction, became in the main a portrait of Thackeray's stepfather, Major Carmichael-Smyth, though his personal appearance was suggested by Colonel Carmichael, Mary Graham's heavy dragoon of a husband.[21]

§ 4

Scattered and haphazard memories of people and events do not make a novel, not even a scrambling, shapeless novel, like many written in the Victorian Age. What is needed is a plot or a theme—some unifying principle. Thackeray was too good an artist to be unaware of this, even though he often let the conditions under which he wrote—haste, fatigue, laziness, ill health—obscure his plan; and it was just the task of finding some unifying principle for *The Newcomes* that was taxing his wits in July 1853. Lady Ritchie tells us that one day at Berne (which he reached on 6 August) he strayed off by himself into a little wood, and that there, in solitude, 'the story was actually revealed to him'.[22] It sounds like a mystic experience; probably it was nothing more remarkable than the process which Lady Ritchie later referred to as 'marshalling the various impressions which had come to him from time to time'.[23] Remarkable and mysterious this process is, undoubtedly; but it is not uncommon. Every artist, every man of science, every thinker, is familiar with the moment when, after weeks or months of trial and error, all the scattered fragments of the puzzle come together in your mind, and the design, hitherto nebulous or even invisible, stands out sharp and clear. By the time this happened to Thackeray in Switzerland, he had already completed two monthly numbers of *The Newcomes* (Chapters I–VI), and was struggling with a third, and if he had not so far had a vision of the book as a whole, it is little wonder that the writing he had done seemed to him stupid, hardly better than 'a repetition of past performances'.[24]

What is probable is that not merely a story but a theme was revealed to him in the little wood; or rather, that he suddenly became fully conscious of the theme he had been bodying forth half-consciously in the pages written, and that in a flash which seemed an inspiration he saw how the principal story, which was to turn on Clive and Ethel, could be twisted to exemplify the theme still further. At this time he was churning over in his mind memories more recent than the ones out of which the book was supposed to grow. He was writing to the Baxters constantly; he was getting letters from them; he was talking about them to all the Americans that he chanced to fall in with during his tour of the Continent. Above all, he was fretting lest his charming but provoking Sally should, at any moment, out of pique or a sudden whim, throw herself away upon a man unworthy of her. As a débutante she had made her mark in a city where wealth greatly mattered; he had watched her making it. She enjoyed success; she enjoyed power; she had no desire to revert, through marrying a nobody, to a nobody herself. If she chose her husband merely for his wealth or his position in society, a certain elderly Cupid now in Europe never would forgive her. So at least he thought, and said. How far his motives were disinterested does not matter much. What he thought, he thought emotionally.

Marriage for the wrong reasons—this was the burden of his thinking. It was a theme he had already treated many times in fiction, though only incidentally. It had now become central in his mind. It would unify *The Newcomes*.

He had only to look back over what he had already

written to see that the theme had been dominant there; for had not Thomas Newcome the elder, the north-country weaver who had come to London in a wagon with a few bales of cloth as his sole fortune, entered into two marriages, the first for love, with the lass from his native village, and the second for convenience and business, with the wealthy and imperious Miss Hobson?—had not Thomas Newcome the younger been prevented from marrying the girl of his choice, Léonore de Blois, and been shipped off to India, only to be caught there by the Widow Casey?—and had not the gentle Léonore, descendant of a noble French family, been hurried for safety into a *mariage de convenance* with a man much older than herself, the comte de Florac? Here were three emblems of the theme in as many chapters.

He was at Vevey on 26 July and, writing to Sally Baxter, preached a short, disjointed sermon on the godless, respectable folk of London Society:

They never feel love, but directly it's born, they throttle it and fling it under the sewer as poor girls do their unlawful children—they make up money-marriages and are content—then the father goes to the House of Commons or the Counting House, the mother to her balls and visits—the children lurk up stairs with their governess, and when their turn comes are bought and sold, and respectable and heartless as their parents before them. Hullo!—I say—Stop!—where is this tirade a-going to and apropos of what?—Well—I was fancying my brave young Sarah (who has tried a little of the pomps & vanities of her world) transplanted to ours and a London woman of society—with a husband that she had taken as she threatens to take one sometimes just because he is a good parti. No—go and live in a clearing—marry a husband masticatory, expectoratory, dubious of linen, but with a heart below that rumpled garment—let the children eat with their precious knives—help the help, and give a hand to the dinner yourself— yea, it is better than to be a woman of fashion in London, and sit down to a French dinner where no love is. Immense Moralist! I think I'll call in Anny now, and give her a turn at the new novel.[25] I see a chapter out of the above sermon and you know I must have an i to the main chance—[26]

Whatever else this fragment may reveal about Thackeray,

it reveals unmistakably how closely intertwined in his thoughts *The Newcomes*, Sally Baxter of New York, and the theme of 'marriage for the wrong reasons' had become.

§ 5

The Newcomes has been often damned by good critics for its formlessness. They have missed the clue. Thackeray built it on a theme, and as soon as he saw his way clear— it may very well have been in that wood at Berne—he became relentless in his working out of this dominating theme. He twisted the characters to fit it; he twisted his events into emblems of it. We might even look upon the novel as a series of emblems. After the introduction, in which he thrice underlines the theme, he begins seriously on the story of the young cousins, Clive and Ethel. From a boy-and-girl friendship they pass insensibly to love, love which is presented as deep and permanent in Clive—if anything can go very deep in a youth so wooden and mechanical—but in Ethel, at any rate at first, as shallower and more hesitant. But a marriage between them would have been a marriage for the *right* reasons. Besides, it was not in the Victorian tradition of the novel to marry off your hero and heroine in the first volume. The control of events is, therefore, now entrusted to old Lady Kew, 'the Wicked Fairy', as Thackeray, in a moment of doubt concerning the credibility of his fiction, called her.[27] Lady Kew's interference is effectual. She sets about contriving for her favourite, Ethel, a marriage for the *wrong* reasons, first with another grandchild and favourite, Lord Kew, and then, after the plans for this have miscarried, with the most eligible bachelor and most fatuous nobleman in England, Lord Farintosh. It is one of the worst blunders in the book that Ethel, as presented by Thackeray, should ever have consented to betroth herself to Farintosh. But the reason for it is all too plain. Thackeray is so possessed by his theme that he is quite ready to play fast and loose with his characters. He has already made Lady Ann Newcome two quite different women at different times; he has been careless in his presentation of Lord Kew, and even, less pardonably, in his presentation of old Lady Kew. He now obfuscates Ethel for the theme's sake. She ceases to become a person and becomes a symbol.[28] The delaying of her marriage with Farintosh by temporarily killing off his mother[29] is another weakness in the story; for the incident is so obviously contrived in the interests of the plot that the reader's faith is badly shaken. On the other hand, the final break with Farintosh is admirably worked up to and presented. Indeed, it is one of the master strokes in the plot that this marriage for the wrong reasons should be prevented in the end by the failure of another, the scandalous marriage of Barnes Newcome with Lady Clara Pulleyn. To the casual reader, who wishes, no doubt, to remain absorbed in the story of Clive and Ethel, much of the time spent on the triangle of Barnes, Lady Clara, and Lord Highgate seems time wasted; but the casual reader is not putting himself at the point of view of the author, for whom the theme is the all-important matter, and for whom, therefore, the Barnes–Clara–Highgate story is almost on the same level of interest as the Clive–Ethel story. Effective, too, and ruthless, but for the theme exactly right, is the marrying of the disappointed Clive to Rosey—another marriage for the wrong reasons, and one that offers an ironical comment on the quixotic Colonel and the self-sufficient James Binnie, who united in promoting it.

There is still another marriage for the wrong reasons in the book—Paul de Florac's with Miss Higgs of Manchester. It looks as if Thackeray's first intention had been to offer this too as a moral emblem. At all events he separates the couple, and allows Paul to amuse himself in other quarters. Then suddenly, and for no reason that derives from the characters themselves, he reconciles husband and wife, and assigns them minor roles in the main, Clive–Ethel, plot. This is another twist for the theme's sake. It may well have appeared to Thackeray that he had forced his argument. He had introduced six marriages for the wrong reasons, and had narrowly averted two more. This was writing in italics. If he now conceded that at least one of the marriages had turned out not so badly in the end, he might thereby escape the charge of special pleading. Besides, de Florac was a Frenchman, and so did not matter very seriously.

§ 6

It was in this fashion, then, and for these reasons, that Thackeray shaped his main plot. There is no denying that he was apt to fumble in his handling of Ethel; he scarcely ever showed that certainty of touch with her which he had shown with Beatrix Esmond, Blanche Amory, and Becky Sharp; and the principal reason is the old one, often suggested in this book, that he was not sufficiently detached emotionally from the original of Ethel. Perhaps it was some consciousness of this failure which induced him to elaborate his Don Quixote. The 'dear old boy' who is also 'rather a twaddler'[30] steals the stage from the hero and the heroine. This is a failure in design undoubtedly. As an agent in the main plot, Colonel Newcome had four tasks to perform: he had to behave as a fond and foolish father to Clive, as an affectionate and then disapproving uncle to Ethel, as an uncompromising enemy to Barnes, and as a victim of the horrible Mrs. Mackenzie. But obviously, as the book developed, he acquired far more prominence than his functions in the plot justified. The Colonel ran away with his creator.

Perhaps this was fortunate in the end. Colonel Newcome *made* the book for contemporary readers; and although readers of to-day may be less inclined to accept a *preux chevalier* whose virtues are paraded too ostentatiously, yet (as Elton very justly says) the Colonel survives even this ordeal.[31] The famous death-scene is still famous, and deserves to be. If Thackeray had always written with such simplicity and restraint when a great occasion was presented to him, we, his readers of a century later, would have fewer doubts about his standing as a novelist.

J. J. Ridley is another character who falls outside the scheme of the book. Thackeray himself knew it. 'Why [he asks in the postscript] did Pendennis introduce J. J. with such a flourish, giving us, as it were, an overture, and no piece to follow it?' Thackeray may have known the answer, but I think not. For J. J. Ridley is a wish-fulfilment—nothing more. He represents what Thackeray in some moods would have liked to be—a successful painter, with his hand in perfect control, single-minded, untroubled by the doubts, spiritual timidities, and recurrent vacillations that his author suffered from. But Clive and Pendennis were also incarnations of Thackeray, and it must have seemed, even to a man so self-centred, that a third incarnation, if elaborated, would have been too much. Hence his postponement of the Ridley story—a postponement, as it happened, till the Greek Calends.

On the other hand, it must have been in order to underline his main theme by contrast that Thackeray made so much of the happily married Pendennises in the second half of *The Newcomes*. No other justification seems possible, and to readers of to-day even this fails. The married Laura is intolerable.

XVI. THE REMINISCENTIAL MANNER

As I survey it now, the curtain is down, and the play long over; as I think of its surprises, disguises, mysteries, escapes, and dangers, I am amazed myself, and sometimes inclined to be almost as great a fatalist as Monsieur de la Motte, who vowed that a superior Power ruled our actions for us, and declared that he could no more prevent his destiny from accomplishing itself, than he could prevent his hair from growing. (*Denis Duval*, p. 469.)

§ 1

It has become a commonplace of criticism to say that Thackeray has the air of a man remembering. Herman Merivale, Percy Lubbock, Oliver Elton, Lord David Cecil —each in his own way makes the same point. Thackeray's writings, says Lord David Cecil, resemble 'the memories of an old man looking back, disillusioned but not embittered by experience, in the calm summer twilight of his days'.[1]

Thackeray avows the method himself, several times. 'I believe a man forgets nothing', says Barry Lyndon on revisiting his old home; and although the book in which this remark occurs is an early one, written before Thackeray had learned by experiment and failure that peculiar reminiscential manner which so well expresses his withdrawn, hesitant, sceptical, yet sensitive and at times sentimental attitude of mind, the remark might be chosen as a motto for his work. With it we may compare not only the passage from *Denis Duval* but three others.

The first is from *The Newcomes*:

This narrative, as the judicious reader no doubt is aware, is written maturely and at ease, long after the voyage whereof it recounts the adventures and perils.[2]

180

The second is from *Philip*, which, like *The Newcomes*, purports to be written by Arthur Pendennis:

> The story came to me piecemeal; from confessions here, admissions there, deductions of my own . . . but the story is as authentic as many histories, and the reader need only give such an amount of credence to it as he may judge its verisimilitude warrants.[3]

The third is the opening of the *Roundabout* 'On a Joke I once heard from the late Thomas Hood':

> The good-natured reader who has perused some of these rambling papers has long since seen . . . that the writer belongs to the old-fashioned classes of this world, loves to remember very much more than to prophesy, and though he can't help being carried onward, and downward, perhaps, on the hill of life . . . he sits under Time, the white-wigged charioteer, with his back to the horses, and his face to the past, looking at the receding landscape and the hills fading into the grey distance.[4]

No one has better conveyed the effect of Thackeray's manner of writing than he has done here himself through an image. He sat under Time, with his face to the past.

It was partly, too, because he felt compelled to keep on striking what Elton calls 'the note of the memoir' that he indulged so often in a kind of fictional ventriloquism. If we look back over the whole range of his novels and short tales, from *Catherine* at the beginning to the unfinished *Denis Duval* at the end, we notice how often he is tempted to interpose between himself and his readers a supposed narrator—a sort of dummy on his knee, into whose mouth he can project his own voice slightly muffled. As a man, Thackeray was self-conscious: he enjoyed no success, for example, as an after-dinner speaker. As a novelist, even as an essayist, he was also self-conscious. To efface himself completely was distasteful to him, for it gave his vanity no chance; and therefore the method which Mr. Aldous Huxley has labelled 'the God's-eye view' did not satisfy him. He claimed the right to annotate his fiction, and indeed exercised the right too freely. On the other hand, it embarrassed him to stand unaccompanied and undisguised on an open platform; for at heart he was timid and uncertain. So he went on looking for a compromise. Notwithstanding his defence of egotism and 'the right line " I "',[5] he preferred to bestow, at the very least, a fictitious name upon the 'I'. Even the 'I' of the *Roundabout* papers in the *Cornhill* had to be 'Mr. Roundabout'.

He reveals his attitude very plainly in one of his letters to the Baxters of July 1853, when he is struggling hard to get *The Newcomes* under way: 'Mr. Pendennis is to be the writer of his friend's memoirs and by the help of this little mask (wh. I borrowed from Pisistratus Bulwer I suppose) I shall be able to talk more at ease than in my own person. I only thought of the plan last night and am immensely relieved by adopting it.'[6] To the Perry sisters, two days later, he says: 'Mr. Pendennis is the author of the book, and he has taken a great weight off my mind, for under that mask and acting, as it were, I can afford to say and think many things that I couldn't venture on in my own person, now that it is a person, and I know the public are staring at it.'[7]

That is Thackeray all over. He wishes to have it both ways, demanding the right to annotate, but afraid to speak too openly in his own person. It was no new attitude in him. He had always been like that, even before the public learned to stare at him. That is why, while still only an obscure journalist, he became so fertile in the invention of pseudonyms.[8] That is why, also, long before he thought of using Pendennis as the pseudo-author of *The Newcomes*, he seemed more at ease when he could hand a story over to some memoirist within it. This trick grew upon him. Pendennis reappeared for *Philip*, and would almost certainly have taken over the novel on the life of J. J. Ridley that was promised, actually begun, but discarded. *Lovel the Widower* was dribbled out by the garrulous Mr. Batchelor. Then, at the end, the attractive admiral, Duval (a more genial, less melancholy Esmond), set about his own biography with a very sure hand.

But, from this point of view, *The Virginians* is the most revealing of the novels. Written between *The Newcomes* and *Lovel the Widower*, it shows Thackeray struggling against inclination and habit: he is trying to tell a plain tale plainly, but cannot; and so he reverts from time to time to a method that he finds more congenial—first, in the long narrative-memoir of Harry Warrington, then in the long narrative-memoir of George Warrington, and finally in the rambling diary of George Warrington.

Indeed, in only two of his major works—*Vanity Fair* and *Pendennis*—does Thackeray dispense with a dummy. The first is from this point of view (as well as from others) something of a triumph. Even so, it shows signs of strain now and then;[9] and, as I pointed out earlier, when the story reached Pumpernickel, the author could not any longer keep himself out of it.[10] As for *Pendennis*, Thackeray was in it all the time, only very slightly disguised as Pen. The book is so evidently autobiographical in substance that the reader hardly notices that it is not autobiographical in form.

Few of Thackeray's minor characters illustrate his ventriloquial habits better than the society gossip, little Tom Eaves, who knows everything, who never takes an active part in any story, but who pops up as chorus when the author needs him. Tom Eaves slips unobtrusively round the corner into a narrative for the first time in *Vanity Fair*, and just at the moment when Thackeray has begun telling us about Gaunt House and the scandalous behaviour of its noble owner. His appearance is as casual and unprepared for as that of a minor character in *War and Peace*; he whispers his scandal and then vanishes again. Little Tom Eaves ages. He lives long enough, however, to play a similar minor part in *Pendennis, The Newcomes*, and *Philip*. He is the Creevey of the novels. Thackeray himself is the Greville.

But a Greville with a difference. Thackeray does not

give the impression of jotting down immediately, the same
evening, his account of what has happened; he gives the
impression that he has let it all settle and arrange itself in
memory, that he is writing of it a long time afterwards, at
leisure.

§ 2

And that is in fact what he was doing. He filled his
books with people, places, and episodes that he took from
his own private and personal experience.

No serious student of Thackeray has failed to notice
this. Helen Pendennis derives from Mrs. Carmichael-
Smyth; Fairoaks and Chatteris in *Pendennis* derive from
Larkbeare and Exeter in Devonshire; the pigeoning of the
wretched Dawkins, as related by Yellowplush, derives
from the pigeoning of William Makepeace Thackeray
while still an inexperienced undergraduate at Trinity
College, Cambridge. These are obvious examples. I have
discussed them, and many others, in earlier chapters.

Thackeray's contemporaries were as well aware of his
tricks as we are. Trollope remarks that he 'in a way more
or less correct, often refers in his writings, if not to the
incidents, at any rate to the remembrances of his own
life'[11]—guarded phrasing, designed, one supposes, not to
hurt the feelings of Thackeray's daughters. Marzials
stresses how autobiographical both *Pendennis* and *Philip*
are,[12] and this appears so obvious to Merivale that he
entertains 'a secret belief . . . that young Thackeray wooed,
loved, and lost an Emily Fotheringay'.[13] Berdmore regrets
Thackeray's habit of using well-known figures out of real
life as the basis of his characters.[14] Most significant of all is
the comment of Edward Fitzgerald, who certainly knew
more about Thackeray's private life than the bulk of his
other friends, and who objected to *Lovel the Widower* for
the excellent reason that the author was 'always talking so
of himself'.[15] Even Saintsbury (not quite a contemporary,
to be sure) calls attention to 'that intense intimacy'
always to be discovered between Thackeray's life and his

writings,[16] and has to admit that 'Thackeray sometimes sailed a little too near the wind' in using club acquaintances as models.[17]

Saintsbury did not wish to admit it. In discussing *Pendennis* he insists that the correspondence between life and fiction is never exact. 'Thackeray,' he says, 'like all the greatest artists, took hints, but did not brook dictation, from his sitters and his scenes.' Therefore, he continues, the reader may at any time find himself 'sliding off solid fact into fiction'.[18] It is clear from the context, however, that what Saintsbury really objects to is a slip in the opposite direction—from the solid fiction of the novels into an unstable world of half-fiction based on them. He calls this 'unwarranted and unwarrantable' in a biography of the novelist, and refers contemptuously to a German monograph that tried to build up the life of Thackeray from the evidence of his fiction, thereby revealing in its author 'a complete and disastrous misapprehension of Thackeray's art and genius'.[19]

I will not defend or attack the German monograph, which I have not seen. But I have tried in this book to show that Thackeray very often did 'brook dictation from his sitters'. That was his chief infirmity, and it is for that reason, more than for any other, that we cannot rank him among 'the greatest novelists'. Saintsbury is almost certainly right about them. They take hints from experience; they reproduce the quality of it; they re-fashion the details. They are masters of their experience. They shape it into something rich and strange. Thackeray could do the same—sometimes. He re-shaped his experience of the various models—two, three, it does not matter how many there were—that he used for Becky Sharp, so that the woman in the novel became a new creation, unhampered by the accidents of real life. But this he was incapable of doing when his relationship to the living original of a character in fiction was predominantly emotional. The principal witness in support of this charge is his mother. The effect she produced upon his fiction—

direct when he chose to portray her as Helen Pendennis; indirect, though little less powerful, when he touched, even lightly, on the Mother–Child theme—was disastrous. Disastrous, too, in varying degrees, were his other obsessions with people—his wife, his mother-in-law, Jane Octavia Brookfield, William Brookfield (after the quarrel), and Sally Baxter.

Thackeray was above all a novelist who remembered. He would certainly have proved a better one had he learned to forget as well.

APPENDIX A

THE CHIEF EVENTS OF THACKERAY'S LIFE

1811   Born (18 July) in Calcutta.

1815   Death of his father, Richmond T.

1817   Sent home to England. Mother remains in Calcutta.
Sent to first school, the Polygon in Southampton. Very unhappy there.
Mother marries Capt. Henry Carmichael-Smyth in India.

1819   Sent to Walpole House, a school in Chiswick.
Mother returns with her husband to England.

1822   Sent to the Charterhouse. Bullied there.

1825   Carmichael-Smyths take small country house, Larkbeare, in Devon.

1828   Removed from the Charterhouse.

1829   Goes up to Trinity College, Cambridge.

1830   Removed from Cambridge, where he had (in the opinion of his guardians) been wasting his time.
Sent to learn German at Weimar.

1831   Returns to England. Admitted to Middle Temple. Begins study of law.

1832   Comes of age, throws up law, and goes to Paris, ostensibly to study French literature.

1833   Returns to London. Associated with firm of bill-discounters.
Becomes part-owner of, and edits, the *National Standard*.
Loses nearly all that was left of his patrimony.

1834   The *National Standard* fails.
Studies art in Paris.

1835   The Carmichael-Smyths leave Larkbeare and take a house at 18 Albion Street, Hyde Park, London.
Still studying art in Paris.

1836   Publishes first book, *Flore et Zéphyr*, a complete failure.
Stormy wooing of Isabella Shawe in Paris.
Marries Isabella Shawe in Paris.
Appointed Paris correspondent of the *Constitutional*, a new Radical daily in London, in which Major Carmichael-Smyth has invested heavily.

1837   Returns to London to work on the *Constitutional*, which is steadily losing money.
Birth of daughter, Anne (afterwards Lady Ritchie).

The *Constitutional* fails. Major Carmichael-Smyth, in danger of arrest for debt, slips away to Paris, where his wife joins him, and where they continue to live for many years.

Takes house at 13 Great Coram Street, Brunswick Square, and begins to write for his life.

The *Yellowplush Correspondence* begins (in *Fraser's*).

1838   *Catherine* (in *Fraser's*).

Birth of second daughter, Jane.

Troubles with his mother-in-law from time to time.

1839   Death of second daughter, Jane.

1840   Birth of third daughter, Harriet Marion (Minny), afterwards Mrs. Leslie Stephen.

A Shabby Genteel Story (in *Fraser's*).

The Paris Sketch Book.

Wife begins to go insane (schizophrenia), and makes two attempts at suicide. Takes her to Cork, to be near her mother and sister. Mother-in-law behaves shamefully. Takes wife to Paris, and places her in *maison de santé*.

Serious financial straits, and has to borrow pretty heavily.

1841   *The Second Funeral of Napoleon* and *The Chronicle of the Drum.*

Tries hydropathic treatment for his wife in Germany.

The Great Hoggarty Diamond (in *Fraser's*).

Meets Jane Octavia Brookfield, wife of Rev. William Brookfield, curate of St. James's Church, Piccadilly.

1842   Lets 13 Great Coram Street to Colonel Charles Carmichael (Major Carmichael-Smyth's brother) and his wife Mary (*née* Graham), T.'s cousin. Lives with them there as guest or lodger.

Begins to contribute to *Punch.*

Tours Ireland.

1843   Gives up 13 Great Coram Street.

Fitz-Boodle Papers (in *Fraser's*).

The Irish Sketch Book.

Takes rooms in Jermyn Street.

Joins *Punch* Table.

1844   *Barry Lyndon* (in *Fraser's*).

Tours Mediterranean and Palestine.

Settles for a time in Rome.

1845   Returns to London, and takes rooms at 88 St. James's Street.

Sends first draft of early chapters of *Vanity Fair* (not under that name) to Colburn the publisher, who keeps but does not publish it.

Brings wife to England, and places her with a family in Camberwell.

1846 *From Cornhill to Cairo.*

Snobs begin in *Punch.*

Takes house at 13 Young Street, Kensington, and brings daughters from Paris to live with him.

Mrs. Perkins's Ball (first Christmas Book).

Begins rewriting *Vanity Fair.*

1847 *Vanity Fair* runs throughout year in monthly numbers.

Friendship with Jane Octavia Brookfield grows warmer. Husband makes first protest.

Falls out with John Forster.

Our Street (second Christmas Book).

1848 Sees more and more of Jane Octavia Brookfield throughout the year.

Finishes *Vanity Fair.*

Becomes a lion in London society.

Begins *Pendennis.*

Pendennis, first monthly number, appears in November.

Dr. Birch and His Young Friends (third Christmas Book).

1849 Jane Octavia Brookfield's uncle protests against T.'s seeing so much of her.

Visits Paris and meets Mary Carmichael again.

Dangerous illness, which interrupts publication of *Pendennis* for three months.

Rebecca and Rowena (fourth Christmas Book).

1850 Intimacy with Brookfields unabated.

Examiner and *Morning Chronicle* attack him for belittling men of letters.

Finishes *Pendennis.*

The Kickleburys on the Rhine (fifth Christmas Book).

1851 Working for lectures on English Humorists.

Delivers lectures for first time in London.

Continental tour with daughters.

Quarrel with Brookfield. Agrees to see no more of Jane Octavia. Time of severe grief and pain.

Begins *Esmond.*

Lectures in English provincial cities and in Scotland.

Resigns from *Punch.*

1852   Continues lecturing.

Finishes *Esmond*.

Esmond published.

Sails for America on lecturing tour.

Meets Baxters in New York. Loses his heart (in some sort) to Sally B., in whom he finds a great resemblance to Beatrix Esmond.

1853   Finishes lecturing tour in America, and returns to London.

Takes daughters on continental tour, and begins *The Newcomes*.

Back and forth between London and Paris all the autumn.

First monthly number of *The Newcomes* (October).

Takes his daughters to Rome.

1854   Serious illness in Rome.

Begins *The Rose and the Ring*.

Returns to London, and moves to 36 Onslow Square, Brompton.

The Rose and the Ring published.

1855   Continues travelling about.

Finishes *The Newcomes*.

Writes *Four Georges*.

Sails for America on second lecturing tour.

Excuses himself from being present at Sally Baxter's wedding.

1856   Returns to England.

Begins *The Virginians*, but lays it aside.

Much on the Continent.

1857   Delivers *Four Georges* in London and other parts of the country.

Asked to stand as parliamentary candidate for Edinburgh, but declines.

Stands for the City of Oxford as Independent, but is defeated.

First monthly number of *The Virginians* (November).

1858   Quarrel with Edmund Yates and estrangement from Dickens.

Much on the Continent.

1859   Accepts editorship of the *Cornhill Magazine*, to be started by Smith, Elder & Co.

Finishes *The Virginians*.

Busy with preparations for the *Cornhill*.

1860 First number of the *Cornhill* appears (January).

   First *Roundabout* and first instalment of *Lovel the Widower* (both in *Cornhill*).

   Buys 2 Palace Green, Kensington.

   Now often ill.

1861 *Philip* begins as serial in *Cornhill*.

   Major Carmichael-Smyth dies.

1862 Resigns editorship of the *Cornhill*.

   Finishes *Philip*.

   Moves into 2 Palace Green. Housewarming party with amateur performance of *The Wolves and the Lamb* (original dramatic form of *Lovel the Widower*).

1863 Anne Thackeray's *Story of Elizabeth* appears in *Cornhill*, and is attacked in *Athenaeum*. T. quarrels with National Shakespeare Committee in consequence.

   Begins *Denis Duval*.

   Writes last *Roundabout*.

   Dies (24 December).

APPENDIX B

WORKS REFERRED TO IN TEXT

(*With short titles used in Notes*)

A. THACKERAY'S OWN WORKS

Biographical Edition, ed. Anne Ritchie, 13 vols., Smith, Elder & Co., London, 1900.

I. *V.F.*	*Vanity Fair.*
II. *Pend.*	*Pendennis.*
III. *Yellowplush*	*Yellowplush Papers*, &c.
IV. *B. Lyndon*, &c.	*The Memoirs of Barry Lyndon*; *The Fitz-Boodle Papers*, &c.
V. *Sketch Bks.*, &c.	*The Paris Sketch Book*; *The Irish Sketch Book*; *Notes of a Journey from Cornhill to Grand Cairo*, &c.
VI. *Cont. to* 'Punch', &c.	*Contributions to* 'Punch', &c.
VII. *Esmond*, &c.	*The History of Henry Esmond*; and *The Lectures.*
VIII. *Newcomes*	*The Newcomes.*
IX. *Christmas Bks.*	*Christmas Books*, &c.

X. *Virgs.*   *The Virginians.*

XI. *Philip,* &c.   *The Adventures of Philip*; and
                         A Shabby Genteel Story.

XII. *Lovel,* &c.   *Lovel the Widower; Roundabout*
                         Papers; Denis Duval, &c.

XIII. *Ballads,* &c.   *Ballads and Miscellanies.*

The Orphan of Pimlico, and other Sketches, Fragments and Drawings, with some notes by Anne Isabella Thackeray, London, 1876.

Stray Papers, being Stories, Reviews, Verses and Sketches (1821–47), ed. Lewis Melville, London, 1901.

B. THACKERAY'S LETTERS

Amer. Family   *Thackeray's Letters to an American Family,* with an Introduction by Lucy W. Baxter, London, 1904.

Collection   *A Collection of Letters of W. M. Thackeray,* 1847–1855, 2nd edit., London, 1887.

Lambert   Catalogue: Library of late Major Wm. H. Lambert, Pt. II, N.Y., 1914.

Ray   *The Letters and Private Papers of William Makepeace Thackeray,* collected and edited by Gordon N. Ray, 4 vols., Harvard U.P., 1945–6.

C. OTHER WORKS

Ballantine, Mr. Sergeant: *Some Experiences of a Barrister's Life,* 2 vols., London, 1882.

Berdmore, Sept.: 'Thackeray', *Westminster Review,* N.S., xxvi, July 1864.

Brontë Corr. The Brontës: Their Lives, Friendships, and Correspondence, 4 vols., Shakespeare Head Press, Oxford, 1932.

Brookfield Circle. Charles and Frances Brookfield: *Mrs. Brookfield and her Circle,* London, 1906.

Brown. *Letters of Dr. John Brown,* ed. his son and D. W. Forrest, London, 1907.

Brown and Lancaster. Brown, John, and Lancaster, Henry H.: 'Thackeray', *North British Review,* xl, Feb. 1864.

Cecil, Lord David: *Early Victorian Novelists: Essays in Revaluation,* London, 1934.

Crowe, Eyre: *With Thackeray in America,* London, 1893.

Early Victorian England, 1830–1865, ed. Young, 2 vols., O.U.P., 1934.

Edinburgh Review, lxxxvii, Jan.–April 1848.

APPENDIX B

Ellis, G. U.: *Thackeray*, Great Lives Series, London, 1933.

Elton, Oliver: *A Survey of English Literature, 1830–1880*, 2 vols., London, 1932.

Elwin, Malcolm: *Thackeray, a Personality*, London, 1933.

Elwin, Whitwell: *Some Eighteenth-Century Men of Letters*, with a Memoir, ed. Warwick Elwin, 2 vols., London, 1902.

Fields, James T.: *Yesterdays with Authors*, Boston, 1872.

Fitzgerald, Edward: *Letters and Literary Remains*, ed. W. A. Wright, 3 vols., London, 1889.

Fitzpatrick, W. J.: *The Life of Charles Lever*, with an Appendix by Major D[wyer], 2 vols., London, 1879.

Hannay, James: *Studies on Thackeray*, London, n.d. [? 1868].

Hodder, George: *Memories of my Time*, London, 1870.

Jeaffreson, J. Cordy: *A Book of Recollections*, 2 vols., London, 1894.

Laughton, J. K.: *Memoirs of Henry Reeve*, 2 vols., London, 1898.

Levy, Goldie: *Arthur Hugh Clough, 1819–1861*, London, 1938.

Linton, Mrs. Lynn: *My Literary Life* (*Reminiscences of Dickens, Thackeray, George Eliot*, &c.), London, 1899.

Locker-Lampson, Frederick: *My Confidences, an Autobiographical Sketch, addressed to my Descendants*, London, 1896.

Lucas, E. V.: 'Thackeray at the *Punch* Table', *Loiterer's Harvest*, London, 1913.

Lytton, Earl of: *The Life of Edward Bulwer, first Lord Lytton*, 2 vols., London, 1913.

Mackay, Charles: *Forty Years' Recollections of Life, Literature, and Public Affairs, from 1830 to 1870*, 2 vols., London, 1877.

Masson, David: *Memories of London in the Forties*, arranged for publication by his daughter, Flora Masson, Edinburgh & London, 1908.

McCarthy, Justin: *Reminiscences*, 2 vols., London, 1899.

Melville, Lewis: *William Makepeace Thackeray*, 2 vols., London, 1910.

Merivale, Herman, and Marzials, Frank T.: *Life of W. M. Thackeray*, London, 1891.

Ritchie: *Letters of Anne Thackeray Ritchie*, selected and edited by her daughter, Hester Ritchie, London, 1924.

Ritchies in India, ed. Gerald Ritchie, London, 1920.

Rosebery, Lord: *Miscellanies, Literary and Historical*, 2 vols., 5th edit., London, 1922.

Sadleir, Michael: *Bulwer, a Panorama*, London, 1931.

Saintsbury, George: *A Consideration of Thackeray*, O.U.P.,1931.

Shorter, C. K.: *Charlotte Brontë and her Circle*, London, 1896.

Spielmann, M. H.: *The hitherto Unidentified Contributions of W. M. Thackeray to* 'Punch', London, 1899.

Stevenson, A. L.: '*Vanity Fair* and Lady Morgan', *P.M.L.A.*, xlviii, June 1933.

Swinnerton, Frank S.: 'W. M. Thackeray', *Great Victorians*, ed. H. J. Massingham and Hugh Massingham, London, 1932.

Trollope, Anthony: *Thackeray*, English Men of Letters Series, pocket edit., London, 1925.

Vizetelly, Henry: *Glances back through Seventy Years*, 2 vols., London, 1893.

Whibley, Charles: *William Makepeace Thackeray*, Modern English Writers Series, London, 1903.

Wilson, D. A.: *Carlyle to Threescore-and-Ten (1853–1865)*, London, 1931.

Wilson, J. G.: *Thackeray in the United States*, 2 vols., London, 1904.

de Wyzewa, T.: 'A propos du centenaire de William Makepeace Thackeray', *Revue des deux Mondes*, 6me période, 81me année, tome 5, 15 sept. 1911.

Yates, Edmund: *His Recollections and Experiences*, 2 vols., London, 1884.

Young, G. M.: *Victorian England: Portrait of an Age*, O.U.P., 1936.

APPENDIX C

NOTES AND REFERENCES

CHAPTER I

1. Lucas, 39 f.

2. Mackay, ii. 285

3. See especially: Brown, 95; Ballantine, i. 135; Fields, 22 and 32 f.; Hodder, 239; *Brontë Corr.* iii. 76; Shorter, 416; Wilson, *Thackeray in U.S.* i. 136 f.; Trollope, 119; Locker-Lampson, 305; Yates, *passim*.

4. See especially: Merivale and Marzials, 146 f.; Shorter, 426 f.; Vizetelly, i. 325; Lynn Linton, 63; McCarthy, i. 39 f.

5. Op. cit. 247.

6. Ibid. 76.

7. 'W. M. Thackeray', *Great Victorians*, 519.

8. But the chief events of his life are chronicled, for reference, in Appendix A.

CHAPTER II

1. Ritchie, 124.

2. 'On a Peal of Bells' (*Round.*), *Lovel*, &c. 377.

3. W. M. T. to E. F., 27 Oct. 1852, Ray, iii. 98 f.

4. *Newcomes*, 270.

5. *Lovel*, &c. 339.

6. *Ritchies in India*, 12.

7. 'On a Peal of Bells' (*Round.*), *Lovel*, &c. 377. See also 'The Notch on the Axe' (*Round.*), ibid. 355.

8. 'On a Peal of Bells' (*Round.*), loc. cit.

9. Int. *Newcomes*, xviii, and Ray, i. 9 n.

10. *Pend.* 19.

11. Ibid. 566.

12. 'Humourists', *Esmond*, &c. 551.

13. *V.F.* 345.

14. *Sketch Bks*, 49.

15. 'Irish Melody', poking fun at Lalor Sheil, an Irish speaker on behalf of Catholic Emancipation.

16. Ray, iii. 93 f.

17. *V.F.* 624.

18. Ritchie, 53.

19. There is evidence in his diary for 1832 (Ray, i. 185–238) that as a young man in Paris he was not quite so chaste as the heroes of his novels.

20. In *A Shabby Genteel Story* he denounces seduction as 'this supreme act of scoundrelism' (*Philip*, &c. 43), and in reviewing Bulwer's *Ernest Maltravers* for *Fraser's* he takes the novelist very sharply to task for allowing Ernest to seduce his pupil, Alice (*Stray Papers*, 294).

21. 'Humourists', *Esmond*, &c. 609.

22. *Newcomes*, 388.

23. *Pend.* 154.

24. Ibid. 494.

25. 'The Last Sketch' (*Round.*), *Lovel*, &c. 186.

26. 'Strictures on Pictures', *Ballads*, &c. 265.

27. 'Serenade', ibid. 113.

28. *Esmond*, 381.

29. Ray, ii. 661.

APPENDIX C

30. *Esmond*, 393.
31. See especially: *Virgs.* 108, 114, 649.
32. 'Denis Duval', *Lovel*, &c. 475.
33. *Pend.* 230.
34. Ibid. 510.
35. Fitzgerald, i. 141.
36. 'Cornhill to Cairo', *Sketch Bks.*, &c. 697.
37. Ibid. 694.
38. *Newcomes*, 51.
39. 'Cornhill to Cairo', *Sketch Bks.*, &c. 702.
40. Ray, ii. 204.
41. Ibid. 209.
42. Ibid. 205 ff.
43. Locker-Lampson, 306.
44. Merivale and Marzials, 13.
45. Brown and Lancaster tell the story of the walk which Thackeray took one Sunday evening in winter with two Edinburgh friends. There was a memorable sunset, and a wooden crane on Corstorphine Hill stood outlined against the sky, taking on the form of a cross. Thackeray 'gave utterance in a tremulous, gentle, and rapid voice, to what all were feeling, in the word "Calvary". . . . All that evening he was very gentle and serious, speaking, as he seldom did, of divine things—of death, of sin, of eternity, of salvation; expressing his simple faith in God and in his Saviour.'
46. Jeaffreson, i. 225.
47. Saintsbury, 270.
48. Ellis, 92.
49. Elton, ii. 254.
50. Ray, ii. 581.
51. Ibid. 662 f.
52. Ibid. 663.
53. *Pend.* 615.
54. Op. cit., *Esmond*, &c. 723.

CHAPTER III

1. Hannay, 35.
2. Brown and Lancaster, 229.
3. Brown, 111.
4. Levy, 152.
5. Ray, i. 6 f.
6. Int. *Newcomes*, xvii.

7. 'On Being Found Out' (*Round.*), *Lovel*, &c. 289 f.; 'On Letts's Diary' (*Round.*), ibid. 339.

8. Int. *Newcomes*, xvii; 'On Letts's Diary', loc. cit.

9. Ray, i. 3 f.

10. As quoted by Melville, i. 25.

11. Trollope, 4.

12. Whibley, 58.

13. 'From Cornhill to Cairo', *Sketch Bks.*, &c. 620 f.

14. 'Thorns in the Cushion' (*Round.*), *Lovel*, &c. 212.

15. *Lovel*, &c. 67 f.

16. Hannay, 37.

17. When Lord Brougham was caught in the act of doing this, he lost face.

18. As quoted by Kellett, *Early Victorian England*, ii. 18.

19. Loc. cit.

20. Till 1843 the novelist called himself Edward Lytton Bulwer; then, on inheriting Knebworth, he changed his name to Edward Lytton Bulwer-Lytton. He became a baronet in 1837, and was raised to the peerage as Baron Lytton of Knebworth in 1866.

21. Lytton, i. 548.

22. *Stray Papers*, 300.

23. *Yellowplush*, 364 f.

24. Ibid. 371, 376.

25. Sadleir, 210.

26. Ibid. 250 ff.

27. Ibid. 254.

28. Mr. Sadleir is not to be held responsible for this point, though he very rightly emphasizes the importance of the relations between Bulwer and his mother.

29. 'Catherine', *B. Lyndon*, &c. 542.

30. So Castiglione in *The Courtier*.

31. e.g. his use of the mock-heroic while Macshane is riding to Worcester, and the episode of Macshane and the horse.

32. Int. *B. Lyndon*, &c. xix.

33. Elton, ii. 237.

34. 'Humourists', *Esmond*, &c. 427 f.

35. Ibid. 446.

36. Hannay, 66. Remember that Hannay had a right to be heard, since he contributed most of the notes to these lectures when they were published.

37. Ibid. 65 f.

38. Saintsbury, 203.

39. Lucas, 30.

APPENDIX C

CHAPTER IV

1. Int. *Philip*, xl f.
2. Ray, i. 182.
3. 'De Juventute' (*Round.*), *Lovel*, &c. 235 f.
4. Diary, 1832, Ray, i. 197.
5. Ibid. i. 244 f.
6. Ibid. ii. 32.
7. Ibid. i. 225.
8. Account Book for 1833, Ray, i. 504.
9. Ibid. 504 f.
10. Whibley, 130.
11. Merivale and Marzials, 236.

CHAPTER V

1. Diary, 1835, Ray, i. 286.
2. W. M. T. to I. S., 21–25 April 1836, Ray, i. 311.
3. Ibid. 303 f.
4. Ibid. 309.
5. W. M. T. to J. O. B., 19–22 December 1848, Ray, ii. 475.
6. *Virgs.* 690.
7. *Philip*, 490.
8. Wilson, *Thackeray in U.S.* i. 104.
9. '. . . my vanity would be to go through life as a gentleman—as a Major Pendennis you have hit it.' W. M. T. to J. O. B., 12–13 March 1849, Ray, ii. 511.
10. W. M. T. to S. S. B., 26 July 1853, ibid. iii. 297.
11. 'Snobs', *Cont. to* 'Punch', &c. 419.
12. *Newcomes*, 475.
13. *Amer. Fam.* 6 f., 86 f., 92.
14. Ritchie, 2.
15. See note 2 (this chapter).
16. *Philip*, 326.
17. Wilson, *Thackeray in U.S.* i. 57.
18. W. M. T. to Jane S., 19 September 1848, Ray, ii. 431.
19. *Collection*, 144.
20. Merivale and Marzials, 30.

CHAPTER VI

1. *Philip*, 293.
2. See especially: 'Snobs', *Cont. to* 'Punch', &c. 370; 'Fitz-Boodle', *B. Lyndon*, &c. 418; 'Irish Sk. Bk.', *Sketch Bks.* &c., 518.
3. Wilson, *Thackeray in U.S.* i. 327 f.

4. Ray, i. 438.

5. Ibid. 367.

6. Ibid. 433.

7. Ibid. 474.

8. Ibid. 476.

9. Ibid. 479.

10. Ibid. 485.

11. See especially *Lovel the Widower*.

12. 'Brown's Letters', *Cont. to* 'Punch', &c. 662.

CHAPTER VII

1. This failure seems to have brought them pretty low in money. The Major would have been liable to arrest for debt if he had remained in London.

2. Ray, i. 353.

3. Dwyer (Fitzpatrick, ii. 410) says that Thackeray was vain of his French accent.

4. e.g. 'She was a perfectly good-natured and simple soul, and never made him a single reproach' ('Ravenswing', *B. Lyndon*, &c. 408); '. . . his father answering to him all questions connected with it.' (*V.F.* 433.)

5. e.g. 'There were colloquies, assignations, meetings on the ramparts, on the pier, where know I?' (*Philip*, 293); 'The factor comes of to pass—no letter this morning.' (Ibid. 463.)

6. Wilson, *Thackeray in U.S.* i. 229.

7. 'Paris Sk. Bk.', *Sketch Bks.*, &c. 143.

8. Ibid. 144.

9. 'Snobs', *Cont. to* 'Punch', &c. 380.

10. 'Jerome Paturot', *Ballads*, &c. 385.

11. 'Snobs', *Cont. to* 'Punch', &c. 378.

12. Whibley, 48.

13. Saintsbury, 22.

14. de Wyzewa, 461, 463.

15. Int. *B. Lyndon*, &c. xx f.

16. Fitzpatrick, ii. 407 ff.

17. Malcolm Elwin, 135.

18. 'Irish Sk. Bk.', *Sketch Bks.*, &c. 349.

19. Ibid. 325.

20. Masson, 244 f.

21. 'Snobs', *Cont. to* 'Punch', &c. 362.

22. *Virgs.* 161.

23. Melville, i. 125.

CHAPTER VIII

1. Preface to *Orphan of Pimlico*, vi.
2. Melville, i. 109.
3. 'Strictures on Pictures', *Ballads*, &c. 268.
4. 'Pictorial Rhapsody', ibid. 328.
5. Ibid. 329.
6. Int. *Cont. to* 'Punch', &c. xxxvii.
7. Lambert, 43; Ray, iv. 419.
8. 'May Gambols', *Ballads*, &c. 425.
9. Ibid. 426; 'Mr. and Mrs. Frank Berry', *B. Lyndon*, &c. 490.
10. 'Picture Gossip', *Ballads*, &c. 452.
11. 'Second Lecture on F. A.', ibid. 277.
12. Whibley, 30.
13. Sadleir, 252.
14. 'Picture Gossip', *Ballads*, &c. 457.
15. 'Paris Sk. Bk.', *Sketch Bks.*, &c. 48.
16. Ibid. 51.
17. Ibid. 56.

CHAPTER IX

1. 'Dr. Birch and his Young Friends', *Christmas Bks.* 96.
2. 'Kickleburys on the Rhine', ibid. 199.
3. The exasperated Thackeray, in a letter to the man who had just seen *The Second Funeral of Napoleon* (1841) through the press for him, asks rhetorically how he is to do this.
4. 'Snobs', *Cont. to* 'Punch', &c. 311.
5. Ibid. 344, 368, 373.
6. Ibid. 461.
7. Berdmore, 173.
8. 'Brown's Letters', *Cont. to* 'Punch', &c. 617.
9. Loc. cit.
10. 'On a Chalk Mark on a Door' (*Round.*), *Lovel*, &c. 285.
11. 'Brown's Letters', *Cont. to* 'Punch', &c. 624.
12. 'Immense Opportunity', *Punch*, 5 July 1845.
13. Spielmann, 133.
14. Whibley, 84.
15. Wilson, *Thackeray in U.S.*, ii. 36 f.
16. Fitzgerald, i. 193.
17. Ray, ii. 683.
18. Ibid. 644.
19. Ibid. 665.

20. Merivale and Marzials, 147.
21. 'Leech', *Ballads*, &c. 488.
22. *V.F.* 79.
23. Young, *Portrait of an Age*, 15.
24. Ray, ii. 761.
25. 'Before the Curtain', *V.F.* xliii.
26. *V.F.* 174.

CHAPTER X

1. '*Vanity Fair* and Lady Morgan', *P.M.L.A.*, xlviii, 2 June 1933.

2. See especially: 'Fitz-Boodle Papers', *B. Lyndon*, &c. 319.

3. See especially: Ray, i. 376 f.; ii. 149. Thackeray facetiously signed one of his unprinted letters 'Sidney Morgan', and a letter to the artist Doyle, 'Sydney Morgan' (Lambert, 50, 63).

4. Int. *V.F.* xxx.

5. Ray, i. clvii n.

6. For biographical details see Ray, i. clvii–clx.

7. W. M. T. to J. O. B., 30 June 1848, Ray, ii. 394.

8. Thackeray, the publishers, and Mrs. Procter were alike concerned at first about *Vanity Fair*, which was not selling as well as they had expected. Mrs. Procter accordingly told Abraham Hayward to write a puff of it, and even (at great length) what to say (Ray, ii. 312 ff.).

9. *Edinburgh Review*, lxxxvii, January 1848, 54.

10. Whitwell Elwin, i. 155.

11. *V.F.* 8.

12. Whibley, 93.

13. *V.F.* 415.

14. Ibid. 422.

15. Ibid. 483.

16. Ibid. 486.

17. Whibley, 96 n.

18. *V.F.* 509 f.

19. Ibid. 130 f.

20. Ibid. 302 f.

21. Ibid. 474 ff., 487 ff.

22. Ibid. 491.

23. Ibid. 407.

24. See especially ibid. 22.

25. Ibid. 25.

26. Ibid. 124.

27. Ibid. 75.

28. Ibid. 175.
29. Ibid. 173.
30. 'Humourists', *Esmond*, &c. 486.
31. Young, *Portrait of an Age*, 14 f.
32. Int. *Newcomes*, xxxix.
33. See especially: the scene in which Becky arrives for the first time at Sir Pitt Crawley's London house; the scene in which Sir Pitt asks her to marry him; the scene in Brussels in which she defeats the panic-stricken Lady Bareacres; and the scenes in which she overwhelms the virtuous ladies of Gaunt House.
34. *V.F.* 521.

CHAPTER XI

1. Saintsbury, 183.
2. *Pend.* 467.
3. Hannay, 12.
4. 'On a Peal of Bells' (*Round.*), *Lovel*, &c. 384.
5. W. M. T. to J. O. B., 7–9 Oct. 1848, Ray, ii. 436 and n.
6. Fitzgerald, i. 193.
7. To use the same woman for two contrasting characters was the sort of sardonic joke that would have appealed to Thackeray, so long as he was not attached to the woman.
8. See p. 104 above.
9. W. M. T. to J. O. B., 4–5 Feb. 1849, Ray, ii. 505.
10. Ibid. ii. 501.
11. Ibid. i. 369.
12. Ibid. ii. 501.
13. Ibid. 504 f.
14. Whibley, 145.
15. Loc. cit.
16. Cf. the Thackeray–Brookfield situation, as outlined in Ch. XIII below.
17. Ray, iii. 288.
18. 'Dignity of Literature', *Ballads*, &c. 632.
19. *Brontë Corr.* iii. 316.
20. *Pend.* 618.
21. Op. cit. 61.

CHAPTER XII

1. Ray, ii. 513 f.
2. Ritchie, 103.
3. 'Humourists', *Esmond*, &c. 530.

4. Whibley, 176.
5. Ibid. 172.
6. Trollope, 162.
7. Ibid. 167.
8. *Brontë Corr.* iii. 324.
9. Ibid. iv. 67.
10. *Brookfield Circle*, 388.
11. 'Sketches & Travels in London', *Cont. to* 'Punch', &c. 629; 'Charity & Humour', *Esmond*, &c. 715.
12. 'Humourists', *Esmond*, &c. 424; 'Charity & Humour', ibid. 715 f.
13. 'Four Georges', *Esmond*, &c. 672.
14. 'Humourists', *Esmond*, &c., 580.
15. 'Nil nisi Bonum' (*Round.*), *Lovel*, &c. 178.
16. 'Humourists', *Esmond*, &c. 534.
17. Ibid. 578 f.
18. Ibid. 580.
19. See p. 89 above.
20. 'Humourists', *Esmond*, &c. 581.
21. Ibid. 582.
22. Loc. cit.
23. Ibid. 600.
24. Ibid. 595 f.
25. 'Four Georges', *Esmond*, &c. 650.
26. Ibid. 651.
27. See especially: *Yellowplush*, &c. 348 ff.; 'Snobs', *Cont. to* 'Punch', &c. 311 f.
28. 'On a Peal of Bells' (*Round.*), *Lovel*, &c. 377.
29. Elton, ii. 247.
30. Mackay, ii. 297.

CHAPTER XIII
1. Ray, iii. 183.
2. W. M. T. to J. O. B., 8 June 1849, Ray, ii. 548.
3. Lambert, 45.
4. Ray, ii. 584.
5. Lambert, 42.
6. Ibid. 43.
7. Ibid., facsimile facing 46; Ray, ii. 493.
8. *Esmond*, 309.
9. Lambert, 45; Ray, iv. 425.
10. Ibid. ii. 793.
11. Lambert, 52; Ray, iv. 428.

12. Lambert 53; Ray, iv. 429.
13. Loc. cit.
14. Lambert, 53; Ray, iv. 430.
15. Lambert, 53; Ray, iv. 431.
16. *Philip*, 503.
17. Lambert, 53 f.; Ray, iv. 431.
18. Lambert, 53 f.; Ray, iv. 432.
19. Lambert, 53 f.; Ray, iv. 433.
20. Brown, 321.
21. Lambert, 56 f.; Ray, iv. 437.
22. Whitwell Elwin, i. 157.

CHAPTER XIV

1. W. M. T. to Mrs. C.-S., 13 March 1852, Ray, iii. 24.
2. W. M. T. to Lady Stanley, 28 Oct. 1851, ibid. ii. 807.
3. Ibid. iii. 49.
4. *Esmond*, 167.
5. Ibid. 359 f.
6. Ibid. 351.
7. At one point Esmond writes: 'We read in Shakespeare (whom the writer for his part considers to be far beyond Mr. Congreve, Mr. Dryden, or any of the wits of the present period), that . . .' (130). It is unlikely that Esmond would have held such an opinion in the early eighteenth century; and in any case Dryden and Congreve were not wits of the period in which he, long retired to Virginia, was supposed to be writing the book. At another point, the Dowager Lady Castlewood of Chelsea breaks into exclamations like 'Oh, flames and darts!' and 'Oh, darts and raptures!' (219). This is too obviously borrowed from Restoration Comedy to sound natural in its context.
8. Ray, iii. 38.
9. *Brontë Corr.* iii. 315.
10. *Esmond*, 166, 176.
11. Ibid. 135.
12. Ibid. 153.
13. Ibid. 164.
14. Ibid. 196.
15. Ibid. 198.
16. Marzials and Merivale, 176.
17. Loc. cit.
18. *Brontë Corr.* iii. 314. There is no such episode in the printed version of the book, but since Charlotte Brontë can

hardly have imagined it, we must conclude that the manuscript she was allowed by George Smith, the publisher, to read, did contain such an episode, and that Thackeray deleted it afterwards. Did he do so as a result of her objection, passed on to him by Smith? We have no information.

19. Rosebery, i. 68.

20. Brown and Lancaster, 237.

21. Loc. cit.

22. See p. 23 above.

23. Ray, ii. 815.

24. Whibley, 189.

25. Saintsbury, 194.

26. Of young Frank, Thackeray remarks: 'Nor is he the first lad that has been spoiled by the over-careful fondness of women.' (303.) Cf. George Osborne and Arthur Pendennis. Thackeray wanted an excuse for his own early follies, and concluded that he had been spoiled by his mother.

27. *Esmond*, 140.

28. Charlotte Brontë is worth quoting again. 'No character in the book strikes me as more masterly than that of Beatrix. . . . So much does she sometimes reveal of what is good and great as to suggest this feeling; you would think she was urged by a Fate. You would think that some antique doom presses on her house, and that once in so many generations its brightest ornament was to become its greatest disgrace. . . . Proud, beautiful and sullied, she was born what she becomes, a king's mistress.' (*Brontë Corr.* iv. 19.)

CHAPTER XV

1. Crowe, 20.

2. Ray, iii. 154.

3. Ibid. 183.

4. See his drawing of himself in this role on the flap of an envelope (*Amer. Family*, facing p. 31).

5. Ibid. 58, 70; Ray, iii. 261.

6. *Amer. Family*, 75; Ray, iii. 280.

7. *Amer. Family*, 80 f.; Ray, iii. 283 f.

8. *Amer. Family*, 6.

9. Ibid. 123 f., 125.

10. *Amer. Family*, 178 f.; Ray, iv. 278 f.

11. *Amer. Family*, 179; Ray, iv. 279.

12. Int. *Newcomes*, xxii f.

13. Loc. cit.

14. 'Diary for 1853', Ray, iii. 668.
15. W. M. T. to J. O. B., 21–23 Jan. 1853, ibid. 183.
16. 'Diary for 1853', ibid. 668.
17. Ibid. 288.
18. *Amer. Family*, 89; Ray, iii. 299.
19. Whibley, 212.
20. Masson, 244 f.
21. Int. *Newcomes*, xxxvii; Marzials, 103; Ray, i. cxi, cxvi.
22. Int. *Newcomes*, xxii.
23. Ibid. xxviii.
24. Ray, iii. 287.
25. Anne Thackeray had now become his amanuensis.
26. *Amer. Family*, 86 f.; Ray, iii. 297.
27. *Newcomes*, 401.
28. 'I know that [Thackeray] meant to like Ethel', says Saintsbury (218), 'and that he thought he ought to like her; but I am not so sure that he thoroughly did. And so he has left her a little "betwixt and between". Sometimes . . . she is all right. Elsewhere I am not so sure of her. For anybody else, "*Pass!*" but for Thackeray, "*Query?*".'
29. Immediately after he had killed off Farintosh's mother, he forgot that he had done so. 'By a most monstrous blunder, Mr. Pendennis killed Lord Farintosh's mother at one page and brought her to life again at another.' (*Newcomes*, 804 f.)
30. W. M. T. to Mrs. Procter, Ray, iii. 341.
31. Elton, ii. 244.

CHAPTER XVI

1. *Early Victorian Novelists*, 78.
2. *Newcomes*, 237.
3. *Philip*, 121.
4. Op. cit. (*Round.*), *Lovel*, &c. 261.
5. 'On Two Children in Black' (*Round.*), *Lovel*, &c. 181.
6. *Amer. Family*, 87; Ray, iii. 297 f.
7. Lambert, 56; Ray, iv. 436.
8. Here is a probably incomplete list of Thackeray's pseudonyms: Michael Angelo Titmarsh, Charles James Yellowplush, Ikey Solomons, Major Gahagan, George Fitz-Boodle, Miss Tickletoby, Spec, Our Fat Contributor, Paul Pindar, The Mulligan, *Punch*'s Commissioner, Fitzjames de la Pluche, Frederick Haltamont de Montmorency, Pleaceman X, Fitzroy Clarence, Hibernis Hibernior, Leonitus Androcles Hugglestone, John Corks, Folkestone Canterbury, Brown the Elder, Mr.

Snob, Solomon Pacifico, Goliah Muff, Gobemouche, Thaddeus Molony, Théophile Wagstaffe.

9. Thackeray is not uniformly successful in *V.F.* in conveying the sense of time passing. In Ch. X, for example, the reader gets a sudden jolt in the middle of a paragraph when the author remarks of Becky: 'Before she had been a year at Queen's Crawley she had. . . .' This would probably have been better managed if Thackeray had allowed himself a dummy.

10. See p. 102 above.

11. Trollope, 49 f.

12. Merivale and Marzials, 101.

13. Ibid. 56.

14. Berdmore, 172 f.

15. Fitzgerald, i. 275.

16. Saintsbury, 129.

17. Ibid. 127.

18. Ibid. 188.

19. Ibid. 171.

INDEX

Names of real people appear in small capitals, names of characters in fiction in ordinary type, and names of books, journals, &c., in italics.

T. = Thackeray.

INDEX

CHESTERFIELD, LORD, 138.
Children's voices, 86.
CHRIST, JESUS, 25 f., 27, 88, 196.
Christian Year, The, 17.
Christianity, 'Gothic', 27.
Chronicle, the *Morning*, 36, 128.
Clapham Sect, the, 18, 173.
Classical education, T. on, 33.
Clavering, Sir Francis (*Pend.*), 120, 126.
Clavering, Lady (*Pend.*), 126.
Clevedon Court, Somerset, 141, 165.
CLOUGH, ARTHUR HUGH, 27, 30, 133.
Cockney, T. a 'mutinous', 33.
Code, the Victorian, 3, 42, 67, 68, 146.
COLENSO, BISHOP, 1.
Coming of age, T.'s, 52.
Commentary in T.'s novels, 113 ff., 157, 182.
Compensations, T.'s psychological, 12.
CONGREVE, WILLIAM, 133.
Constitutional, the, 60, 75, 128.
Contrast in *V. F.*, principle of, 105 f.
Cornhill Magazine, the, 1, 47, 75.
Cornhill to Grand Cairo, 24 f., 33.
Costigan, Capt. (*Pend.*), 81, 112, 171.
Costigan, Milly, the Fotheringay (*Pend.*), 17.
Crawley, Miss (*V. F.*), 106, 113 f.
Crawley, Mrs. Bute (*V. F.*), 106.
Crawley the Elder, Sir Pitt (*V. F.*), 105.
Crawley the Younger, Sir Pitt (*V. F.*), 106, 114.
Crawley, Rawdon (*V. F.*), 105, 106.
Creation, T.'s powers of, 125 ff., 127 f., 172.
CREEVEY, the Diarist, 183.
CROWE, EYRE, 64.
Cruelty of women, 22 f., 161 f.
CRUIKSHANK, GEORGE, 84.
Cynicism of T., alleged, 3 f., 5, 42, 101.

Dawkins (*Yellowplush*), 55 f.
Death, of Helen Pendennis, 15 f.; T. on, 145; of Jane T., 65; of Sally Baxter, 170; of Colonel Newcome, 178.
DECAISNE, the painter, 16.

Degree, living according to our, 93 f.
Denis Duval, 107, 180, 182 f.
Deuceace (*Yellowplush*), 55, 56.
DICKENS, CHARLES, 18, 91, 100, 101, 117, 119, 127, 131, 172.
Didactic note in Victorian writing, 99.
Dignity of Literature, The, 128 ff.
Discounting bills, T. engaged in, 53.
'Discriminated occasions' in T.'s novels, 43, 116 f., 155 ff., 202.
'Discursive' Muse, T.'s, 115 f.
Dissociation in T.'s character, 4 f., 15 f., 22, 23, 24 f., 40 f., 45 f., 76, 78, 82 f., 88.
Distance, aesthetic, 6, 54 f., 160.
Dobbin, William (*V. F.*), 102, 106, 109, 110.
Domestic servants, T. on, 93 f.
Don Quixote and *Newcomes*, 172, 173.
'Dramatic' in T.'s fiction, 116 f., 119 f.
Drawing, T. and, 51, 84 f.
DRYDEN, JOHN, 30, 31.
Dummy, T.'s use of, 102, 126, 171, 179, 181, 182 f.
Duty, T. on love and, 147, 152.
Duval, Mme (*Denis Duval*), 23.
DWYER, MAJOR, 79 f.

EASTLAKE, SIR CHARLES L., 86.
Eaves, Tom (*V. F.*, *Pend.*, *Newcomes*, *Philip*), 183.
Education, T. on Classical, 33.
Egocentricity of T., 5 f., 61 f., 96, 184 ff., *et passim*.
Eighteenth Century, Victorian attitude towards, 138.
ELIOT, GEORGE, 163.
ELTON, SIR CHARLES, 141.
ELTON, OLIVER, 27, 43, 178, 180, 181.
ELWIN, WHITWELL, 3, 4, 108, 138, 153.
ENCYCLOPAEDISTS, THE, 76.
Epistles to the Literati, 38.
Ernest Maltravers, 37.
Esmond, Beatrix, *see under* Beatrix.
Esmond, Harry (*Esmond*), projection of T., 145 f., 165; discriminated occasions for, 155 f.; love story with Rachel central theme of book, 160.

INDEX

Esmond, opening scene, 112, 155; as memoirs, 107, 126; the writing of, 154, 159, 170; saddened by Brookfield quarrel, 154; 'the very best I can do', 154; discriminated occasions often 'posed', 155 ff. commentary in, 157; perfect long speech, 157; style of, 158 f., 204; *Spectator* paper in, 159; history and, 159 f.; Charlotte Brontë on, 159, 163, 204 f.; plot of and sub-plot in, 160; 'distance' achieved by historical setting, 160; objections to, 163, 164; 'triplicity' in, 165.

ETTY, WILLIAM, 85, 88.

Evangelicalism, and Bechers, 9; in *Vanity Fair*, 18; in *Pendennis*, 18; and Mrs. Carmichael-Smith, 17 f., 22; in *Newcomes*, 18, 173.

Evasiveness, T.'s, 4, 182.

Examiner, the, 128.

Fairoaks, 17.

FANSHAWE, MRS., 149.

Fareham, Bechers at, 8 f.; T. plans to use for *Newcomes*, 170; T. uses for *Roundabouts*, 172.

Farintosh, Dowager Lady (*Newcomes*), 177, 206.

Farintosh, Marquis of (*Newcomes*), 176, 177.

Fashion in fiction, T. and the, 115 f.

FAWCETT, HENRY E., 49.

'Fecundity of imagination', T. says he lacks, 127 f., 172.

Fiction and Life, in T., 6, 47, 54 f., 61 f., 107 f., 120 f., 170, 172 f., 184 f.

FIELDING, HENRY, moral theory, 5; irony of, 42, 43; compared with T., 5, 88, 105; Charlotte Brontë on, 133; T. on, 19, 118, 133, 134, 135 ff., 138.

Fitz-Boodle, George, 103 f.

FITZGERALD, EDWARD, friendship with T., 4, 51; on T.'s religion, 24; on lionizing of T., 97; on T.'s use of his own life for fiction, 184.

Florac, Paul de (*Newcomes*), 78, 177 f.

Flunkey, the little bit of the, 96 f., 98.

Foker (*Pend.*), 55, 126.

Foker, Lady Agnes (*Pend.*), 127.

FONBLANQUE, ALBANY, 81.

FORSTER, E. M., 6.

Fotheringay, the (*Pend.*), 17, 120, 121, 123, 126, 184.

Fraser's Magazine, 37 ff., 85, 128.

French, the, T. on, 75 ff.; attitude to sex and marriage, 77 f.

French language, T. and the, 76.

Fun, Truth, and Love, 28, 100.

Gallicisms in T., 76, 199.

Gambling, T.'s, 50 ff.

Gaunt Gaunt, Plantagenet (*Dr. Birch*), 90.

GAY, JOHN, 135.

Gentleman, T. on the, 90 ff., 118; T. as, 40, 94, 98.

GEORGE I, 139.

GEORGE II, 139.

GEORGE III, 139.

GEORGE IV, 139 f.

Georges, The Four, 134, 137 ff.

GOLDSMITH, OLIVER, 21, 51.

Good-bye, T.'s avoidance of saying, 11.

GRAHAM, MARY, *see under* CARMICHAEL, MARY.

GREVILLE, the Diarist, 183.

Gulliver's Travels, 44.

Gumbo (*Virgs.*), 82.

HALLAM, HENRY, 145.

Hamilton, Duke of (*Esmond*), 155, 157 f.

HANNAY, JAMES, 30, 31, 35 f., 40, 44, 45, 46, 119, 197.

Hare Court, T. studying law at, 51.

Hatherley's School of Art, 172.

HAYES, CATHERINE, 79.

HAYWARD, ABRAHAM, 107 f., 201.

Heart, the important factor in Art, 86.

HELVÉTIUS, CLAUDE A., 76.

Higgs, Miss (*Newcomes*), 78, 177.

Highgate, Lord, formerly Jack Belsize (*Newcomes*), 150, 177.

History, and *Esmond*, 159 f.

Hobson, Miss (*Newcomes*), 175.

HOGARTH, WILLIAM, 135.

211

INDEX

MILL, JOHN STUART, 27.
MILLMAN, DEAN H. H., 27.
Mirobolant (*Pend.*), 78.
MITFORD, MARY RUSSELL, 163.
Mohun, Lord (*Esmond*), 155,
161.
Money, T. and, 47, 48, 53 f., 131,
138 f.
MOORE, PETER, 12, 48.
'Moralities', T.'s, 41 f.
Morgan (*Pend.*), 120, 126.
MORGAN, LADY, 103 f., 201.
Morning Chronicle, the, 36, 128.
Mother, and child, 16 f., 88, 111,
157, 186. (*For T.'s mother see*
CARMICHAEL-SMYTH, ANNE.)
Mothers-in-law, T. on, 48, 69 ff.
Esmond marrying his m.-in-l.,
164.
Museum, the, 35.

Namby-pamby, T. on the, 87.
Narrator, T.'s use of imaginary,
102, 126, 171, 179, 181, 182.
National Standard, the, 35, 37,
53.
NEAVES, CHARLES, LORD, 30, 45 f.
Newcome, Lady Anne (*New-
comes*), 176.
Newcome, Barnes (*Newcomes*),
61, 150, 177, 178.
Newcome, Clive (*Newcomes*),
projection of T., 170, 172 f.,
179; ' barber's block', 172;
story of, 174, 176, 177, 178.
Newcome, Ethel (*Newcomes*),
and Sally Baxter, 62, 170;
story of, 61, 174, 176, 177, 178;
T. fumbles over, 176 f., 178,
206.
Newcome the Elder, Thomas
(*Newcomes*), 175.
Newcome the Younger, Thomas,
the 'Colonel' (*Newcomes*),
financial failure, 56; and Don
Quixote, 172, 173; originals
of, 173; marriage, 175; steals
the stage, 178.
Newcomes, prudery and, 19;
Sally Baxter and, 62, 168,
169 f., 174 f.; theme of, 62,
78, 107, 174 ff.; opening
scene, 171; early plan for, 170,
172; contracted for, 170;
difficulty at the beginning,
167, 171 f., 173 f.; preface to,
171.

Newgate School of Fiction, 41 f.
New Monthly Magazine, 95.
Nose, T.'s broken, 32 f.
Novel, T. and the, 48, 98 f.;
Newgate School, 41 f.; anony-
mity in, 6; imaginary narrator
in, 102, 126, 171, 179, 181 f.;
creation in, 108, 112, 125 ff.;
panoramic, 114 f., 119; remi-
niscential or memorial, 180 ff.
Nudes, T. on, 85, 88; Queen
Victoria and, 88.

O'Dowd, Mrs. (*V. F.*), 81.
Old Testament, 1, 25 f.
Opening scenes, T.'s, 112, 171.
Optimism, Victorian, 101.
Osborne the Elder, George
(*V. F.*), 105.
Osborne the Younger, George
(*V. F.*), 16, 105.
Overwriting, T.'s, 11, 16, 109,
120, 157.
Oxbridge, *see under* Cambridge.

Painting, T. on, 84 ff.; T.'s own,
84 f.
Panoramic writing, in *V. F.*,
114 f.; in *Pend.*, 119.
Paris, T. and, 50, 53, 57 ff., 75 f.
Paris Sketch Book, 56, 75, 78.
PARSONS, THOMAS W., 96.
Partings, T. on, 11.
Patrimony, T.'s, 48.
Pendennis, Arthur, (*Pend.*, *Newcomes*, *Philip*), and T. himself,
15, 17 ff., 69, 118 f., 126, 179;
l'homme sensuel moyen, 118;
as narrator of later novels,
102, 126, 171, 179, 181, 182.
Pendennis, Helen (*Pend.*), and
T.'s mother, 15 f., 21 ff., 121,
157; and Fanny Bolton, 22,
120; jealousy of, 23; infuriating but central, 125.
Pendennis, Major (*Pend.*), eye
for a scamp, 50, 55; resembles
T., 61, 198; breakfasts, 112,
119; and Morgan, 120; a
triumph, 125.
Pendennis, prudery and, 19 f.;
opening scene, 112; Cam-
bridge chapters in, 54 f.;
reference to Catherine Hayes,
79; contains more of T.'s best
work than any other novel,
119; disjointed, 119, 120; lack

INDEX

Servants, T. on domestic, 93 f., 134.

Sex, T. and, 19 ff., 77 f., 88, 117, 164, 195; the French and, 77 f.

SHAKESPEAR, GEORGE, 31.

Shandon, Capt. (*Pend.*), 81, 120.

Sharp, Becky (*V. F.*), *see under* Becky.

SHAWE, HENRY, 73.

SHAWE, ISABELLA, afterwards MRS. THACKERAY, T.'s wooing, 48, 57 ff., 63 f.; character of, 58, 64 f., 67; insanity, 66; and Amelia, 65, 107 f., 110; and Charlotte Baynes, 65; and Rosey Mackenzie, 65, 172; T.'s attitude to, 83; and Mary Graham (Carmichael), 122.

SHAWE, JANE, 58, 65, 71.

SHAWE, COL. MATTHEW, 57, 63.

SHAWE, MRS., the mother-in-law, 48, 57 ff., 66, 70 ff., 83, 173.

'Sheaves' scene in *Esmond*, 162 f.

Sheepshanks, Lady Jane (*V. F.*), 18, 106, 109 f.

SHEIL, RICHARD LALOR, 36, 81.

Sheppard, Jack, 41.

Sibwright, Percy (*Pend.*), 127.

Simcoes, the (*Pend.*), 18.

SKELTON, JOHN HENRY, 37.

SMITH, GEORGE, 47.

SMITH, the MISSES, 121.

SMOLLETT, TOBIAS, 135.

Snob, meaning of word, 91 f.

Snobbishness, T. accused of, 4, 96, 98; in Victorian England, 92, 95, 96.

Snobs, The Book of, 4, 28, 61, 82, 90 f., 93, 96, 99.

Society, T. lionized by, 97 f.; T. breaking up framework of, 99, 100; influence on Victorians, 100.

Southdown, Lady (*V. F.*), 18, 106.

Spectator paper in *Esmond*, 159.

SPIEGEL, MELANIE VON, 50.

Spiggot, Jack (*Snobs*), 61 f.

'Spiritual sensuality', T.'s, 144.

STEELE, RICHARD, 135, 159, 161.

STELLA, SWIFT and, 44.

STERNE, LAURENCE, 133, 137, 144.

STEVENSON, LIONEL A., 103.

Steyne, Marquis of (*V. F.*), 105 f., 111.

Stonehenge, Lady (*Brown's Letters*), 69, 73 f.

Strictures on Pictures, 16, 85.

Strong, Chevalier (*Pend.*), 126.

Style, T.'s, 11, 15 f., 109, 119, 158 f.; Bulwer's, 39.

SWIFT, JONATHAN, 30, 42, 43 ff., 133, 134 ff., 159.

SWINNERTON, FRANK, 5.

Sympathy and satire, 30 ff., 45 f.

SYNGE, W. W. F., 60.

Tapeworm (*V. F.*), 102.

TAPRELL, WILLIAM, 51.

Temple, Middle, T. entered at, 51.

Temps, le, 30.

TENNYSON, ALFRED, 121.

THACKERAY, ANNE (née BECHER), *see under* CARMICHAEL-SMYTH, ANNE.

THACKERAY, ANNE, afterwards LADY RITCHIE, and her grandmother, 7 f.; birth, 70; on her father's drawing, 84; on possible original of Becky, 104; and Brookfields, 147; on early plans for *Newcomes*, 170, 173; amanuensis for T., 175.

THACKERAY, REV. FRANCIS, 48.

THACKERAY, HARRIET MARION (MINNY), afterwards MRS. LESLIE STEPHEN, and her grandmother, 7 f.; birth, 66, 70.

THACKERAY, JANE, death, 65; birth, 122.

THACKERAY, RICHMOND, life in India, 9; death, 10; will, 48.

THACKERAY, WILLIAM MAKE-PEACE, the Elder, 10, 12.

Theatres, T. and, 51, 53.

Times, The, on T., 3; on Macaulay, 36.

TOLSTOY, LEO, 5, 183.

Tom Jones, 5, 19, 118, 135 f.

Trinity College, Cambridge, 49.

TROLLOPE, MRS., 37.

TROLLOPE, ANTHONY, 82, 133, 184.

Truth, love, and fun, 28, 100.

Tuft-hunting, T.'s excuse for, 98.

TURNER, DR., 31.

Tutelary spirit, T.'s, 12, 14 ff., 29.

Twisden, Agnes (*Philip*), 61.

Unconscious mind, T.'s, 108 f.

'Uncouth raptures', T.'s, 144.

University life, T. on, 54 f.

215

INDEX